SCHOOLING DECISIONS:
THE ORIGINS AND CONSEQUENCES OF SELECTION AND STREAMING IN IRISH POST-PRIMARY SCHOOLS

Copies of this paper may be obtained from The Economic and Social Research Institute (Limited Company No. 18269). Registered Office: 4 Burlington Road, Dublin 4.

Price IR£11.00

(Special rate for students: IR£5.50)

Damian Hannan is a Research Professor at The Economic and Social Research Institute. Maura Boyle is a former Research Assistant at the ESRI. The paper has been accepted for publication by the Institute, which is not responsible for either the content or the views expressed therein.

SCHOOLING DECISIONS: THE ORIGINS AND CONSEQUENCES OF SELECTION AND STREAMING IN IRISH POST-PRIMARY SCHOOLS

DAMIAN F. HANNAN
with
MAURA BOYLE

© THE ECONOMIC AND SOCIAL RESEARCH INSTITUTE
DUBLIN, 1987

ISBN 0 7070 0094 7

Acknowledgements

We are greatly indebted to the many individuals and organisations who contributed to making this report possible, particularly to the Principals and Guidance Counsellors in the sample of post-primary schools who provided the main information on schooling practice on which this report is based. In addition, we wish to acknowledge the generous co-operation and support of the Department of Education in this research.

Critical comments on earlier drafts of this report were given by the internal ESRI referees and by an anonymous external referee. In addition, Adam Gamoran of the University of Wisconsin, Pat Clancy of UCD, Tom Kellaghan of the Educational Research Centre and Sr. Nano Brennan of the CMRS made very valuable comments and criticisms. Denis Conniffe and Brendan Whelan suggested useful modifications of the statistical analysis of Chapter 5 which considerably improved it, while Brendan Halpin provided valuable programming assistance. To these and to all other readers of earlier drafts we are extremely grateful.

Finally, we would like to sincerely thank Mary Cleary and other members of the Institute clerical staff who typed the various drafts of this report and proof read the final draft. We would also like to thank Mary McElhone who copy edited and processed the final document. To all these individuals and others too numerous to mention we are extremely grateful. Much of the value of the report derives from their help and criticism, any remaining errors of interpretation or omission remain the responsibility of the authors.

CONTENTS

LIST OF TABLES

LIST OF FIGURES

LIST OF CHARTS

GENERAL SUMMARY

Introduction: Objectives of Research and Approach Used

1.   This is a study of the social organisation of schooling – of the way curricula and instructional units are organised within schools. It deals with the method by which the curriculum is allocated to different categories of pupils, the underlying reasons why schools vary in this respect, and some of the effects of that variation on pupil attainments.

2.   Most school effectiveness studies assume that schools allocate their teaching resources relatively homogeneously to all pupils. In fact, within most Irish schools, the total stock of curricular and instructional resources is quite differentially allocated to distinct categories of pupils.

3.   This research into that differential allocation process, has 3 objectives: (i) It describes the main characteristics of schooling practice in a sample of Irish post-primary schools. If possible its aim is to derive a typology of schooling practice, or of the form and ways in which instruction is provided. (ii) It attempts to account for, or explain why, schools differ so widely in these practices. (iii) It examines some of the main effects of such schooling differentiation on pupil attainment levels. Schooling practice, as used here, refers to the following 5 characteristics of the way instruction is organised within schools: (a) pupil categorisation – mainly whether pupils are assigned to classes on the basis of perceived "ability" or not; (b) whether the curriculum is differentiated by such pupil class characteristics or not; (c) extent of curricular choice left at the individual pupil-teacher level; (d) extent of subject-teacher and parental involvement in subject/level choices; and (e) extent to which pupils are constrained or restricted in their social interaction with their classmates.

4.   The word "streaming" is usually used to refer to the organisation of classes on the basis of the assessed "ability" or performance of pupils: a hierarchy of homogeneous ability classes. But such rigid streaming of pupils may or may not be accompanied by rigid curricular differentiation – assigning Honours levels and a highly academic curriculum to the upper streams and a Pass level curriculum and vocational subjects to the lower streams. Equally, subject/level choices by pupils may be minimised or maximised in such schools, and subject teachers may or may not be involved in any subject/level choicemaking that occurs. Pupils may also be highly restricted in their school interactions to their assigned classmates or not.

5.   Greater flexibility in resource use and more sophisticated timetabling is required in schools with less rigidly differentiated instructional processes. However, the presence of such management expertise does not guarantee effective mixed-ability teaching or more flexible curricular and instructional processes; nor indeed does its absence guarantee rigid streaming. The reasons for variation in curricular and instructional practices by schools are much more complicated and deep-seated.

6.   Schools stream, it is usually asserted, because they believe strongly that it is in the interests of the majority of their students to do so; particularly so in schools which are perceived to have wide variances in the ability levels of their pupil intake. Many school decisionmakers in these circumstances believe that the less able pupils would suffer in mixed ability classes because of their constant performance comparisons to higher performing pupils to which they would be subject. It is also asserted that high ability pupils would be held back by being put in with slow learners, with the pace of instruction and difficulty of topic having to be tailored to the average, or even the slowest, learner in the class. In other words, grouping by ability occurs because of the belief that it leads to better learning outcomes for most students, particularly those at the extremes.

7.   Given this belief in the beneficial effects of streaming, one would expect that the tendency to so differentiate the schooling process would depend mainly on the degree of actual ability and social variation amongst pupils. These are what one could call "technical-rational" reasons for streaming and curricular differentiation: greater pupil numbers, greater actual differentiation in the social statuses and ability levels of intake pupils, as well as greater variation in the expected or planned output of schools — from aspiring apprentices leaving at Group Certificate level to University entrants from Leaving Certificate Honours levels. Generally these are some of the usually accepted reasons for its occurrence. However, we will argue strongly that these are not the main reasons why it occurs, nor indeed are the expected effects of "streaming" as beneficial as its proponents often argue.

8.   It is, on the contrary, argued here that the main underlying reasons for greater differentiation in the schooling process are institutional or volitional rather than technical, in the sense discussed above; being chosen by school decisionmakers rather than being determined or imposed by circumstances. It is proposed that these "choices" have more to do with the original "charters" or acquired social functions of schools — primarily their choice of clientele (sex and social class) and their choice of, or priority placed on, type of output; the guiding philosophy of the authority running the school being of central importance in these respects.

9. From a review of the research literature, it is also proposed that contrary to some of the commonsense rationales for streaming, the main outcome of more rigid pupil and curricular differentiation is much greater polarisation in educational attainments than occurs in less rigidly differentiated or more mixed ability schools, without any compensating average attainment advantage. There is also the related viewpoint that much of the deleterious effects of rigid schooling differentiation occurs as an organisational side effect of increased schooling differentiation and stratification of classes, obviously not one that is intended but one, however, which is very difficult to avoid — even when its dangers are fully appreciated.

Methods

10. The study is based on the extensive records of school characteristics gathered in the course of our previous study — *Schooling and Sex Roles* (1983) — in a sample of 95 post-primary schools. Interviews with Principals, Guidance Counsellors, as well as with a small sample of highly knowledgeable informants who had played central roles in the Irish second-level system, provide the main sources of information about the operation of Irish schools in this study. In addition, interviews with over 3,500 Leaving Certificate pupils and around 5,000 Intermediate Certificate pupils provide the basic information about pupil achievement.

Results

11. There is wide institutional diversity in Irish second-level schools, and this has substantial effects on the nature of schooling provided. Besides the threefold distinction between Secondary, Vocational and Community/ Comprehensive schools there is considerable variation in the originating charters, as well as acquired educational and social roles, of Secondary schools. These result in large differences in the social class, sex and ability intake of different schools as well as differences in both the chosen and acquired social placement or social mobility functions of schools. These variations are described in detail in Chapter 2.

12. There is equal diversity in the manner in which schools within our sample organise their instruction and differentiate their curriculum. Only around 1 in 5 of these schools at Intermediate Certificate level had purely mixed ability classes. The great majority streamed or "banded" their pupil intake. The extent of streaming, however, declines substantially at the senior cycle level. Curricular differentiation — in the level and type of subject allocated to classes — is equally pronounced. Higher (streamed) classes are allocated Honours levels and more academic subjects, while lower ability

classes are allocated Pass levels and vocational type subjects. Coinciding with this higher pupil and curricular differentiation is equally restricted choice making by pupils and limitations on teacher and parental involvement in any schooling choices that do occur. In highly streamed schools where the curriculum is highly differentiated, schooling decisions tend to be very centralised and schooling processes routinised. In mixed ability schools, on the other hand, with little or no curricular differentiation, there tends to be a wider diversity and greater flexibility in decisionmaking.

13. The 5 different dimensions of schooling differentiation, therefore, are highly interrelated and, in fact, form a single unidimensional scale or ordered typology – from most to least differentiated. This scale varies from the 7 schools – out of 80 with 2 or more classes – which are very highly streamed and have very rigid curricular differentiation to 11 schools at the other extreme which are completely mixed ability with no curricular differentiation. In addition to the top 7 highly streamed schools there are also 25 schools which are highly "banded" or loosely streamed and which have less rigid curricular differentiation. These leave more subject/level choice making to the individual pupil, and have somewhat less centralisation of decisionmaking than in the former case. Together this makes for a total of 40 per cent of all larger schools which have highly differentiated schooling provision. Almost half the schools then fall between the two extremes of rigid differentiation or mixed ability provision. These mostly have loose banding, some, but not very rigid, curricular differentiation, some centralisation and limitation on subject/level choice making by pupils, and moderate segregation and ranking of pupil classes. Although, therefore, the great majority of schools do "stream" in some sense, there is great variation in the stringency with which they do so. These variations in schooling practices, as well as the consistency with which they are related, are analysed in detail in Chapter 3.

14. "Environmental" and "technical" factors – the usual rationales given for streaming – have very low correlations with the rigidity of streaming and curricular differentiation. Institutional, social and cultural factors have a much greater influence. The most rigid schooling differentiation is most characteristic of boys' Secondary schools, particularly those which have acquired a sponsoring social mobility, role for lower middle or upper working class boys with ability and ambition. Rigid and loose banding is characteristic of large Vocational and Community/Comprehensive schools. In both cases the relationships are clearly the result of value priorities and policy decisions. At the other extreme the most "mixed ability" schools, with least curricular differentiation and most widespread choice making, is most characteristic of girls' middle class Secondary schools; and to a lesser extent of upper middle

class boys' Secondary schools also. The relationships to these social and institutional variables are too clear-cut not to reflect clear differences in ideology and policy; outcomes of "choice", not imposed by environmental constraints. Chapter 4 deals with this in detail.

15. Increasing levels of rigidity and differentiation in the schooling process have no discernible positive effects on average attainment levels, as judged from the experiences of the total entry cohort to a school. The evidence indeed suggests a slight negative effect: on increased dropout rates, on the average attainment levels of the entry cohort and on the percentage going on to University. These negative effects are minor, however. Increasing differentiation, however, has a very pronounced polarisation effect on pupil attainment levels — judged by all measures of attainment which characterise the total entry cohort, and even of the proportion that survives to the Intermediate Certificate examination. We do not have the necessary data to test the hypothesis, but it appears as if increased attainments by highly placed classes are being bought at the cost of lower attainments by lower streams or bands in most streamed or highly "banded" schools. On average, therefore, the overall effect is negative.

However, the increased variance in highly streamed schools can occur in different ways. And it appears that in a small minority of schools that higher attainments in higher streams are not being purchased at the cost of lower attainments in the bottom streams; both the average attainment level and the variance in attainment are increased. The opposite syndrome of effects, however, is equally likely to occur — though equally as infrequent; increased proportions of pupils with lower attainments without any compensating growth in higher attainments. The study, however, was not designed to provide the necessary evidence to test for or explain why these discrepant outcomes occur. These results are discussed in detail in Chapter 5.

16. Since this is a long and, at times technically complex study, interested readers who may find the conceptual and methodological discussions too off-putting but who wish to get a more complete picture of the study than is given in this General Summary may need some guidance. There are summaries provided at the end of each chapter which, when combined with the first few introductory pages of each chapter, provide a more detailed overview of the study. In addition, Chapter 6 provides a much more detailed overall summary of the orientation and results of the study than is given here, as well as detailed conclusions drawn from these results. Chapter 1 is essential reading for all those who wish to get a clear view of the conceptual and methodological approach adopted in this study and Chapter 2, as a whole, is recommended to all readers.

Chapter 1

THE ORGANISATION OF POST-PRIMARY SCHOOLING IN IRELAND: A CONCEPTUAL APPROACH

Introduction

In our previous publication, *Schooling and Sex Roles*, (1983), we analysed the main "schooling differences" that distinguished boys' from girls' second-level education. There it became apparent that these differences were long established and were highly institutionalised — i.e., that different kinds of schools were being systematically organised for different kinds of pupils and to achieve different educational and social goals. Second-level schooling occurs within around 800 separate organisations which vary in size from less than 50 pupils to over 1,200. Despite a similarly constraining environment within which they work — a central source of and similar levels of funding, a relatively common curriculum and individual subject syllabi, a common regime of public examinations — schools vary widely in their individual curricula, in the way their subject offerings and teaching resources are organised and allocated, as well as in the effectiveness with which this is done (Hannan, Breen, and Murray, Watson, Hardiman and O'Higgins, 1983; Madaus, Kellaghan *et al.*, 1979).

What was most striking about these results was that this organisational and curricular variation appeared to be to a large extent under the control of individual school decisionmakers, or to be functions of the founding charters of specific school types (Hannan, Breen *et al.*, 1983, pp. 156-197). Thus in our analysis of the curricula provided in second-level schools a clearly "chartered" Vocational and Comprehensive curriculum was characteristic of both these school types; but within Secondary schools the curricula provided, although highly correlated with school size and the pupils' sex and social class characteristics, were obviously also highly influenced by the "chartering objectives" (e.g., the original or founding educational objectives of the religious order running the school) as well as to the management policies of individual schools. This variation was not due to external constraints such as school size or resource availability (ibid., pp. 156-197). In addition it was also very clear that curricular change over time — both in the structure and size of the curriculum provided — was only marginally related to changes in a school's resources, being deter-

1

mined more by the actual use made by school managements of their resources (ibid., pp. 198-224). Moreover, our results clearly indicated that, within broad constraints set by the Department of Education (Rules and Programmes for Secondary Schools, and for the Day Vocational Certificate Examinations), which indicate the minimum number and identity of subjects that have to be taught, Secondary school principals have wide autonomy in curricular decision making. The curricula of Vocational and Community/Comprehensive schools are much more determined by central policy (ibid., pp. 82-88). There was wide variation, therefore, in the nature of the curricula provided by schools. And that variation appeared to be largely responsive both to a school's founding charter and to school decisionmakers' views of the needs and demands of the clientele being served and the educational objectives being sought or achieved.

Such discretionary differences amongst schools in their curricula is not the only, even the main, distinction in schooling practice. They appear to differ even more markedly in the way they sort or categorise their pupil intake. At one extreme are schools where there is an unquestioning and unproblematic acceptance of highly differentiated "streaming" or "tracking" arrangements — where pupils are assessed on their educational ability or performance on, or previous to, entry, and allocated to hierarchically ordered classes on this basis. Schools then distinguish amongst these classes in terms of the type and level of subject allocated to them on the basis of a belief in the beneficial effects of maximising the "fit" between "type of pupil" and type of curriculum: "fitting" pupils into preset curricular-pedagogical boxes. At the other extreme are a small number of schools which have almost no classes at all; where there is very wide choice of subjects/levels left to individual pupil choice, on the basis of a philosophy or view of education which treats individual differences amongst pupils in a more individually developmental way: fitting the curriculum and pedagogy to variable pupil competencies and needs.

Although privately legitimised or rationalised, no doubt, within the school or group of associated schools, these varying schooling practices and their associated philosophies or ideologies of education have not been publicly debated in Irish education. Such streaming, "tracking" and associated curricular differentiation practices, have been the subject of great debate and controversy in the US, Great Britain and most European countries, at least since the early 1960s. (See Yates, 1966; Dahllof, 1971; Jencks *et al.*, 1972; Newbold, 1977; Kelly, 1978.)

"Streaming" had become almost universal in the Britain of the early 1960s, having developed mainly after the Hadow Report of 1926 which advised the establishment of second-level education for all (Yates, 1966; Kelly, 1978). Previously the "standards" system was used in primary schools

— a system of grouping based on equal performance, not age. This had meant that children moved from grade (or standard) to grade on the basis of attaining a certain performance level, being kept back until they reached the necessary standard. The growing popularity of grouping by year of age or entry age — following criticism of grouping by standard, with too much age variation within classes — coincided with the growing use of "intelligence tests" to group pupils of similar ages by their level of "general ability". This increasing development of streaming practices in both primary and second-level schools was officially advocated in a number of British reports in the 1920s and 1930s. (See review by Kelly, 1978; and Yates, 1966.) In the United States such "streaming" or "tracking" practices were equally widespread in both grade schools and second-level schools in the 1950s and 1960s — the practice being favoured by an overwhelming majority of teachers (NEA, 1968; Jencks et al., 1972, pp. 33-34).

From the early 1960s onwards, however, this practice of "streaming" or "tracking" came under sustained attack because of its socially divisive and educationally unequal effects. First, no clear evidence existed to support the posited intellectual or cognitive development advantages of teaching homogeneous ability groupings over heterogeneous ones. The evidence here was highly inconclusive (see reviews by Yates, 1966; Barker-Lunn, 1970; Jencks et al., 1972; Kelly, 1978). As Jencks et al. (1972, p. 108) summarised their review of the research literature at that time: "ability grouping sometimes helps disadvantaged students, sometimes hurts them, and sometimes has no effect. The same appears to be true of advantaged students. Nobody knows when tracking will produce one effect or another". So, in terms of cognitive development or achievement gains, there is no consistent evidence that "streaming" or "tracking", combined with differential instructional processes, has an overall advantage for a school's pupils. Indeed reviews of the recent research literature generally conclude that "ability grouping" or "tracking" has no "main effect" — or overall average advantage (Hallinan, 1987, p. 42; Good and Marshall, 1984; Persell, 1977).

There is, however, clear evidence of the polarising effects of curricular differentiation or "track placement" (i.e., in a college or university preparatory course, a vocational-technical course, or a "general" academic course, etc.), on levels of educational or academic aspiration and achievement. (Jencks et al., 1972, p. 157; Heynes, 1974; Yuchtmann and Samuel, 1975; Persell, 1977; Alexander and McDill, 1976; Kerckhoff, et al., 1982; Shavitt, 1984; Good and Marshall, 1984; Hallinan, 1984 and Hallinan and Sorenson, 1985.) These differential effects on educational/occupational achievement appear to be most marked where official institutional differences in educational provision exist as in Israel (Yuchtmann and Samuel, 1975) or Britain (Kerckhoff *et al.*, 1982) or presumably Ireland. Here, where there are clear institutional differences between Secondary/Grammar and Vocational/Technical schools, as well as curricular and certification differences, starting social background and ability inequalities — which are important in allocating pupils to schools, or streams or tracks within schools — become considerably exaggereated or reinforced in their effects. The differential chartering, labelling and socialisation effects of the different school or "track" types, reinforces originating status differences (see Heynes, 1974; Yuchtmann and Samuel, 1975; Alexander and McDill, 1976; Kerckhoff *et al.*, 1982; Shavitt, 1984; Hallinan, 1984 and 1985). Such categorical distinctions operate as "important institutionalised mechanisms for social selection and channelling as well as allocation of rewards" (Heynes, 1974, p. 449).

In addition, the segregation and differential ranking of "ability groups" within schools has clear social and social psychological effects. As Simpson (1981) argues, where school systems contain many different avenues of unrestricted achievement for pupils, pupils do not tend to cumulate consistent judgements of self worth across the different subject areas to form a single general evaluation — since individuals may excel in one area and fail or do badly in others. So, in mixed ability schools/classes, where there is considerable "setting" of optional subjects and levels, with attendant wide choice of subjects/levels, and where individual pupils are encouraged to maximally develop their individual capabilities, the various areas of individual achievement will be much less correlated than in schools organised differently.

> To the extent that classroom instruction is organised so as to create multiple performance dimensions, multiple bases for evaluating and comparing performances will exist, and global comparisons of the type providing a singular, dispersed stratification order will be inhibited (Simpson, 1981, p. 122).

(See also Blau, 1977.) Since individual pupil differences are valued and their expression facilitated in such "mixed-ability" schooling a single formalised basis of evaluating or ranking pupils does not exist.

In most streamed schools, on the other hand, the personal achievement model assumed is one of "general ability" — with pupils' different intellectual abilities seen as ordered along a single dimension. Pupils are assigned to ranked (streamed) classes on that basis, with curricula and classroom instruction allocated accordingly. Student performance in the different areas of the curriculum are constrained to coalesce, and a singular stratification order will be encouraged. Besides the administratively determined consistencies in achievement across different curricular areas, which are maximised in highly streamed schools, such schools also encourage the formation of closed class groupings of peers who take the maximum number of subjects together. As a result, reference group judgements are much more consistent and cumulative within any streamed class, and the associated peer group, than within "mixed-ability" classes or schools. In "mixed-ability" schools considerable variation exists even in the identity of peers taking the various optional subjects or levels together — and as a result neither interpersonal ranking nor individual self judgements cumulate in the same consistent way as in highly streamed schools.

The rigid streaming of classes has been shown, therefore, to have the potential for substantial differentiation or polarisation effects on pupils' achievements as well as aspiration levels, as well as on the cultural and social life and development of pupils (see Hargreaves, 1967; Lacey, 1970; Rosenbaum, 1976; Campbell, 1981; Shavitt, 1984; Oakes, 1985). The effects on lower ability classes appear to be particularly marked, especially on pupils' educational aspiration levels, on the development of differential peer group structures and culture and on levels of self confidence and educational self competence. At its most extreme many studies show that such streaming practices concentrate and constantly reinforce negative feedback for the lower streams, and senses of graded achievement and success for the upper streams, along a set of corresponding dimensions of educational achievement. Such streaming practices appear to generate in some settings highly consensual and constantly reinforcing hierarchies of achievement and educational status within the pupil population, and create cultural and social boundaries or barriers between differentially ranked classes of pupils. (See especially, Simpson, 1981; Rosenbaum, 1976.) As Kerckhoff (1986, p. 856) summarises his recent study:

> Students in remedial classes lose a great deal of ground (at least in reading), students in low ability groups lose ground and students in high ability groups increase their average performance level beyond that exhibited by comparable students in ungrouped schools settings. The losses by students in low ability groups, combined with gains by students in high ability groups, make the overall effect of ability grouping very striking.

However, not all studies come to the same conclusion as Jencks *et al.*, (1972) have pointed out.

Study Objectives

Our main objective in this study, then, is to describe some of the central dimensions of such "schooling practices" in our sample of Irish second-level schools — if possible to derive a typology of "schooling-practice" processes: the different ways in which schools organise the process of "schooling" their pupils. We are particularly interested in the way pupil categorisation/allocation practices are related to curricular allocation practices, as well as to pupil-teacher interaction over subject and level choices, etc. A second objective is to attempt to account for that variation; why some schools stream rigidly while others adopt a mixed-ability approach. Do environmental pressures or, what we could call "technical" factors — like increasing school size, particular levels of educational disadvantage in their clientele or much wider ability variances in their pupil intake — account for this school variation? Or to what extent do basically institutional factors — related essentially to the basic organisational charters of schools, or the underlying educational/mobility objectives these schools seek to achieve — determine a school's "processing" characteristics? A third objective is to evaluate some of the main educational achievement consequences of such variations in the schooling process.

The primary objective of this study, therefore, is to develop a valid and reliable typology of "schooling practices" in our sample of schools; and to do so in ways which help both to illuminate our understanding of them, as well as provide an effective conceptual tool for analytical and policy evaluation purposes. By "schooling practices" we mean: (a) those pupil categorisation and pupil-to-class allocation procedures employed by schools; (b) the differential way the curriculum is allocated to these classes of pupils; (c) the breadth and choice in the curriculum on offer and the extent to which the "choice" of schooling applied to pupils is imposed by the school or negotiated by interaction between pupils, teachers, and parents; and (d) the extent to which pupils form into "closed" class groupings. It is, therefore, a much wider and more complex process than that indicated by whether the school "streams" its pupil intake by their assessed ability levels or not. Having done so, such schools may or may not rigidly differentiate their curricula, or may or may not leave a high level of subject/level choice at the individual pupil and subject-teacher level, and may or may not "construct" classes of pupils which maximise the formation of within-class interpersonal relations and minimise interaction between different classes of pupils. As we shall see, these various dimensions of schooling practice are intimately intercorrelated, and these inter-relationships may have quite unintended consquences which may well override original intentions.

Treating Schools as Work Organisations: What Conceptual Approach to Use

Schools and schooling have been so much a part of our lives in modern society that we take both concepts ("schools" and "education"), and the organisations and processes they describe, so much for granted that our use and understanding of both words is so infused with our presumptions and values that the words themselves almost impede insight and understanding.

To speak about schools as work organisations akin to factories, state bureaucracies or business organisations might seem, therefore, to many people to be both a far-fetched and a distasteful analogy. Surely one cannot speak about "processing" human beings as one might process raw materials within a factory without seeming to deny the humanity of pupils and teachers and the special and intimate socially interactive nature of the schooling process? Obviously it is not our wish to do either. In fact, quite the contrary. Our intention is to seek additional insight into the ways in which schools as organised work systems come to decisions which in large part shape and form the humanity of their pupils. These "decisions" often emerge as the result of long chains of minor, apparently unconnected, choices; the eventual outcome never being directly envisaged or intended. The current "schooling process" may often, in fact, be the result of decisions made decades in the past, being kept in place more by inertia and the implicit administrative and sectional interests served rather than by the result of any conscious plan or strategy.

Even where the schooling process has been consciously organised to achieve specific objectives — like "ability grouping" to maximise achievement in examinations by the top performers — the consequences of what may appear to be minor subsidiary decision (like the rules governing the takeup of honours and pass levels, or restrictive time tabling) might well result in unintended and unwelcome student achievement or behaviour outcomes that negate the original intention.

We need, therefore, a conceptual approach which allows us both to be able to escape from the presumptions underlying our taken-for-granted views about current schooling practice, as well as provide us with the conceptual tools to explicate the underlying organisational bases of schooling decisions. Given, therefore, the wide variation in "schooling process" that we have observed we take it that the decision in favour of one particular method of "processing" or "schooling" rather than another has many features in common with analogous "processing" decisions in other kinds of organisations. We hope the reader will bear with us while we try to lay out what seems to us the most useful approach to both describing the essential common features of the process itself as well as the basic considerations that might lead organisations to choose one particular processing arrangement rather than another. We feel strongly that, used intelligently and sensitively, such a conceptual approach can be extremely useful in analysing what goes on within schools as organisations.

One of the most illuminating and influential studies of schools which treated them as very complex social systems was that by Colin Lacey (1970), in which many of the most important schooling processes emerged as unintended organisational consequences rather than as ones resulting from design.

A study of a modern British boys' grammar school, he defined it as a "professionalising" school — one acting as a community's or society's agent of socialisation and social placement, providing channels of mobility for and socialisation into the national professional and managerial class for highly selective groups of students. The grammar school itself selected its own intake and provided a very complex and differentiated socialisation experience for its intake — which, as Lacey points out, predated the school itself, in that a considerable amount of anticipatory socialisation had already occurred before entry: "the process of selection for the grammar school, from a hierarchy of junior schools, ensures that the intake to the grammar school consists of boys who have been used to playing the "best pupil" role in the junior school and who have thought of themselves as grammar school pupils" (op. cit., p. xv). Once selected, however, the grammar school rigidly differentiated its pupil intake, allocating the categorised pupils to hierarchically organised classes which were assigned different curricula and instructional programmes of varying difficulty and status.

This differentiation of pupils by their presumed learning capabilities, as well as expected adult roles, is arranged through hierarchically organised classes of pupils whose relative status is mainly a function of the school's dominant academic goals and values. This differentiation of the student body almost inevitably leads to an equivalent development of a student stratification order. Students' own peer groups gradually become almost exclusively limited to school friends and gradually, within the school, to friends within each class boundary — as these boundaries rigidify and become stratified. A polarisation of student peer cultures develops, the top class's highly attached to the school's core values, the bottom class's position developing out of its failure and alienation from the school's core values: and, therefore, tending to be quite antischool. Most of these outcomes are unintended effects of the way the school is organised. In this particular case these consequences are highly responsive to the quite severely differentiated schooling arrangements imposed by school management and supported by the teachers. An extremely complex process of peer group formation, of teacher student interaction, of attachment to and alienation from the core values and the central objectives of the school then develops in ways that were clearly unintended but were organisationally predictable (Lacey, 1970, pp. 49-94).

This very schematic outline of Lacey's model of organisational differentition and student achievement polarisation will guide much of what follows. It is, however, too restricted in scope to fit our purposes. He was dealing with a case study of an individual school. We are dealing with a national sample of all types of Irish schools — only some of which are very selective secondary schools with characteristics close to Lacey's formulation, but with almost as many which suffer badly from the "cream off" effects of such selective academic schools. Secondly, our interest is in describing and explaining the wide variety of differentiation practices that occur within Irish schools, only a small proportion of which would fit Lacey's model. Finally, we are interested in explaining why schools vary so much in their differentiation practices, as well as evaluating the consequences of such wide variation for student achievement. For this purpose we need a much more generalised organisational model than that provided by Lacey — although the insights provided by Lacey's study will inform much of the analysis, as it has so much of recent sociological work in this area. The most useful organisational model for our purposes is that proposed by Perrow (1967, 1970).

In describing the organisation of schooling we wish to focus attention on the *work* that organisations do — the way in which pupils are "processed" within the school — i.e., what Perrow (1967, 1970) calls the "technology" of the school. Although Perrow's model was mainly developed for materials processing or manufacturing concerns it has been adapted for "people processing" organisations like hospitals, schools or administrative organisations and it is, of all organisational models, the most useful and illuminating one for our purposes; i.e., for developing a critical understanding of the underlying structure of the wide range of schooling practices employed in Irish second-level schools. Since the main objective of this research is to describe and bring order to, (i.e., to "dimension") the relatively wide variance in schooling provision and practice present in Irish second-level schools the emphasis in the conceptual approach is being put on the nature of the work process employed as well as on the underlying reasons why school organisations might choose one strategy rather than another.

The Technological Perspective: Schools as Organisations

For Perrow, "organisations are viewed as systems which utilise energy in a patterned, directed effort to alter the condition of basic materials in a predetermined manner" (Perrow, 1965, p. 913). As applied to schools, viewed as "processing" organisations, pupils (the "raw material") are taken in and a series of instructional processes are applied to them so as to bring about desired learning outcomes — the "goals" of the schools as an organisation. The technique or complex of techniques employed to alter the basic "raw materials" (pupils) to achieve anticipated goals — "how work is done" — is the main defining characteristic of organisations according to Perrow (1965, p. 916).

Two aspects of this work process are of critical importance.

(1) the number of "exceptional cases" encountered in the work, or the degree to which these do not allow the creation of routinised work

solutions. Such "exceptions" may be due to the nature of the raw material itself — the objective degree of variation in it; but more frequently it is due to the nature of the concepts and values applied to the "measurement" of that variation. As to organisations dealing with human beings — like schools — the extent to which individual pupils are treated as fitting within a small set of educable categories, or considered as unique individual personalities, is more a function of educational philosophy or ideology than any "objective" variation involved. At one extreme there are schools, for instance, where classifying their "raw material" into a small number of types, each of which is "schooled" differently, is a totally unproblematic process. The validity of the procedure is completely taken for granted. But at the other extreme are a small number of schools where the unique personality of each child is paid attention to, and such ways of "typing" pupils and assigning such pupil types to selected curricula are rejected as almost immoral.

(2)   The nature of the "search process" which is undertaken by the individual "worker" in deciding what process is applied to what type of material. (a) At one extreme such work process decisions are not left to the individual worker, the process being decided upon centrally and its application has become highly routinised. At this extreme the "search process" is conducted on a logical analytical basis, using "well understood" and widely accepted models of analysis agreed within the organisation. Here an unquestioned routinisation of the schooling process often occurs. (b) But at the other extreme, where each individual pupil is treated as a "special case", the "search process" is one which draws on the residue of unanalysed experience, intuition or professional competence of workers (teachers), and decisions are negotiated at an interpersonal pupil-teacher level.

Treating schools as organisations, therefore, two aspects of their "technology" are important: the degree to which individual pupils are perceived as "exceptional cases", or as belonging to one of a small number of educable categories using widely accepted typologies; and the nature of the "search process" itself, particularly the degree to which processing exceptions when they occur can be analysed or dealt with in an administratively centralised and routinised manner. Generally, the greater the extent to which pupils are categorised rigidly using familiar and widely accepted categories, the more likely it is that there will be a routinised or centrally organised "search process". The greater the use of streaming/tracking procedures within schools, for instance, the lower the choice of subjects/levels left at the individual pupil-teacher-parent level.

Most organisations — and schools are no exception — seek to minimise "work effort" and, therefore, tend to routinise or normalise: to reduce the number of "exceptional cases" and the complexity and difficulty of the "search process". There will be a tendency, therefore, to order and categorise pupils, and to simplify and routinise the whole work process applied to them. Increasing experience and knowledge will be used to improve efficiency and reduce the tension, worries and work effort involved in the whole work process; i.e., to reduce the extent of individuality perceived in the "raw material" and to simplify the complexity of the "search process" applied. The reduction of uncertainty, ambiguity and unpredictability in the work process becomes an aim or interest to most workers involved. Schools are subject to those pressures like any other organisation, and their inchoate and hidden effects can often be as important as conscious plans in shaping an organisation.

There is a clear relationship between the nature of the "work process" or task-structure of organisations like schools and the nature and structure of interpersonal relationships within them, as well as the co-ordination and control of work activities. In cases where many "exceptional cases" occur, or are allowed to occur, in the basic "raw materials" (pupils); and where the nature of the individual case is not "well understood", so presenting many occasions for exceptional handling; the search process cannot be conducted using centralised and formal methods. The discretion of those who do the work in this case must be high. And the co-ordination of work in such cases can only be through consultation, feedback, discussion, etc. In schools, for example, where pupil ability categories are not employed and each pupil is treated as a special case to be catered for individually, it is not possible to routinise or centralise decisions. Here high teacher/pupil/parent involvement and autonomy is necessary. On the other hand, in cases where there is perceived to be a uniform, stable pupil intake ("raw materials"), whose relevant nature is perceived as well understood, thus enabling pupils to be handled with few exceptions occurring (and the few exceptions which do occur can be handled centrally and formally), one might expect to find lower discretion among teachers, a well programmed production process with a very clearcut division of labour and co-ordination of work effort through formal planning and a centrally controlled and programmed structure of tasks and roles. For example, in schools which stream their pupil intake rigidly and treat the resultant ability categories as non-problematic, schooling options are to a large extent centrally controlled or determined with little discretion left at a pupil-teacher level.

Where the "task structure" on the other hand is flexible and polycentric — e.g., mixed-ability classes with considerable subject/level choices at pupil/

teacher level – this has obvious implications for both the division of labour and hierarchical structure of the school: it is looser and more flexible. But also in this kind of school one would expect to find substantial discussion about the values, goals and direction of development of the organisation – i.e., an "open system" perspective. The basis of interaction in a more rigid, controlled and task structured school on the other hand, would be more likely to be focused on work or task identification and implementation, with highly routinised procedures and a more hierarchical structure. Going in a "streaming" or "mixed-ability" direction is likely, therefore, to have very complex, emergent, organisational effects.

To conclude, therefore, what Perrow's perspective suggests is that particular school organisation decisions about its "work process" have clear implications for other aspects of its operation – which may not only be unforeseen but may even be unwelcome when the original decisions were being taken, particularly implications for the nature of social relations within the school. In addition it emphasises the role of "choice" in establishing a school's working process. The importance of choice is brought out much more clearly by Child (1972), however.

Strategic Choice

Perrow's emphasis on the nature of the "transforming" work process within organisations also implicitly emphasises the role of choice and power within organisations in determining the work process outcomes. The model of "strategic choice" proposed by Child (1972), complements Perrow's analysis in many respects. Child suggests that a major factor which had been ignored by earlier theories about organisations, including the technology model, is "the essentially political process, whereby power holders within organisations decide upon courses of strategic action" (1972, p. 1). Child takes his concept of "strategy" from Chandler, who defines it as "the determination of the basic long-term goals and objectives of an enterprise, and the adoption of courses of action and the allocation of resources necessary for carrying out these goals" (Chandler, 1962, p. 13). Thus, changes in the size, environment and technology of an organisation can stem from an unplanned adaptation to environmental pressures or from conscious modifications of such long-term goals to changing environments, as well as from strategic choices about how to achieve these changing goals. According to Child, the conditions of environment, size and technology – previously seen as some of the main determinants of organisational function – can be seen as multiple points of reference or constraint in the process of strategic decision-making – not, in themselves, determining the organisational outcomes. And in many respects, in any case, size, environment and technology are themselves open to choice. For example, schools *chose* not to grow beyond a particular size or, alternatively, *chose* an aggressive expansionist policy as the total number of pupils seeking post-primary education expanded rapidly over the 1970s. Many schools also clearly planned what kind of teachers to employ and what kind of subjects to add to the curriculum as pupil numbers increased; others, however, showed no evidence whatsoever of planning in this expansionist period (see Hannan, Breen *et al.*, 1983, pp. 198-218).

Arguments placing primary importance on environmental factors in organisational functioning, for instance, according to Child, fail to take account of decisionmakers' ability to take positive steps to define and manipulate their own corners of the environment. For example, schools can often carve out their own particular environments with respect to clientele: i.e., fee paying or selective but "free" Secondary schools. Furthermore, depending upon their goals, decisionmakers may choose either to ignore or restrain certain developments within the environment. Aldrich and Pfeffer (1976), in what they term the "Resource Dependence Model", point out the importance of environmental contingencies and constraints, but emphasise the importance of the exercise of strategic choice between various courses of action. Madaus, *et al.*, (1979, 1980), also point out that what schools choose to do with their resources and facilities is as critical as the presence or amount of such resources and facilities.

Thus, to an important extent, the "choices" made by an organisation's decisionmakers are extremely important "as to where the organisation's operations shall be located, the clientele it shall serve, or the types of employee it shall recruit determine the limits of its environment — that is, to the environment significant for the functions which the organisation performs" (Child, 1972, p. 10). Boundaries between an organisation and its environment are further defined by the kinds of relationships which decisionmakers choose to enter with equivalents in other organisations. Child suggests that in view of all these essentially strategic and political factors, environmental conditions cannot be regarded as a direct source of variation in organisation structure. Child similarly sees size and technology as being a function of choice, rather than being primarily constraints on choice. Taking Perrow's model, for example, the definition of the nature of the raw material (and the subsequent technological implications of such a definition) often lies in the hands of certain decisionmakers within the organisation. Strategic choice, then, must be incorporated into any theory of organisations, according to Child, if one is to recognise "the essentially political process in which constraints and opportunities are functions of power exercised by decisionmakers in the light of ideological values" (1972, p. 16).

An important criticism of Child's model is that it assumes that decisionmakers are easily identifiable, and that goals are easily determined, and not conflicting. With regard to the latter, and particularly in relation to educational organisations, the determination of clear goals is likely to be a problematic task. "The education policy formation system deals with complex multi-dimensional problems. Its goals are instrumental and expressive, some of them are tangible and some intangible and difficult to define in operational terms. Some of the goals lack general consensus and conflicting views prevail about what goals to pursue and in which priority" (Elbaim-Prior, 1973).

Perrow's distinction between "official goals" and "operative goals" (1961, p. 885) provides a useful framework for dealing with this problem. Official goals are often purposely vague and general. They do not generally closely reflect actual ongoing work and behaviour within the organisation. They do not specify with any clarity the way in which choices among alternative ways of achieving even official goals are to be made; not to mention priority amongst multiple goals, whether official or unofficial, pursued by different groups within the organisation (i.e., the "operative goals" of different groups). And characteristics of the chosen "technology" or work process, according to Perrow will itself have a determining influence on the identity of the controlling group in the organisation; who, in turn, will have a substantial influence on any proposed changes in operative goals. Thus, in organisations where the production of goods or services cannot be carried out in a routinised manner, the dominant group is likely to be the relevant professionals — for example in acute hospitals. Where the production process is routinisable, control will most probably be in the hands of the more experienced and senior administrators — as in most administrative organisations, for instance.

In the case of schools, therefore, some of the main characteristics of the work process are chosen, not determined. But, once a particular model of schooling has been adopted — for example, rigid streaming — that solution has a substantial influence on who the main influential groups or important actors in the school will be, as well as the nature of social relations, and of authority or power relationships within the school.

In the discussion thus far a number of separate dimensions of the schooling (work) process have been dealt with:

(i) The way the pupil intake, the school's "raw material", is understood, described and categorised. Schools obviously vary widely in the extent to which they "select" their pupil intake, as well as the way they categorise them. They also vary widely in the criteria they use in allocating pupils to different categories/classes, as well as how permeable or open class boundaries are. The nature and extent of such category differentiation is one of the main variables we are interested in in this study. (ii) Secondly is the extent to which, having created explicit pupil categories with clear boundaries between classes of pupils, the school also makes rigid and clearcut distinction between the types of subjects or levels it applies to each category of pupils. (iii) Thirdly, schools vary widely in the extent to which school decisionmakers, like the principal, vice principal or career guidance teacher, etc., monopolise the decisions as to which pupil or which category of pupils is assigned each teaching process or curricular package. In some schools this decision is centralised; in others this decision is left at the individual pupil or subject teacher level, or based on interaction between pupils, teachers and parents. At one extreme are schools which centrally impose a quite different type and level of curriculum to the top and bottom streams, while at the other extreme are schools which leave almost all such decisions to be negotiated between the individual pupil, her/his parents and individual subject teachers, etc.

Theoretically these three sets of variables are necessarily closely correlated. Rigid pupil categorisation makes little sense without subject/level distinctions being applied to different categories. If both of these distinctions hold for a school this entails both centralisation of decisionmaking and a considerable reduction of individual pupil's and individual teacher's autonomy in determining which schooling process (subject type and level, etc.) will be applied to each pupil. Such a centralisation of decisionmaking is bound to have significant effects on other areas of pupil/teacher interaction and relationships, as well, of course, as influencing the interaction of teachers with each other and with school administrators, etc. If, for instance, pupils are rigidly categorised by their perceived "ability" levels, and if the school has a widely agreed upon and well understood and standardised teaching process applied to these different "ability" groupings, very little discretion is left at the individual pupil, teacher or parent level. Such decisions as to what kind of treatment to apply to what category of pupils are made at central level by the principal, vice principal or career guidance teacher usually. The co-ordination or integration of all work activities here is made possible by a highly differentiated division of labour and by a control system which is quite hierarchical. If, on the other hand, pupils are treated as unique individuals, for whom the school tries to maximise quality and "choice of treatment", a lot of discretion has to be left to the individual pupil and the individual teacher. In this situation the co-ordination of work efforts to reach agreed goals across all teachers can only be by "feedback" or consultation: i.e., by negotiated mutual adjustment between a relatively large number of actors. The overall nature of the decisionmaking and social organisation of the school will, therefore, be highly influenced by the nature of the work process employed (Perrow, 1972). There is, then, a substantial element of choice as to which schooling strategy to employ but once chosen and put into operation, many consequent "decisions" are largely pre-empted.

The conceptual approach adopted here, therefore, views schools as organisations for getting schooling or educational work done — for mobilising, and combining resources (teachers, rooms, teaching materials, etc.) in a particular work process with the objective of bringing desired change to their intake pupils. The actual social arrangements entered into amongst people to achieve these objectives are — for analytical purposes only — seen as dependent on the work process or "technology" chosen. To a variable extent these emergent social arrangements may have educational consequences which are not intended. Child's (1972) paper combined with Perrow's (1967, 1972) conceptualisation of the work practices of an organisation allow us to examine schooling arrangements, therefore, as partly resulting from decisions taken by power holders in the light of their objectives and values, and their perception of the nature and extent of environmental constraints and resources; but partly also as determined or highly influenced by purely organisational constraints, which may not be foreseen when initial decisions are being taken.

Such central organisational "decisions", however, may have been taken a long time in the past, the school continuing in present channels with objectives and working practices which have remained unchanged, unchallenged and unproblematic for quite some time. The extent to which a school is so characterised in circumstances where the external environment, its own "market", and "educational technology", has changed considerably, indicates the dimensions of organisational adaptability and effectiveness — ones, however, not covered in this study.

Organisations generally seek to minimise uncertainty and work effort. There is a general tendency, therefore, to "make normal" the work of the school — to simplify and order, to categorise and standardise: i.e., to define a "normal" student, and a range of acceptability around the norm, to standardise and to make unproblematic the whole teaching process, routinisation being an almost inevitable tendency as organisations mature. Personnel in schools which stream their pupil intake and which differentiate the curricular offerings according to widely accepted rationales, obviously have a much easier life (with accepted "solutions" to most "problems" that arise) than those in schools which seek to treat each individual pupil as a unique personality. These have a much more elaborate and difficult "search process" to go through each time a unique schooling solution has to be found to the problem posed by the "education" of each individual pupil.

To draw this discussion to a close we may crudely categorise schools according to the two following dimensions of their basic working processes (or "technology"). Figure 1.1 provides a simplified "ideal type" classification of schools' working process or arrangements. The two diagonal cells of the table (cell A and D) provide idealised solutions.

Figure 1.1: *Basis of Categorising Schooling Arrangements*

Degree of standardisation of pupil "raw material" inputs:	*Degree of standardisation and differentiation of techniques performed on the pupil "raw material". (The "Search Process" (Perrow, 1972))*	
	(i) LOW	*(ii) HIGH*
(i) LOW:	A or Montessori or many Upper Middle Class Grammar Schools	B
(ii) HIGH:	C	D Highly streamed schools with highly differentiated and standardised curricula

Type A schools are at one extreme: where each individual pupil is treated as a unique personality, and a unique solution to her/his schooling is sought so as to maximise the achievement of the individual pupil's abilities, aptitudes and unique personal qualities. In some cases clearcut educational philosophies and teaching-learning procedures have been developed and implemented in particular schools — as in Froebel or Montessori schools, or in some upper middle class grammar schools. In these kinds of schools individual pupil and teacher choice is maximised and a considerable autonomy is left at the pupil-parent-teacher interaction level.

At the other extreme are the Type D schools — with highly standardised (streamed) categories of pupils and highly differentiated curricula applied to each class of pupils. In these kinds of schools very little leeway is left at the individual pupil-teacher level: who teaches what class, and which pupil takes what subject or teacher is, by and large, determined by central decisionmakers.

These are obviously two extreme examples. It is also possible to get a moderate to high degree of pupil categorisation by ability and yet to allow a moderate degree of choice to each streamed class or category of pupil — i.e., Type C schools; although Type B schools cannot logically occur. The two extreme types are emphasised only to illustrate the intrinsic interrelationships amongst different dimensions of schooling practice. In Chapter 3 we will explore this in greater detail.

As we shall see below there are likely to be quite distinct social and institutional reasons why different schools make different schooling choices.

Why Do Schools Vary in Their Work Process?

In examining the choices actually made by schools about the curriculum and the type of schooling offered, it became quite clear in our earlier study (Hannan, Breen *et al.*, 1983, Chs. 4 to 7) that wide divergences occur amongst school-owning authorities in those respects — whether VECs or religious orders, or Comprehensive/Community schools. Different educational goals may be articulated in the institutional charters of the various school organisations: e.g., the Vocational Education Act of 1930 or the original charter of a religious order, etc. In addition there is variation in the regulations governing the different school types. In other words different school-owning authorities have quite different objectives or reasons for being in education in the first place, and different formal/informal constraints influence their actions. In addition the social class orientation of a school-owning authority (or the consequence of having a particular social class mix in the school intake) will also have almost inevitable consequences for the type of education provided — both in terms of the objectives being pursued, the resources available, and the outcomes expected. Sex of pupil is likely to have even more determinative effects in these respects, as was made clear in our previous report.

Some other major sources of variation are obvious: the extent of turnover in a school's management, such that schools with frequent turnover are more likely to have both more opportunities to innovate and change both the goals and means of education, but are also more likely to have closer monitoring of their work by higher authorities (the head of the religious order, for instance). Changes in the external environment of schools — by changing from being a single sex to a coed school, for instance; or changes in the intake mix of schools; or changes in the number and kind of the inflow of pupils, and so on, force constant reconsideration of curricular/institutional goals and objectives. As a result openness to innovations or new ideas in education — such as the critiques of streaming and movement toward mixed ability teaching — are more likely to be characteristic of schools which face such constant external change, or benefit by more frequent changes in senior management personnel.

We can summarise the discussion about the underlying reasons for variation in the schooling process applied within schools in terms of two contrasting sets of hypotheses: (1) *"Technical-rational"* reasons, where it is hypothesised that the underlying work process applied is "well understood" and widely accepted. Here the main reason for variation in the work process is, therefore, technical: i.e., concomitant variation in the intake "raw material" — the "ability" or aptitude ranges of pupils, with an appropriate and widely agreed upon work process applied to each defined ability/aptitude category. Here, therefore, the wider the ability/aptitude and social class range in the pupil intake the greater the differentiation made amongst pupils and the greater the associated differentiation in the curricula applied. So, larger schools and schools with wider ability and social class intakes will force schools toward differentiation and standardisation of their work processes and operating procedures. If we assume that the schooling process applied is an outcome of rational-technical decisionmaking, the underlying rationalities for which are widely accepted amongst school decisionmakers, then the different "techniques" or work processes used by schools will be applied in the same way and for the same set of "technical" reasons across all/most schools. These "technical-rational" reasons are usually the main reasons given by school authorities for streaming or curricular differentiation.

The educational process, however, is *not* based on such a scientifically or technically validated methodology in this sense at all. So to universally apply such a view — given its objective invalidity — would require a very high degree of value and belief consensus on a particular set of educational/pedagogical theories amongst school decisionmakers. This, in fact, does not exist. Such a consistent set of beliefs may, however, exist within particular organised groups of schools, particularly those which have a central organising authority.

(2) The alternative view is that the "schooling process" is not well understood or universally "rational" in the above sense. To be valid, such a "technology" would have to be based on an explicitly articulated and scientifically validated theory about the schooling process which had been shown to have clearly predictable outcomes with different types of inputs and work processes, etc. This is not so. On the contrary, it is mainly *social or institutional forces* which determine which "schooling process" is applied to what types of pupil intake. Whereas medicine and hospital practice, for instance, to a large degree fits the former model — or through the power and influence of organised professional bodies has been made to fit that model — schooling practice is not of the same order. The relevant collectivity, usually the State, lays down the broad framework of rules and procedures which govern education and which enforce compulsory adherence to these standards both by the general public — through compulsory attendance laws, for instance — and through school regulations. Within this broad framework of provisions and regulations, however, individual schools have wide freedom of choice. Within these degrees of freedom it is mainly structured differences in the philosophical and ideological approaches to education, and the roles that the relevant school or schools play in social and occupational placement for their pupils, that mainly determine "technological" choice. What school decisionmakers conceive to be the basic social categories into which their pupil intake are sorted (by gender, social class, "ability"/"aptitude", etc.), as well as the, usually implicit, social destinations toward which these pupil categories

are assumed to be moving (Leaving Cert./University, or early dropout and unemployment), are the main factors determining the degree of standardisation of the schooling process.

Within this latter perspective, schools are seen as organisations with unclear and varying goals, conflicting demands, a "technology" or work process whose characteristics and outcomes are unclear, and neither fully predictable nor can they be scientifically validated. Within this perspective the pursuit of a clear set of underlying goals for the organisation is not its central defining characteristic or the driving force behind the work performed. Besides the unintended organisational consequences of explicit school organisation (Lacey, 1970) that emerge over time school organisational behaviour is in large part *institutionally* determined, first by conformity to State determined regulations and provisions (about the curriculum, the qualifications of the teachers employed, the timetable, the nature of school facilities, etc., as well as a minimum set of regulations for grading and categorising pupils); secondly, within the wide range of possibilities allowed, by the founding and historically acquired "charters" or "missions" of the different school-owning authorities and the communal or societally agreed upon definitions of what it is they are supposed to be doing (see Meyer, 1970; Kamens, 1977). These "definitions" are sometimes formally or even legally defined (as in the 1930 Vocational Education Act and Memo V40), but more often than not they are the "social residues" or "implicit charters" resulting from the historically acquired roles which different schools or different school-owning authorities have carved out for themselves. In Chapter 2 we examine these different institutional charters and historically acquired roles in detail but here we want to indicate their main characteristics and implications.

Meyer and Rowan (1977, 1980) proposed, rather radically, that schools have their greatest effect not through the socialisation effects they have on the content of knowledge, attitudes and skills transmitted to their pupils but by the school's legitimising role in bestowing a new educational and social status on graduating pupils, or by oversight on early school leavers. Schools have agreed "chartering rights" — roles in sorting and categorising each generation of new adult entrants to the society — which they have been given by, or have acquired within, their society. And, over the past century particularly, different types of second-level schools have been publicly assigned, or have acquired, different roles in these respects which are publicly recognised within the society.

The educational process is not, therefore, determined by "rational-technical" responses to market demands or even to State regulation. Such State regulations as exist leave wide degrees of freedom to individual schools. Nor is the schooling process applied a necessary technical response to the variance in the educable characteristics of pupil input, nor even the technical requirements of desired "outputs". Education, unlike medicine, is not based on scientifically or technically validated and rationalised procedures and bodies of knowledge which are mediated through a powerful professionally organised body. Such a "technically" based consensus on "processing" is not present in education and, even if it was, the teaching "profession" is not sufficiently powerfully organised to impose such a unified practice.

In the Irish case three different school types exist with quite different "chartering rights" and educational and social objectives: Secondary (grammar) schools, Vocational schools and Comprehensive/Community Schools.

In 1980/81 around 56 per cent of boys and 74 per cent of girls went on from Primary to Secondary schools. Although privately owned and managed, these schools are mainly financed and considerably regulated by the State. Their origins — for a minority of upper middle class fee-paying schools, but also a number of diocesan schools — go back as far as the eighteenth century: as either élite upper class or upper middle class "prep" schools or as Catholic junior religious seminaries. Almost universally they provide an academic type education suitable for third-level (University) entry or for direct entry to intermediate level non-manual occupations which do not require third-level qualifications for entry: i.e., "professionalising" schools in Lacey's (1970) sense.

Almost half the boys going to Secondary schools attend ones run by the Christian Brothers. Their founding charter and historically acquired educational function is now directed mainly to educating either upper working class (the education of the poor being one of their founding goals) or lower middle class pupils, using primarily an academic curriculum. They provide an important channel for upward social mobility for able working class boys or boys from small farming backgrounds. Similarly nearly half of Secondary school girls attend schools run by the Mercy order — whose founding charter and acquired educational role is, in many respects, similar to that of the Christian Brothers. But both of these teaching orders have over time acquired particular social class clienteles and orientations, and social mobility functions, which are not always in keeping with their charters but which nevertheless are quite distinct from other religious orders. The Jesuits, for instance, or the minority of Protestant schools, have founding charters, class orientations and acquired social mobility or class maintenance roles which are quite different from the former two religious orders.

Vocational schools cater for around a third of the entry cohort of boys but only 17 per cent of girls. As their original founding charter (the Vocational Education Act, 1930 and Memorandum V40, 1942) intended and as their gradually acquired role clearly manifested, Vocational schools provided "continuation education" and vocational preparation courses for boys entering mainly skilled manual and technical occupations and for girls entering clerical and service employment in the age group 14-16. Prior to 1967 they were, in fact, precluded from providing the sort of academic education characteristic of the Secondary school sector. However, from 1967 onwards, but gathering momentum from the mid-1970s, Vocational schools have come increasingly to acquire a much more comprehensive curriculum and educational function — teaching the full set of academic courses up to the Leaving Certificate where the size of school is sufficient to provide the necessary resources (see Hannan, Breen *et al.*, 1983, pp. 84-92; Coolahan, 1981; Atkinson, 1969).

The newer "Comprehensive" and "Community" schools are fully publicly-owned like Vocational schools, except that they are not under the control of local educational authorities. In design and function they approximate closely the Comprehensive school systems of Britian and the Continent (see Yates, 1966; Kelly, 1978). They are usually situated in "greenfield sites" on the edges of growing urban areas, or result from amalgamations of Secondary and Vocational schools in small towns throughout the country. They cater for roughly 10 per cent of all second-level pupils — though the proportion is growing rapidly. They apper to have a clear comprehensive curricular and instructional philosophy which is shared amongst nearly all the Community/ Comprehensive schools. Only the Vocational schools, when they get equally large, approach the same type of curricular comprehensiveness (see Hannan, Breen *et al.*, 1983).

Amongst our second-level schools, therefore, there are three separate institutional types with different historical roots. These have quite distinct initiating charters and different social and educational objectives. They also tend to have different governing structures and relationships with the State's Department of Education; and, to a large extent, different outcomes. What is most relevant — from the point of view of the "work process" carried out within them — is that they have historically oriented themselves toward different social groups and play different social placement or social mobility roles. In other words these different school types, either through their initial explicit "charters", or arising from their historically acquired roles within their local communities, serve quite distinct educational and social mobility functions: expediting the mobility of able working or lower middle class youth in some cases, consolidating the position of the upper middle class in other situations, or ensuring access to skilled manual apprenticeships or clerical jobs for pupils from working class or small farm origins in other cases. As a result it is very likely that the internal working arrangements of these schools — their "technology" — will closely reflect, or be predicated upon these different "charters" or "missions". Within this framework, therefore, internal work practices will reflect these differential institutional forces and the larger social role of the school, rather than be the result of straightforward "technical" determinations.

To conclude, then, we assume that under "technical-rational" assumptions the degree of standardisation of pupils/curricula, and the associated degree of centralisation of schooling process decisionmaking, would be a function of:

(i)   Size of school: the larger the school, or the number of pupils accepted in any one year, the greater the differentiation.

(ii) Extent of variance in the ability levels of pupils, or in the social class of the pupil intake: the greater the variance the greater the differentiation.

(iii) Extent to which the school serves all pupils in the area or community, or occupies only one niche for itself amongst a number of schools competing for pupils in the same catchment area: the greater the specialisation the lesser the differentiation.

Under institutional assumptions on the other hand, we would expect that such variation in the degree of standardisation of the schooling process is a function of:

(a)   The explicit "charter" of the governing authority of the school.

(b)   The main social placement (mobility) function of the school: i.e., the "mission", or social objectives served by the school, and the associated need to segregate pupils on the basis of the different educational channels or socialisation processes perceived as being required to serve a number of different objectives.

(c)   The existence of an organised consensus on the philosophical or conceptual approaches to instructing/learning within an organised set of schools — for example, Christian Brothers, Community schools, Vocational schools. We would expect, therefore, much greater consensus amongst such an organised grouping of schools on the schooling process, than across a similar set of schools owned by different authorities, but with the same pupil intake characteristics.

(d)   The sex of the pupil body and the predominant sex of the teaching body. Boys' education, for instance, is generally treated in Ireland in a much more instrumental, purposeful and in a more technically directed way than is girls' education. The latter is perceived by school authorities, parents and teachers to serve much wider and less directly occupationally relevant functions (Hannan, Breen et al., 1983). So, even given the same ability and social class ranges, one would predict much less standardisation of, and variance in, the schooling process in girls' than in boys' schools.

Data and Methods

The data used to test the falsity or validity of these hypotheses come from the detailed national survey of post-primary schools carried out for the *Schooling and Sex Roles* study in 1981. Detailed information was obtained from a national sample of 95 post-primary schools which were randomly selected to be representative of all Irish post-primary schools. (See Hannan, Breen *et al.*, 1983, pp. 26-29.)

Ninety five principals and 68 career guidance teachers were intensively interviewed about the provision and organisation of their schools, and almost 10,000 pupils in these schools were interviewed about their perceptions and experience of schooling in all of these schools. The coverage and accuracy of the information provided was cross-checked and this information was supplemented where necessary from other sources.

The interviews with principals and career guidance teachers were extremely detailed, the interviews varying in length from 1½ to 2½ hours for the more detailed interviews with principals. It is mainly this information given by principals — cross-checked where possible against information provided by career guidance teachers — that provides the main data for this study. The principal's questionnaire is provided in Appendix 1. It provided information on 8 main areas of school functioning: (a) the guiding philosophies and goals of the organisation operating the school (Qs 6-12); (b) the organisation and decisionmaking structure of the school (Qs 13-19); (c) the teaching and other resources of the school and their organisation (Qs 20-30); (d) curricular provision and its allocation rules (Qs 31-39, 48-52, 55, 61-62, 69); (e) pupil selection and allocation criteria (Qs 40-47, 53, 54-60); (f) pupil organisation and control (Qs 64-70); (g) pupil intake characteristics (Qs 71-75); (h) parental involvement in schools (Qs 76-77); and (i) principal's own educational career, etc. (Qs 78-87). The quality of the information provided appeared to be very high, but its validity was assessed by extensive cross-checking. In many cases, however, in the following analyses we use indices or scales constructed from these responses rather than raw responses — so that only data that are consistent and reliable, and have high cross validity are used. We are then highly confident of the reliability and validity of the data available. These interviews with principals provide most of the detailed results for Chapters 3 and 4 and much of Chapter 5.

For the detailed analyses of the effects of streaming and curricular differentiation in Chapter 5 we use, in addition, data provided by the national sample of Intermediate and Leaving Certificate pupils interviewed in 1981: a total of 5,166 Intermediate Certificate and 3,967 Leaving Certificate pupils (see Hannan, Breen *et al.*, 1983, pp. 27-29, for details of samples and copy of interview schedule, pp. 332-351).

Chapter 2

PART I

THE INSTITUTIONAL BASES OF THE SECOND-LEVEL SYSTEM

Our main objective in this chapter is to explicate the institutional bases of second-level schooling in Ireland which underlie the varying tendencies of schools to differentiate their schooling processes. We first deal with the different founding "charters" which Secondary, Vocational and Comprehensive/Community schools have: the explicit goals or objectives they were set up to achieve; and the different curricular, instructional and pupil categorisation processes implied by these charters. Secondly, we examine the distinct roles or "missions" which different Secondary schools have acquired over time as they adjusted or adapted to emerging environmental "niches": e.g., changes in their pupil composition, changes in parental demand or expectations, and changes in the wider economic and institutional "demands" about the nature of their outputs. These different emergent roles, or functions, that schools acquire are likely to be just as important as explicit charters in influencing the type of education they provide.

The main sources of information used will be previously published work on the history and structure of the second-level system (mainly Atkinson, 1969; McElligott, 1966; Coolahan, 1981), and new information gathered in the course of our previous study (Hannan, Breen *et al.*, 1983) from school Principals and Career Guidance teachers. In addition, we carried out extensive interviews with a large number of key informants and influential persons in the educational sector on the nature and characteristics of the educational system. And finally, data on the social composition, educational and occupational characteristics and achievements of pupils in a national sample of second-level schools will be used. Part II of this chapter reports the results of detailed interviews and surveys about these issues carried out with a national sample of school decisionmakers and pupils in 1980.

This informational base will be interpreted primarily using a conceptual framework which views schools and schooling not as technically determined organisational responses to "market forces", but rather as institutions with varying "charters" adapting or fitting their behaviour to societal or institutional expectations, regulatory demands and certification rules. It is our hypothesis, therefore, that it is mainly because different types of second-level schools have different charters, vary systematically in their "choice" of pupil intake, and have chosen or acquired different educational and social placement functions in the society that they differ so widely in their schooling processes. Such variations in "charters" and functions is highly predictive of the extent to which schools differentiate their pupil intake and their curricular offerings, and aim to bestow quite different types of educational status outcomes on their varying pupil categories.

Such wide variance between schools in their schooling process is, we suggest, mainly a function of the way in which school decisionmakers interpret their chartering, classification and certification functions. So within the organisational perspective adopted here, the type of schooling provided is regarded mainly as an outcome of the interaction of the following four inter-linked variables:

1.   The main educational and social objectives sought by the school authorities; or the educational outcomes toward which the school is directed or around which it is organised. This is mainly determined by its "chartered" or institutional objectives.

2.   The sex of the pupils involved. Girls' schools, as we saw in the previous report (Hannan, Breen *et al.*, 1983) aim to achieve quite different outcomes and they utilise quite different curricula and educational allocation processes than boys' or coed schools. The pressure to sort, categorise, differentiate or specialise amongst girls is significantly lower than amongst boys.

3.   The main social class orientation of the school — indicated by the predominant social class origins of the pupil body. Schools providing for upper middle class pupils provide a quite different educational process to those provided for lower working class pupils. Irish schools are quite highly differentiated in their social class intakes.

4.   The extent to which such decisions as the above, as well as decisions such as the type of streaming practices adopted by the individual school, remain with the principal or at the individual school level. Individual schools which are part of larger corporate bodies are often constrained by decisions taken by superordinate authorities or highly influenced by dominant and often taken-for-granted practices within the larger organisation.

Our main argument then is that it is the particular organisation of these variables within a school — sex, social class, educational goals and objectives pursued, and the extent of incorporation of principals within larger organisations with varying chartered objectives — that explains the type of schooling process supplied. In the following we will examine each of these characteristics of schools in turn using the detailed data available from our national post-primary schools' study. But first we provide a brief historical sketch of the different origins and "chartering" objectives of different types of Secondary schools, as well as Vocational and Community schools.

Institutional Diversity: Historical Origins and Current Structure

Like many other European countries, Ireland has a number of parallel second-level school systems each of which has distinct historical origins and different educational functions (Yates, 1966; Archer, 1979; Elvin, 1981). The main distinction lies between the publicly owned and maintained schools, most of relatively recent origin — the Vocational, Comprehensive and Community schools — and the much older privately owned, independent, but now almost exclusively publicly funded, Secondary schools.

This tripartite system has developed or, more accurately, emerged without any clear overall plan or centrally determined governmental control. Unlike British educational reform, for instance (Norwood Report, 1941), the allocation of children to the different school types locally has never been attempted through public or corporate control. Nor has such selection been based on any educational or pedagogical theory as in Britain or Israel where pupils are (or were) assessed publicly on their general academic ability and previous attainments (see Yates, 1966; Kelly, 1978; Grey, McPherson and Raafe, 1983); although such an implicit policy did exist up to the 1960s reforms when pupils had to pass the Primary Certificate examination (or an equivalent) to be a "recognised pupil" in a Secondary school.

In most communities or catchment areas, therefore, a division of labour emerges from the free competition of these different schools with each other on the basis of class, sex and educational specialisation. The Secondary schools mainly furnish places for children from dominantly middle class or upwardly mobile working class families. They provide a general or academic education biassed toward third-level entry, and perceived as a gateway toward professional or white-collar employment. Vocational schools cater dispro-portionately for children from working class origins or from small farm origins. Traditionally they oriented their programmes for the higher achievers toward achieving skilled manual apprenticeships for boys and clerical positions for girls. Middle class parents generally tend to see these schools as inferior substitutes for their children. Comprehensive and Community schools have quite comprehensive catchments and serve comprehensive educational objectives.

Unlike Britain, however, places available in Secondary (grammar) type schools have not been explicitly nor publicly rationed. Indeed since the rapid expansion of second-level education from the late 1960s onwards the great bulk of the increase in participation has occurred in Secondary schools (Hannan, Breen *et al.*, 1983, pp. 88-115). Only in boys' Secondary schools has rationing occurred — mainly because they did not expand their provision at anything like the same pace as girls' or coed Secondary schools.

Between 1963 and 1980 for instance, Secondary schools increased their intake of pupils from 43 to 65 per cent of the total cohort leaving Primary schools, taking slightly more girls than boys. Vocational schools simply held their share of around one-third of the boys' cohort but lost out significantly amongst girls, dropping from about a quarter to less than one-sixth of the entry cohort. In the same period Comprehensive and Community schools increased their share of the intake from 0 to 10 per cent of the cohort. In other words, the growth in the number and proportion of the cohort going on to second-level schools over the past 20 years has been almost exclusively catered for by the expansion of the privately-owned Secondary school sector, which provides a much more academically directed education than either of the other two school types. The enormous expansion in the State's investment in second-level education then has mostly been handed over to be managed by private Secondary schools which are not directly under public control.

Almost a third of the cohort did not go on to second-level schools at all in the mid-1960s. These were primarily from working class and small farm origins and also suffered from more serious educational disabilities than those who had gone on (OECD, 1966; Rudd, 1972; Swan, 1978). Since Vocational and Secondary schools were distinguished by quite different social class and educational disability clienteles in the 1960s it is very likely that the bulk of those lower ability and lower social status children, who had previously dropped out at primary level, went on to the Vocational rather than the Secondary schools. So that over time it is likely that the Vocational school system has, in relative terms, become more disadvantaged.

In the following sections we examine each of these three different school types in turn — paying particular attention to their different institutional origins and current practices.

Secondary Schools

Previous to the relaxation of the Penal Laws in the 1780s Secondary education remained under the exclusive control of the established Anglican (Church of Ireland) Church. The relatively small number of Protestant schools in the country catered almost exclusively for the Protestant upper and upper middle class, providing a classic grammar school type of education which, besides preparing people for orders, taught for entry to professional and Government service as well as solidifying the religious and cultural position of the upper middle class (see Atkinson, 1969; McElligott, 1966). With the relaxation of the Penal Laws, Catholic schools started to be founded. From the late eighteenth century these were mainly established by the Catholic diocesan authorities and by indigenously developed religious congregations like the Christian Brothers and the Mercy and Presentation Sisters. Most Protestant schools continued to be supported by the State in the form of land grants, rents, etc., and funds from religious taxes, and there continued a relatively close relationship between the State and the established church in which an anti-Catholic and anglicising educational bias was clearly present. As a result Catholic education (and to some extent Presbyterian education) developed in part reaction to what was seen as the religious and cultural proselytising role of the State-supported system.

Throughout the nineteenth century the fear that education might become a State monopoly — one that was perceived by Catholic authorities as both anti-Catholic and anti-Irish — underlay many of the struggles over educational control. And that persistent underlying conflict to a large extent explains the origins of our peculiar Church-State system of shared control of second-level education in Ireland today. With no State endowment both the diocesan authorities and the religious congregations had to find the resources themselves to fund and staff second-level schools. It was mainly amongst the recruits to the new Irish religious teaching congregation, as well as amongst other Catholic religious orders fleeing persecution in France and seeking members and refuge in Ireland, that the Catholic religious authorities found the trained and disciplined manpower and resources to expand their educational provision. (See McElligott, 1966, pp. 56-98; and Atkinson, 1969, pp. 73-89.) It was, therefore, the establishment and rapid growth of the Catholic religious orders and congregations in Ireland in the nineteenth century that explains the growth of second-level education and indeed much of primary education for the Catholic population of the country. Such school personnel were highly committed, highly disciplined and single minded in the pursuit of educational goals. It was a cheap, voluntary and locally-funded method of schooling with minimal State support until the 1870s. It worked very closely with the local clergy and bishops and generally had an uneasy, if not hostile, relationship to the State. Nevertheless, it developed a high level of commitment to serve the public good. And over time it also developed an education which had a very close relationship to public service occupational requirements — particularly after the reforms of civil and public service entry in the second half of the nineteenth century, as well as the growth of the public examination system.

The 1878 Intermediate Education Act gave such schools for the first time a steady, though frugal, financial support and established second-level education in Ireland on a solid foundation. It centralised and standardised the curriculum and examination system and publicly validated educational provision that was in agreement with the Act's provisions. At the same time through maintaining an "at arms length" relationship with the school authorities it left the school under almost complete private control. The State determined and controlled curricula and set examinations centrally. It paid for education through examination results initially, later through the agency of "recognised pupils" — of a specific standard and following specified curricula. Through a common set of rules and regulations (in modern times "The Rules and Programmes" for Secondary schools) governing pupil categories and characteristics, as well as subject and timetable requirements, it effectively controlled the structure and nature of curricula. And through guaranteeing uniform standards in courses, facilities and examinations — through controlling the examination system and, later, through public school inspectors — the State standardised and centralised the Secondary education system. And it did this without taking any of the schools into public control or without exerting any local or central control over entry to the Secondary schools — except in terms of entering pupils having to meet certain minimum educational standards.

And it is this peculiar relationship between Secondary schools and the State which, once they conform to the rules and regulations set by the State, they remain publicly funded but privately controlled, remains true up to the present day. Public policy on second-level education has mainly evolved, therefore, through successive compromises between the State and the different private and religious interests involved in education. Such a relationship at its earlier stage provided an extensive Secondary education system at minimal public cost, staffed by highly committed professional teachers who generally worked tirelessly for the benefit of the community as a whole in ways that would generally have been much less elitist than was true of British grammar school education, for instance.

Such a system, however, does not allow for corporate control or indeed influence over education — as to who is educated, where and how, for example. As a result substantial social class and ability selectivities occur amongst schools due to individual parental choice and individual school decisions — not on the basis of any local or central authority making such decisions. Also, the specific professional powers and responsibilities of lay teachers within schools — who have no local public authority to whom they are responsible and who, up to very recent times, were excluded from managerial positions in schools — have been very slow to develop. In addition there has not developed any powerful regional or national corporate educational bodies concerned mainly with professional educational or pedagogical issues. Most such bodies are concerned with mainly narrow trade union matters or, in the case of the managerial bodies, preoccupied with managerial/control issues. As a result educational policy making has evolved in a very *laissez faire* and less informed way than is true of most other European countries.

A brief discussion of six of the main orders and congregations presently involved in Irish Secondary education follows. Each controls 15 or more schools, and between them they account for 55 per cent of all Secondary schools in the country. The current role of these schools can only be understood in terms of the historical origins and circumstances from which the different congregations developed their traditional apostolate. The information contained in this section comes mainly from historical and biographical sources, but information on current educational policies comes from informal interviews with knowledgeables within the religious orders as well as from formal interviews with school Principals. In the latter case, since it would be difficult to generalise from a small number of interviews with school Principals to the whole educational philosophy of an order or congregation, only where there is general corroboration between the responses to formal interview questions and what emerges from the more unstructured interviews with knowledgeables is such generalisation deemed valid. In the following we briefly discuss these six congregations — in the order of the number of schools they control.

(i) The *Sisters of Mercy* are the largest religious congregation of women in Irish education, owning over 100 schools in Ireland. Fifteen of the schools in our sample are Mercy schools.

The first Institute of Mercy was founded in 1827 in Baggot Street, Dublin, by Catherine McAuley, a very religious and socially concerned woman of considerable means. The Baggot Street house was founded, as were all the future Houses of Mercy, "for the relief, education and protection of the poor". (Draft Constitution of Sisters of Mercy of Ireland, 1983, p. 3.) Besides the provision of a Catholic education for poor Catholic children, Catherine McAuley saw her role in terms of alleviating the suffering of the poor, the main cause of which she saw as ignorance (Burke-Savage, 1950, p. 36).

The curriculum she advocated was primarily pragmatic, geared directly to what she saw would be the requirements of a working-class woman's life. Thus, reading, writing, grammar, spelling, arithmetic and home crafts (i.e., needlework, knitting and simple cookery) comprised her curriculum (op. cit., p. 268). At an organisational level, she chose a flexible localised system of government, which would allow her congregation to adapt itself readily to local needs, unencumbered in the main by a central Mother House. So, compared to other religious congregations, individual school principals or managers would have considerable autonomy.

As we shall see later the contemporary educational philosophy of the Mercy congregation was quite clearly articulated in the present survey. In terms of clientele, there is still an obvious orientation to the under-privileged and the poor. Its educational objectives are quite pragmatic, and it places much less emphasis on formal religious training than do most of the other religious societies. Education is seen in quite instrumental terms, e.g., as a means towards getting exams, getting a job, making a living. This is seen to be best achieved by good curricular and instructional provision. Coupled with this, however, is a concern for the personal development of its pupils and thus pastoral care provisions and the "hidden curriculum" were frequently referred to. The society's working objectives tend to be fairly clearly aligned with its general apostolate, which would suggest that conscious "stocktaking" is a regular feature of its educational practice.

(ii)   The *Christian Brothers* comprise the largest single body of male religious involved in Irish Secondary education, having over 80 post-primary schools in Ireland.

The congregation was founded in Waterford in 1809 by Edmund Rice with the specific objective of educating boys from poor backgrounds. Edmund Rice (1762-1844), from a wealthy background and with a great interest in local charitable work, set up his first school for the education of poor boys in Waterford in 1803. It proved to be auspiciously successful (Atkinson, p. 78) and he quickly extended his work by establishing other schools. Religious vows were taken and in 1820 the Christian Brothers were formally established by a Papal Bull. The rule which was adopted by the Christian Brothers was one very similar to that suggested by St Jean Baptiste de la Salle.

The practical nature of the education provided is exemplified by the early curriculum. Fitzpatrick (1945) describes it as consisting of spelling, reading, arithmetic, geometry, mensuration, bookkeeping, apprenticeship for trades, catechism and moral and religious instruction. In addition to this practical orientation the Christian Brothers have always woven a distinctively nationalistic culture through a usually pragmatic curriculum. The Brothers produced their own textbooks — emphasising Irish culture, history and geography, in opposition to the National Board's textbooks which in earlier years tended to be culturally imperialistic. Almost all early observers of the Brothers, though often critical of their nationalistic orientation were highly impressed with their teaching skills and success.

Today, the Christian Brothers' schools (CBS), with few exceptions, cater mainly for a largely upper working class and lower middle class clientele. Besides catering for boys their educational orientation differs from that of the Mercy and Presentation Sisters in one other important respect. Although the social class composition of their pupil bodies is quite similar, the Christian Brothers have sought both traditionally and in recent times, to provide their pupils with the means for upward social mobility, particularly in regard to those whom they deem to have the greatest "natural ability". The Mercy and Presentation Sisters, even in their pragmatic concerns, tend not to emphasise social mobility as a goal, perhaps as a result of having a mainly female clientele.

At another level, the Christian Brothers continue to be concerned with imbuing in their pupils a knowledge and respect for formal religious faith and doctrine; but, like most boys' schools, are less likely to place such religious teaching within a "personal development" framework.

(iii) The *Presentation Sisters* run over 50 Secondary schools in Ireland, and are thus the second largest congregation of women involved in Irish education, after the Mercy Sisters.

The congregation was found by Nano Nagle who opened her first school in Cork in 1775. She was a native of the city and, like Catherine McAuley, was an idealistic young laywoman with some private wealth to finance her educational schemes for the poor of Cork. As a laywoman she worked for many years establishing schools for illiterate poor children, both boys and girls. She finally decided to adopt religious life in 1776, but only with the provision that the order would remain unenclosed. However, after her death, when application was made for pontifical approval, this was only granted on the basis that solemn vows would be taken and that the rule of enclosure would be preserved. Since Vatican II, however, the congregation has regained a structure and lifestyle more closely aligned with what their foundress envisaged.

Atkinson provides a good account of the education schema of the Presentation Sisters in their early years:

> Religious exercises took up a large part of the school day. However, the practical needs of life were emphasised by teaching not only reading and writing, but needlework, spinning and plain cookery (Atkinson, 1969, p. 75).

Today, the congregation is seen to have clear educational objectives directed at a mainly lower-middle and upper-working class clientele. In our survey, we noted that the Presentation Sisters, like most of the other female religious orders, gave educational priority to the personality development of their pupils, and thus pastoral care and individual development strategies are emphasised. However, unlike the majority of other female orders, but similar to the Mercy Sisters and in keeping with their orientation toward the education of the poor, they tend to couple such goals with quite pragmatic educational goals. As with the Mercy Sisters, there tends to be a clear articulation between all of these goals and the actual schooling process which is used in their schools.

(iv) There are 31 *Diocesan Colleges* in Ireland. Even before Catholic emancipation (1829) a range of Diocesan colleges was established, beginning in Kilkenny with St. Kieran's College in 1783 and in Carlow with St. Patrick's College in 1793. Many of these colleges started off with ecclesiastical departments where young men were prepared for the priesthood. Over time, however, they have developed essentially as grammar schools preparing boys for St. Patrick's College, Maynooth or other major seminaries, as well as providing the same type of education for other boys not going on for ordination. The diocesan schools owe their distinctive educational traditions, therefore, to their origins as minor seminaries: in particular study of the ancient classics has been important in these schools. Even Latin has, however, now been dropped from the curriculum in many of the schools. There has also always been importance attached to achievement in the public examinations. In the past, the diocesan schools operated mainly as boarding schools, requiring that pupils be of fairly well off backgrounds, although fees were subsidised by the dioceses and scholarships were also available. The Free Education Scheme, and the greater predominance of day pupils as the schools lost their unique role as junior seminaries, changed these characteristics of the diocesan schools. Today they cater for a largely middle to lower middle class clientele.

(v) The *De La Salle Brothers* have 17 second-level schools in Ireland. They originated in France towards the end of the seventeenth century; their founder being Jean Baptiste de la Salle. He devoted his life to teaching poor boys, and with a group of like-minded men, founded the "Brothers of the Christian Schools". This too is the title which Edmund Rice adopted for his Christian Brothers, and his constitution is modelled closely on theirs. The De La Salle Brothers first came to Ireland in the late eighteenth century after they had been expelled from France and dispersed to other countries. Their first Irish foundation was in Waterford. The original aims of the De La Salle Brothers, as later for the Christian Brothers, were to provide instruction in the three Rs for the poor, as well as in religious and moral education.

Pragmatism continues to be a major part of the De La Salle Brothers' educational philosophy. However, although similar to them, they tended to be more flexible than the Christian Brothers and have been involved in co-education for some time. Unlike the Christian Brothers also, they tend to stress the personal development and pastoral care of their pupils over and above their formal religious training. Their educational philosophy is generally a conscious, clearly thought out one, which is backed up by actual provisions in the schooling process, using well organised pastoral care programmes and specific curricular provisions.

Like the Christian Brothers, although dedicated to the education of the poor, their clientele tends to be dominantly middle to lower middle class.

(vi) The *Irish Sisters of Charity* run 15 schools in Ireland. Originally its foundress, Mary Aikenhead, was motivated in a similar fashion to her contemporaries, Catherine McAuley and Edmund Rice, to provide services for the poor. Inspired by the work of the French Sisters of Charity, and with a particular interest in orphans, Mary Aikenhead founded the Irish Sisters of Charity in 1815, opening her first school in Gardiner Street, Dublin in 1831. Edmund Rice and his congregation provided pedagogical advice and training for the sisters in their initial years.

Today, perhaps as a result of its less specific charter, the society does not appear to direct itself to any distinctive social group in its educational mission, unlike the Mercy and CBS congregations. Its main distinctive educational emphasis seems to be its concern with the provision of formal religious education, an emphasis unusual among the female religious congregations.

(vii) Besides these 6 main Catholic religious congregations 6 others who operate at least 5 Secondary schools each require some description: the Jesuits and Holy Ghost Fathers, the Presentation Brothers, the Holy Faith Sisters and the Loreto and St. Louis Order. The first two mentioned — Jesuits and Holy Ghost Fathers — have provided a more exclusive grammar school education, mainly for upper middle class boys, and have traditionally been associated with exclusive boarding schools. Their equivalent in girls' education are the Loreto and St. Louis orders, both catering for middle to upper middle class girls. Associated historically with expensive boarding schools they provide a quite academic education emphasising the personal and intellectual development of pupils and the development of accomplishments in music and art (see Atkinson, 1969, p. 77).

Holy Faith Sisters orientated their education to poor girls like the Mercy and Presentation Sisters, though they were also concerned with counteracting prosletism (Gertrude, 1967). The Presentation Brothers developed as an offshoot of the Christian Brothers but, although sharing the same original apostolate toward the education of the poor, they now tend on average to serve a somewhat higher status clientele; and tend also to emphasise the personal development and pastoral care of their pupils to a greater extent.

Summary — Secondary Schools

Within the Secondary sector, therefore, there is wide variation both organisationally and ideologically amongst the religious authorities running schools. Much of this variation is partly the result of the diverse origins, charters and traditions of the various religious orders, which comprise the majority of Secondary school owners and managers.

Organisationally, different religious orders or other school authorities vary in the type of authority structure within which individual schools are incorporated. These range from situations of almost complete autonomy (e.g., Protestant schools, lay Catholic schools), to situations where the school is subject to a highly centralised authority structure, as in Christian Brothers' schools for instance. Of the religious congregations with a number of schools in Ireland, the Mercy Sisters is the least centralised, operating on a federal diocesan basis; while the Christian Brothers is the most centralised. The majority of religious societies have loose hierarchical structures, with National Provincialates usually. Senior school appointments tend to be made by Provincials but, once appointed, Principals tend to enjoy a high degree of autonomy. And, in comparison to other schools, such Principals are usually appointed for set terms so that additional potential for flexibility is built into the structure in this way.

We noted two possible dimensions to a religious congregation's or Order's educational philosophy; first, its social group orientation and secondly the curricular or educational values it wishes to implement or objectives it wishes to achieve. We found that these two dimensions tended to be related to one another in an identifiable pattern. Although all of the religious orders, irrespective of their social group orientation, stressed formal religious training, (the Christian Brothers most so, the Mercy least so), those orders catering for lower middle or working class clienteles tended to emphasise pragmatic educational goals. At the other extreme, the Holy Ghost Fathers, the Jesuits, and the Loreto Sisters tend to cater for an upper middle class clientele and accordingly their educational objectives tend to stress intellectual and personal development goals to a far greater extent.

Vocational Schools

There are 245 Vocational schools in Ireland which provide the general second-level courses for 21 per cent of all pupils at second level, although over 24 per cent of pupils first entered Vocational schools (Department of Education, 1982/83). These schools, however, provide almost 80 per cent of all secretarial, pre-employment and specialist technical courses arranged for second-level pupils. Vocational schools are owned and operated by sub-committees of the relevant local authorities – the Vocational Education Committees.

The seeds of the present Vocational system were sown with the establishment of the Department of Agriculture and Technical Instruction in 1900. One of the aims of the Department was the setting up of a central technical institute in each county. The Vocational Education Act (1930) revised this system, on the basis of recommendations put forward by a Commission of

Inquiry, and thus was formed the legislative basis of the present arrangements. It was under the charters of this Act and subsequent Government memoranda (particularly Memo. V.40, 1942) that the Vocational school system was developed up to the late 1960s.

One of the main functions of the new scheme was to provide "continuation education": "to continue and supplement education provided in elementary schools, and include general and practical training in preparation for employment in trades, manufacturing, agriculture, commerce and other industrial pursuits" (Vocational Education Act, 1930). Vocational education was, therefore, explicitly geared to providing a practical post-primary education for those not going to Secondary schools. As the important Departmental Memorandum (V.40, 1942) put it — "The immediate purpose of day continuation education, as organised under the Vocational Education Act, is to prepare boys and girls who have to start early in life for the occupations which are open to them". These occupations require primarily manual skills, and "continuation courses have, therefore, a correspondingly practical bias": training for skilled and semi-skilled manual occupations for boys and in commercial courses and domestic economy for girls. In both cases the design of the courses was based on a considered evaluation of the educational and training needs of young boys and girls entering the local labour market or the domestic economy. And, this, in terms of the quite marked sex role division of labour that was current at the time, posited a quite separate education for boys and girls. Both social class and sex role distinctions were, therefore, built into the provision of Vocational education from the beginning. Up to 1966 a quite separate curriculum and examination structure existed for Vocational schools — Vocational schools not being allowed and not providing the more academic Intermediate and Leaving Certificate courses.

After 1966, however, with the integration of the Group Certificate and Intermediate Certificate curricula and the provision of these more extended and more academic courses, the relative isolation of Vocational schools markedly declined; so that by 1980/81 approximately 85 per cent of all Vocational schools provided partly or fully integrated junior and senior cycle courses. The curriculum provided, however, is still markedly different from that of the conventional Secondary schools (see Hannan, Breen et al., 1983, pp. 170-190).

That the implicit social class bias in Vocational school provision resulted in quite marked class differentials in school entry has become clear from a number of studies of schools since the 1960s (OECD, 1966; Swan, 1978). The Hannan, Breen et al., (1983) study showed marked differences even in the early 1980s (ibid, p. 90). In addition it was evident that higher ability pupils were being "creamed off" by local Secondary schools, with about

80 per cent of Vocational schools suffering disproportionately from this and taking in a highly disproportionate number of pupils with both literacy and numeracy problems (ibid, p. 91).

Amongst the educational reforms of the late 1960s the attempts to co-ordinate all local schools within a catchment area so as to avoid duplication of effort and maximise comprehensive schooling floundered because of opposition mainly from the Secondary school authorities. They felt there was little to gain in such a marriage of "unequals", where it already was the "superior" partner. As Coolahan points out: "Irish social attitudes still tended to disparage manual and practical type education, and aspiring middle class parents preferred the more prestigious academic type education which led to greater opportunities for further education and white collar employment" (Coolahan, 1981, p. 103).

What happened with the rapid educational expansion that followed the introduction of "free" education in 1967 was that Vocational schools were placed much more directly in a competitive position with local Secondary schools, and usually they (Vocational schools) lost out: except in those few (less than 1 in 4) areas where there was only a Vocational school (White Paper, 1980, p. 6). Clientele self-selection, and the more selective/competitive position of local Secondary schools, meant that Vocational schools tended to attract or receive a disproportionate intake from lower socio-economic groups as well as the least academically able pupils (Swan, 1978; Hannan, Breen et al., 1983, pp. 90-92).

The administration of the Vocational educational system lies with local Vocational Education Committees (VECs), the majority of whom are elected members of the local authority; the others being appointed from local employers, trade unions, religious and other persons interested in education (McElligott, 1966, pp. 104-106; Coolahan, 1981, pp. 96-97). Each Committee is elected or appointed by the local authority and holds office for the same period as the elected authority. Once established, however, the VEC is independent of the local authority. The administration of Vocational schools is attended to by the Chief Executive Officer (CEO) of the VEC. The CEO is responsible to the VEC for the organisation and administration of the scheme and all the schools within its jurisdiction. The chain of authority in the Vocational system then extends from individual school Principal, to Chief Executive Officer of the VEC, to the Vocational Education Committee itself. Where a Vocational school has a Board of Management this represents an intermediate step between Principal and CEO.

The teaching staff of Vocational schools is accredited to the relevant VEC not, as in Secondary schools, to the individual school. And the VEC has the power to transfer teachers, or to spread their services over more than one school within its jurisdiction. Principals and Vice-Principals, however, are appointed to a specific school. The school Principal is at all times subject to the authority of the VEC's Chief Executive Officer, who is entitled to enquire about any aspect of the Principal's administration of the school. Thus they are not as autonomous as Secondary school Principals.

Comprehensive and Community Schools

The development of Comprehensive and Community schools was based on the perceived need to "comprehensivise" local educational provision — accepting contemporary views on educational provision in Britain and Europe, as well as the need to provide post-primary schools in areas where none existed. They were expanded after abortive attempts by the State to increase effective local co-operation between the bipartite Secondary-Vocational system during the 1960s. They were set up to provide pupils with as broad and (as the name suggests) comprehensive a range of subject choices possible, within the one school building. To this end, the curricula incorporated both academic and technical subjects, and rigid streaming practices were to be avoided. In order to make wide choice economically feasible, schools had to be large. This pressure, as well as the overall liberal "ethos" of the whole comprehensive concept, led to a policy of co-education and non-selectivity. In their construction also "streaming" of pupils was explicitly rejected and priority was placed on "mixed ability" teaching. (See Department of Education. 1969.)

The Community school concept was a development of the Comprehensive school philosophy. This entailed the development of the local school as an educational facility at the disposal of the whole local community, as well as being the provider of a comprehensive education for all local second-level schoolgoers. So, as well as incorporating many of the distinctive features of Comprehensive schools, the Community school seeks to liaise closely with the local community through opening its doors to various forms of educational and communal recreational and leisure activities. It also seeks to imbue in its pupils an awareness of "community" and the "responsibilities of citizenship".

Comprehensive schools were introduced in 1963, and the first 3 schools had opened by 1966. Twelve more Comprehensive schools were sanctioned by 1972 — some in areas in which there had never previously been a post-primary school such as new suburbs, but others resulted from the amalgamations of existing schools. After this date no new Comprehensives were approved. From 1972 similar schools which were built became "Community schools". There are some differences in the size and representatives of Boards of Management of both schools — the Comprehensive board being much smaller and less representative — but the main difference lies in the widei communal involvement and responsibility of Community schools (Coolahan, 1981, pp. 219-220). The Board of Management of a Comprehensive or Community (henceforth called "Community" schools only) school appoints teachers and administers the school's budget. It has much the same formal functions as a manager in a Secondary school, but tends to be far more active and powerful. It differs from the Board of Management of a VEC's Community College in that it is not responsible in turn to any higher authority, other than the Department, in the execution of its functions. Community schools, then, have no formal intermediate bodies mediating between the individual school and the Department, as have the majority of Secondary and all Vocational schools.

In Community schools, the Board of Management, or a subsidiary Appoinments' Board, appoints both Principal and Vice-Principal. Often the appointments are permanent, after an initial year-long probationary period; but it is more usual for them to be indefinite. Although there are variations across schools within this sector, Principals tend to have much more limited autonomy than most Secondary or even some Vocational schools. Important decisions are referred to the Board of Management, and some of the major decisions are referred directly to the Department of Education (Hannan, Breen et al., 1983, p. 88). The greater extent to which individual schools in this sector liaise directly with the Department of Education is probably a factor of their having no intermediate body between the school and the Department, as well as the fact that the schools are actually owned by the Department. Schools deal individually with the Department in negotiating the school budget and obtaining services and entitlements.

As to social class intake, Comprehensive and Community schools tend to have broader and more varied intakes than other school types in keeping with their educational objectives, as well as reflecting the fact that they are usually much less subject to competition within their local catchment areas (Hannan, Breen et al., 1983, p. 90).

By 1983 15 Comprehensive and 41 Community schools had been established, catering for 12 per cent of all second-level school entrants in 1981/82 (Department of Education, 1982/83).

PART II

RESULTS FROM SCHOOL SURVEYS ON SCHOOL DIVERSITY: THE DECISIONMAKING AUTONOMY OF PRINCIPALS, EDUCATIONAL/CURRICULAR IDEOLOGY, AND THE SOCIAL GROUP AND ABILITY CHARACTERISTICS OF SCHOOL INTAKE

The following conclusions are based mainly on the extensive interviews which were carried out with 95 school Principals in a national sample of second-level schools in 1981 (Hannan, Breen, et al., 1983, pp. 27-29; see Interview Schedule Appendix I). In addition interviews were also carried out with a smaller sample of 68 Career Guidance Teachers in schools where they were present. Finally interviews were also carried out with a sample of over 5,000 pupils in Intermediate Certification classes, while all Leaving Cert. (N = 3,967) pupils' classes in the sampled schools were also interviewed. These pupil interviews provide the main data on the social class origins of pupils. The results of these various interviews which bear on our main questions are given below: first dealing with the decisionmaking autonomy of Principals, secondly with the curricular/educational ideology and stated educational objectives of the Principals and their schools, and thirdly with the main social group orientation of and actual social class composition of pupils in the various schools. We examine the extent to which the beliefs and values of school Principals, as well as the social group characteristics of pupils in the various schools correspond with the original school "charters" and objectives.

The Autonomy of Principals

Of the three school systems discussed, Principals in Secondary schools have by far the highest level of decisionmaking autonomy about the type of schooling process they provide while Principals in Vocational schools have the least (Hannan, Breen, et al., 1983, p. 88). Community and Vocational school Principals are much more highly constrained by the need to refer decisions to higher school or public authorities than the Secondary school Principals. Most major decisions, especially those involving extra budgetary expenditure or ones involving major organisational changes, have to be referred to the school management board or, for the Vocational schools, to the CEO.

Although Secondary school Principals, on average, have much more autonomy they also show significantly more between-school differences in this respect than is true of Vocational or Community school Principals. There is, as we have seen, already wide variance in the ownership of Secondary schools and in their organisational attributes. Of the 531 Secondary schools, 4 per cent are owned and operated by Protestant and other denominational bodies — but each of these schools operates almost autonomously although strong management boards characterise those schools. Six per cent are owned by lay Catholics, again operating autonomously but generally with weak management boards if any. Almost all of the remainder are owned and managed by Catholic institutes or local diocesan clerical authorities — who vary significantly in their authority structure. There are over 60 such religious institutes involved in Irish education, but 13 of these own and operate around three-quarters of all such schools. Indeed 2 religious institutes, the Mercy Order and the Christian Brothers, own 41 per cent of all religiously-owned Secondary schools in Ireland. If such corporate bodies are tightly co-ordinated and have consistent educational goals, or share consistent educational ideologies, then such groups of schools are likely to resemble each other closely in their schooling practices.

Overall, therefore, almost 3 out of 4 Secondary schools are owned and operated by 13 religious orders, each of whom operate a large number of schools. A school's incorporation within such a large encompassing body not only reduces a Principal's autonomy in most cases but has many other consequences on school goals and operating procedures. Schools which are members of such superordinate organisations have a central authority to refer to, which normally keeps local school needs under review. Such centralised managements also normally transfer Principals and other religious staff from one school to another. They can also, though rarely, be called upon for additional funding. If mainly a teaching religious order, like the Christian Brothers or Mercy or Presentation Sisters, there is, in addition to the normal overseeing of a school's operation, a centralised procedure for the reappointment and transfer of Principals (and some clerical teachers) every five to six years, and moreover the possibility for a fundamental review of the whole Order's teaching work arises in the periodic "chapters" of each order. In some respects, therefore, the very fast reaction of these privately-owned Secondary schools to the Free Education Scheme in 1967 must have been influenced by their organisational advantages over Vocational schools. They have an ownership, management and staff which, in most cases, is single-mindedly dedicated to education and has strong ideological commitments to their particular role in it.

There are various degrees of such hierarchical organisation. For our purposes, the following three encompass most variations:

(i)   the individual school is not a member of any larger corporate grouping, but operates as an autonomous unit;

(ii)   the school is a member of a larger corporate grouping, but this takes the form of a fairly loose federation which exerts minimal control on the individual Principal;

(iii) the school is incorporated into an organised system with a central directive authority, to which individual Principals or local school authorities are responsible.

The following allocation (Chart 2.1) of congregations and other groupings to the categories in our threefold typology, is based on reviews of the literature available and extensive interviews with informants which have been described earlier. Only the larger congregations are categorised.

Chart 2.1: *The Extent of Hierarchical Organisation of School Authorities*

School type	Likely Level of Autonomy of Local Principal		
	Relatively autonomous. Each school is independent	*Large corporate grouping, control with moderate degree of local autonomy (e.g. Federations)*	*Large corporate grouping with central directive authority*
	(High Autonomy)	*(Moderate Autonomy)*	*(Low Autonomy)*
Secondary	(i) All lay Catholic Schools (N = 35) (ii) Most single schools owned by religious orders (N = 23) (iii) Protestant and other denominational schools (N = 23) (iv) Most Diocesan schools	Mercy Sisters (107) Some Diocesan schools	A* *(Moderately Hierarchical)* Presentation Srs. (50) Charity (15) Holy Faith (12) Louis (9) De La Salle Brs. (17) Patrician Brs. (8) Presentation Brs. (8) B* *(Highly Hierarchical)* Jesuits (4) Holy Ghost Fathers (6) Christian Brs. (83) Dominican Srs. (10) Loreto Srs. (10)
Vocational schools			All vocational schools (245)
Community/ Comprehensive schools	Community and Comprehensive schools (N = 56)		

*B schools appear to be more tightly controlled and directed from the centre than A schools.

Autonomous Schools

There is no larger grouping: the individual school acts as an autonomous unit. Into this category fall the Protestant and interdenominational schools, the Jewish and German schools, the lay Catholic Secondary schools, and the congregations with only a single school. The Principals of most lay Catholic schools appear to have the greatest freedom of action, and are answerable only to the parents of their pupils.

Although in some respects the Protestant school system is centralised — by the administration of a number of joint committees — each schoo, to a very large extent, operates independently. Most have independent Boards of Trustees and Boards of Management, however. These, to a large extent, are elected by and co-opted from parents and supporters of the school. The Board of Management appoints the Principal, usually, if lay, to a permanent position. Once appointed, the Head has considerable autonomy, though less so than with Catholic Secondary school Principals because s/he has a local Board of Management to which many non-routine decisions would have to be referred. And, of course, all major items of expenditure, all major alterations of building, or of the teaching and schooling process, would have to be agreed with the Board of Management.

Besides the Protestant schools most other "autonomous" schools are owned and managed as single units and have therefore almost complete autonomy — although in the case of some Diocesan schools the local Bishop may retain considerable power in his own hands.

Moderate Incorporation (Federation)

There are a number of different school-owning authorities which fit within this category: most Diocesan schools which are subject to episcopal control and appointment of Principals, and religious organisations that are organised as federations like the Mercy Sisters.

The most important group of schools in this category — in terms of number of schools and pupils — are those run by the Mercy Order. To some extent, like the Catholic Diocesan colleges for boys, the local Mercy congregations ran their schools as part of an organisation over which the local Bishop had the highest authority. However, since the mid-1960s the Bishop no longer exerts the same control as previously. Generally now all schools and convents within a diocese have been consolidated under a single authority whereas previously a number of Foundations existed within each diocese. There has also been some movement towards interdiocesan organisations. Each diocese is now headed by a Mother General, who is empowered to transfer personnel within the diocese.

Principals, like most other religious orders, are appointed by the religious superiors for a period of 5-6 years. Many school Principals tend to have very wide autonomy, with little interference from central authority in the management of the school. It is indeed sometimes said that Principals are appointed to office on the basis of their adaptability, to maximise the benefits of local autonomy. Even expenditures which require substantial sums of money, or changes in structure of buildings, can be made locally. As well as the Principal, Mercy schools tend to have, almost universally, a separate manager who has financial responsibility. This manager is usually head of the local convent and is appointed by the local Superior. Often managers have previously acted as Principals, so that they and the local convent are available for consultation, advice and support.

Loosely Hierarchical

Here, the school is a member of a broader grouping which has an effective regional or national structure and hierarchical authority, but one which is not highly centralised. A large number of the major congregations involved in education come into this category — Presentation, Charity and Holy Faith Sisters; De La Salle, Presentation and Patrician Brothers.

Presentation Sisters, the second largest women's congregation, had similar diocesan origins and active mission to the Sisters of Mercy, but became more deeply subject to local episcopal authority in the course of the nineteenth century. Within the last decade, however, it has reorganised itself into two provinces in Ireland, and through this escaped the boundaries of local episcopal control. It is, therefore, a nationally organised and hierarchically controlled body, unlike the Mercy congregation for instance. Although it is less hierarchically structured than the Christian Brothers, for example, personnel can be moved from one convent and diocese to another, while school Principals are appointed and transferred from one school to another.

Authority is invested in the religious Superior who appoints the Principal almost invariably for a 5-6 year term. The school has a separate manager-bursar who is also appointed by the religious Superior. The manager is rarely head of the local convent, unlike in the case of the Mercy. Usually the manager has had extensive experience of school management and, living in the same community as the Principal, can generally offer advice and back-up for the Principal. Except for major expenditure and major structural alterations of buildings, all schooling decisions can be made with high local school autonomy.

A similar comment is appropriate to the Irish Sisters of Charity and to the Holy Faith Sisters. In the case of these congregations, some change has occurred in the devolution of authority from a strong central office of Mother General to local communities. Like the Sisters of Mercy, the Sisters of Charity have many other involvements besides schools. The Sisters of Charity and the Holy

Faith and Presentation Sisters all resemble the Sisters of Mercy in their relative lack of surplus resources: all originated as indigenous congregations concerned with the education of the poor, a point which is dealt with more fully in the next section.

The Sisters of the Holy Faith are similarly quite centrally organised, operating on a national Provincialate basis. The levels of authority run from Mother General (national level) to Regional Superior but it is the Mother General who appoints each school Principal, whose office is for an indefinite period. There is a separate manager appointed to each school, with a clear division of labour between her and the local Superior.

The Irish Sisters of Charity tend to be quite highly hierarchically organised also. In Ireland, the Order operates as one unit, with a national Provincial. Appointments of school Principals are made from within the Order, and last for indefinite periods. The Principal, once appointed, has almost complete autonomy except for the limited cases when high expenditure or building alterations are necessary. The Principal is also aided by a separate school manager or bursar, who is usually head of the local convent.

De La Salle Brothers are organised as a national Provincialate, with a national provincial and council structure. Their continental origins appear to have inclined them towards relative freedom at local level, with subsequent diminution of centralising tendencies. It is the religious Superior of the local house who acts as school manager, and who appoints the school Principal, an appointment which is usually for a 6-year term. Most schooling decisions are, therefore, taken at a local level. On the other hand, De La Salle personnel tend to be constantly mobile, and their well maintained link with the international congregation promotes openness to new ideas.

The Marist Brothers similarly operate on a national Provincialate basis, and it is the Provincial who appoints the Principal-Manager of each school. Once appointed, however, the Principal is relatively autonomous and each school more or less operates on an independent basis.

Presentation Brothers, Patrician Brothers and Brigidine Sisters are all indigenous congregations with a diocesan basis of organisation. The Presentation Brothers are organised on a national Provincialate basis. Schools are owned by the congregation's Trustees. The national Provincial appoints school Principals, whose terms of office tend to be an indefinite period not exceeding 10 years. The school has a separate manager (a member of the Order), who is not usually the same person as the head of the local monastery. By and large, however, local Principals appear to be quite autonomous in the day-to-day running of the school.

Highly Hierarchical

The religious institute is a well-organised corporate system, which is highly centralised under a single authority. The chief exemplars of this mode of organisation are the Christian Brothers or the Jesuits or Holy Ghost Fathers. The Dominican and Loreto Sisters are also somewhat similar.

The Christian Brothers, unlike most other indigenous orders, have always been organised as a trans-diocesan congregation. They now form two provinces in Ireland, divided by a line running through Dublin city westwards to Galway. The congregation is tightly organised on a hierarchical national basis. It is not under the control of local Catholic bishops; indeed, in its long history in Irish education, conflicts with local bishops have been quite frequent (see Dowling, 1971). The activities of all members in each province are monitored by the Provincial, with the aim of using each member with maximum efficiency. Members are regularly transferred, and Principals usually spend 6 years in any 1 school. Constant turnover allows a regular reassessment of achievements, and a fresh input from the new Principal. The Christian Brothers are not by any means the only congregation to ensure regular transfers, but they are by far the largest to do so. This requires a consistent and standardised policy for their schools, and an efficient central authority to co-ordinate transfers and oversee continuity. A school Principal, integrated into this larger organisation, is necessarily very sensitive to the traditions and methods of the Brothers. While educational innovation does not usually begin at individual school level, widescale change can be implemented throughout the system in a short period of time.

The Loreto and Dominican Sisters, both congregations of continental origin which had adapted themselves to peculiarly Irish conditions, are not as tightly organised as the Christian Brothers, but they do have a central Provincialate. Rather like the Holy Ghost and Jesuit Fathers, individual Principals have a good deal of freedom, guided by the traditional ethos of their institute. But transfer of personnel and, in some cases, financial co-operation between schools, are centrally organised. The Dominican Sisters' schools are more highly geographically concentrated, facilitating informal as well as formal contacts, but the Loreto schools have various other inter-school ties, such as a common set of exams and a strong games league, which heighten the sense of corporate identity.

The male clerical orders have a strong basis of autonomy and independence. They are usually foreign in origin and international in structure, and schools they operate are often prestigious and fee paying — like those run by the Jesuits and Holy Ghost Fathers. The Holy Ghost Order operates a single national Provincialate, with, however, slightly less perceived centralisation of power than in other religious orders with a similar structure. The formal

governing structure of schools is much like that of other centralised orders
with a Principal appointed usually from within the order for an indefinite
period, although at least 1 school has appointed a lay Principal. The Jesuits
also are organised on a national Provincialate basis. The Irish Provincial
appoints school Principals for a usual 6-year period. There is no school
manager apart from the Principal, and quite often a Board of Management is
referred to for most schooling decisions. In both cases, however, it is not so
much the centralising authority but the unifying ethos and educational
traditions of these Orders — including their obvious middle-class orientation
that has most influence on schooling practice.

This model of the corporate structure of religious orders and of the relative
autonomy of Principals is taken from previously published reports and from
interviews with knowledgeables. In the following table we give the results
from our interviews with the Principals of the various types of schools as to
their views of their relative autonomy. The results strongly support the view
that Vocational and Community school Principals are much more tightly
controlled by authority than the great majority of Secondary school Principals.
But they do not support the hypothesis that the experienced degree of
autonomy of Secondary schools' Principals conforms closely to their degree
of formal incorporation into hierarchically organised religious orders.

Both Vocational and Community school Principals are much more constrained by their need to refer many decisions on a regular basis, on budgetary
and other routine management matters, to their Boards or to the Chief
Executive Officer of the Vocational Education Committee. There are some
differences between counties and individual schools in these respects but,
relative to all Secondary schools, there are significantly greater controls on
their schooling management decisions than is true of all Secondary schools.
Only Principals in those Protestant schools which have school boards, or
schools run by religious orders with small numbers of schools but with a very
clear hierarchical (national Provincialate) structure are equally constrained
by superordinate authority.

Interestingly, however, Principals in the Christian Brothers' schools feel
almost as equally free of such intrusive authority as does the much less
hierarchically structured Mercy congregation. Except for major expenditure
items beyond the normal school budget, or other major decisions such as
alterations in school buildings or changes in subscriptions or fees, etc., most
such Principals feel free to make all other routine and non-routine decisions
within their own schools. Of course such Principals are appointed for a very
short period and operate within the generally clearcut ambit of the order's
educational philosophy and goals. So, compared to the management structure
of Vocational and Community schools — where Principals are appointed for

Table 2.1: *Perceived Level of Autonomy of Principals in Schooling Decisions — in Different Categories of Schools*

School Authority	Perceived Level of Autonomy of Principals*			Total No. of Schools
	1. Almost Completely Autonomous, Except for Major Budget Changes, Building Alterations, etc. (High)	2. Moderately Autonomous Except for Questions Like Fees, Donations, Budget, or Building (Medium)	3. Has to Refer All Non-Routine Items on a Regular Basis to Board, Executive or Religious Superior (Low)	
1. Vocational schools	0	12	14	26
2. Comprehensive/ Community schools	0	5	7	12
3. Mercy Order	9	3	1	13
4. Christian Brothers	8	3	1	12
5. Other Female Religious Orders	10	2	2	14
6. Other Male Religious Orders	5	1	2	8
7. Lay Catholic	0	2	1	3
8. Protestant schools	0	2	1	3
Total	32	30	29	91

$\chi^2 = 43.09$; df (collapsed to 12 cells) = 6; $p < .001$. Data on the Autonomy Scale for 4 schools incomplete.

*This is a highly reliable 6 item Guttman Scale (CR = .92; Coefficient of Scalability = .65) which ranges in score from 1.0 to 7.0. The 6 questions refer to the extent to which the Principal could make certain decisions themselves or had to refer them to higher authorities: (i) 94 per cent and (ii) 93 per cent of Principals respectively said that they themselves made decisions about subject additions to the curricula, provided they remained within the quota; as well as any changes necessary in the way they categorised or allocated pupils to classes; (iii) only 55 per cent, however, felt they could either increase fees, or ask for (increases in) voluntary contributions from parents without referring to higher authorities; (iv) 44 per cent said they could themselves decide to add other subjects to curricula if it involved expenditure above the quota; (v) only 28 per cent reported they could make major alterations in buildings without referring the matter; and (vi) only 6 per cent said that they could incur major expenditures above the normal budget without referring the matter to higher authorities. (See Principal's Interview Schedule, Q.19, Appendix I.)

life, and there is no overarching (total) institutional system to which they belong and within which they have been intensely socialised — CBS Principals are much more likely to share such schooling preconceptions and objectives than are Vocational school Principals.

The experienced autonomy of Principals then gives us a somewhat different ordering of school authorities than that given by the formal hierarchical structure of their organisation. This is particularly obvious in the case of Christian Brothers' schools and Protestant schools. The former are far less directly constrained by their religious authority than the latter are by their immediate school management board. So most serious but ongoing schooling management decisions do not have to be referred to any higher authority by a CBS Principal, but have to be discussed with the Board by Principals in Protestant schools. In fact, by and large, it is the presence of these school level boards of management that exercises the main authority in most Secondary schools, as well as in Community schools, not the superordinate religious authority. As we shall see later, however, being a member of such a large hierarchically organised grouping clearly introduces consistencies in schooling provision and structure — which it is clear, however, cannot be directly attributable to imperative control.

The Social Group Orientation and Educational Objectives of the Different School Authorities

The basic educational objectives or philosophy of any public educational body or of a religious organisation operating schools will amost inevitably shape the values which underlie school Principals' or school authorities' decisions about curriculum content, subject options, ways in which pupils are categorised and allocated to classes, etc. We have clearly demonstrated this effect in regard to subject provision and allocation in our previous publication (Hannan, Breen *et al.*, 1983). Individual school Principals or local school decisionmakers do not normally refer such decisions to higher authority, but make them in the light of those values and objectives to which implicit consent has been given, and indeed, prolonged socialisation guaranteed, by being a long-term member of a religious institute, etc.

Most religious institutes which operate Secondary schools were set up to achieve quite specific missions: whether this be to provide a basic education for the poor, the recruitment and training of young members of their own order, the education of young ladies from mainly middle class backgrounds in intellectual development and social accomplishments, or the development of the intellectual abilities of their pupils to as high a level as possible. Equally Vocational and Community/Comprehensive schools were set up to achieve quite specific social and educational objectives and have quite clearcut chartering missions.

Even though the original inspirational ideals of a religious institute may no longer enliven present educational practice in any detail, it will nevertheless have shaped the development and received culture of the organisation. The pressures to which all schools are now subject, to prepare pupils as well as they can for the public examinations, have had a clear effect on most educational organisations. The rapid decline in recruitment to religious orders, as well as the rapid increase in pupil and teacher numbers has clearly diffused the influence of such founding charters on current school practice. In addition many religious organisations involved in education have recently radically revised their educational charters. Still the weight of historical adaptations of founding objectives is bound to have a very significant influence on the design of educational processes.

The educational priorities of a religious institute and the social stratum from which its pupils are drawn are generally closely correlated. This may be affirmed explicitly by an institute. More commonly, however, individual schools maintain openness of access but, where a choice of school exists within a locality, parental perceptions of the character of the corporate group to which each school belongs and the type of education it provides, usually ensures that a local division of labour emerges amongst schools which differentiates pupils by their social group of origin and type of education provided. This is so particularly where there is a clear social choice — between Vocational and Secondary schools for instance. But even where two or more religious orders operate locally such a social division of labour usually emerges according to parental perceptions of the different schools' traditions.

Protestant schools, not being as locality-bound as others for clientele, are somewhat less subject to parental assessments of this kind. Such schools provide for a small, specific religious group which, although represented in all social strata, are dominantly middle class, even upper middle class, in composition.

Vocational schools in their origins and founding objectives were clearly designed for the education of working class, small farm or lower middle class pupils who either could not afford to, or were not suitably qualified for, Secondary education, and their teaching objectives and curricula were clearly designed to achieve very practical and short-term vocational objectives. And, by and large, as their numbers expanded in most local authority areas from the 1930s to the mid-1960s their role expanded to fill a social and educational vacuum left by the private Secondary schools: i.e., small towns and open country areas not serviced by Secondary schools. They also gradually assumed educational goals and tasks oriented to manual-technical and apprenticeship style training for boys and commercial, service and domestic science specialities for girls. Their assumption of the full second-level educational functions after 1967 — when they were first allowed to educate their pupils for the more academic Intermediate and Leaving Certificate examinations — has usually meant that they gradually comprehensified their curricula and instructional programmes as their pupil numbers increased. In most respects now large Vocational schools are very little different from Comprehensive schools.

The Comprehensive and Community schools, although varying somewhat in their governing structure and educational objectives, are both comprehensive schools which are usually located as sole schools within a local catchment area. They are, therefore, consciously comprehensive in curricular objectives and aim to serve all social groups and ability levels within the community. And as can be seen in our previous publication (Hannan, Breen *et al.*, 1983, p. 90) they generally have a much wider social mix of pupils than other schools. Their original "charter" emphasised comprehensiveness in intake with no selection. It explicitly discouraged streaming and banding practices and encouraged the erosion of the academic/technical differentiation of the curriculum within schools (Atkinson, 1969, pp. 170-172; Coolahan, 1981, pp. 195, 218-220). As an official parental advisory publication put it in 1969:

> Students in these schools are not "streamed". That is to say we do not find separate classes for clever students, or moderately good students, or slow students. Most students, after all, are good at some things and not so good at others. Instead of "streaming" the students, the comprehensive school puts them into middle or "non streamed" classes. (Department of Education, 1969, p. 28)

As we shall see later in this case, as in many others, although the ideal is not achieved it does have a clear impact on schooling decisions.

Any school authority's educational orientation, whether religious or secular, develops out of its original founding aims, although particular historical circumstances along the way may have redirected the course of its mission and its working objectives. None the less, many of the differences which are observable between the educational philosophies of contemporary religious orders, can be accounted for by differences in their original founding aims. There are three main elements of importance in any school authority's educational philosophy:

(a)   the clientele to which the authority directs itself,
(b)   the educational/social goals it pursues, and
(c)   the educational or curriculum content which it deems appropriate for this clientele.

These three elements are, in fact, mutually dependent. The clientele largely dictates the educational/social objectives sought as well as the curricular emphasis, while the curriculum often implies a particular clientele.

In regard to the clientele, the initial aims of a religious order or other school authority tended to define who was to be educated. This may have been a very explicit primary goal of the authority: e.g., as in the case of those orders set up specifically to educate and improve the conditions of the poor (e.g., the Mercy and Presentation Sisters and the Christian Brothers). Those orders involved in the education of the middle or upper middle class tended, on the other hand, not to primarily define their clientele in these terms, rather such a clientele followed on as a result of other more primary aims. For example, many orders' educational involvements were embarked upon with the intention of perpetuating or instilling in their pupils certain values ranging from individual character development to the value of cultural pursuits (e.g., Ursuline). Other orders had specific educational goals such as the achievement of very high intellectual or cultural standards among their pupils, e.g., Society of Jesus, Dominican Sisters. The identification of these orders' schools with such values and goals attracted, as a rule, a more secure middle class clientele, while the primacy of these goals implied a less pragmatic curriculum than that offered to the poor by the orders discussed earlier.

Other orders became involved in education in order to find and prepare suitable recruitment material for their own organisations, thus implying a largely middle to lower middle class pupil body (e.g., the Diocesan colleges and Holy Ghost Fathers). But other teaching orders were specifically invited into Ireland to educate upper middle class pupils who previously had sent their children to Catholic boarding schools in England (e.g., Loreto, Sacred Heart, Religious of Christian Education, etc.).

In the following chart we attempt a classification of educational authorities by their social group orientation. We would like to stress that we make no claim for complete accuracy in this classification. It is being proposed for analytical purposes only in order to explore the underlying reasons for curricular and schooling process differences amongst schools. The information from which it was constructed comes from a number of sources: historical analyses of the origins of Irish second-level education (Corish, 1971; McElligott, 1966; Atkinson, 1969); from documents and histories of individual orders (e.g., Fitzpatrick, 1945; Burke-Savage, 1950); by interviews with informed persons from the individual religious orders and educational bodies, and finally our formal interviews with 95 school Principals. In the following chart then we classify all of the main educational authorities by their predominant social class orientation and their primary curricular emphases.

Besides the relatively greater size of their clientele, Secondary schools have a much older lineage than Vocational or Comprehensive/Community schools and will therefore be dealt with first.

As can be seen from Chart 2.2, and we hope to demonstrate below, Irish Secondary schools are quite clearly differentiated by their mission or their social, educational and religious objectives. Some religious orders – like the Christian Brothers or the Mercy and Presentation orders – were specifically founded to educate the poor, the illiterate and ignorant; or, as the Mercy Constitution puts it, "for the relief, education and protection of the poor". For most of their history and using most of their resources they concentrated their efforts on basic or primary education of the very young. It was only from the end of the nineteenth century onwards – and particularly from the inception of the Intermediate Education Act of 1878 – that they started to provide Secondary education, many of their "Secondary" schools indeed being additions ("Secondary Tops") to their own primary schools.

So the founding objectives of the Christian Brothers, Presentation and Patrician Brothers and of the Mercy and Presentation Sisters, were to serve the interests of the Irish small farm or working class poor. In all areas religious education was very important – particularly in the context of the fear of proselytism which persisted long after the Penal Laws were relaxed or abolished. For such orders, therefore, both formal religious teaching and moral education were very important objectives (Atkinson, 1969).

The female congregations, like those of Mercy or Presentation, however, although stressing religious education to the same extent as their male colleagues, tend in recent times to phrase it more in terms of personal and moral development goals, and within the context of a pastoral care programme.

For most religious congregations concerned with working class and lower middle class girls' and boys' education, a division does exist between both sexes' education in terms of the educational and wider socialisation priorities being pursued: that for boys' education being far more pragmatic, formal and categoric; that for girls' education being more directed toward moral and personal development and interpersonal adjustment.

Unlike these congregations the Diocesan colleges have always been almost exclusively second-level schools, originally devised as junior seminaries. Although having no clearcut social class orientation their academic and economic requirements were such that their clientele were dominated by the sons of middle sized to larger farmers and of the urban middle or lower middle classes. Their curriculum emphasised the teaching of the classics yet, as Atkinson (op. cit., p. 59) says, the model used was, unlike the English grammar school, based on the classical tradition of French educationalists, emphasising as well as the classics, French, History and natural philosophy.

Finally, a number of Secondary schools were specifically set up to serve

Chart 2.2: *Classification of the Social Group Orientation and Educational Ideologies/Objectives of School Authorities*

Educational ideology, philosophy and objectives	Social Group Orientation or Founding Charter Orientation		
	Educational effort directed toward the poor, the illiterate, the ignorant (primarily working class)	Unclear but not explicitly to the poor; implicitly to middle or lower middle class	Explicitly middle class
A. Practical, pragmatic, but with religious education/preparation emphasised.	(i) *Boys' Schools:* Christian Brothers, De La Salle Brothers		
Personal development and pastoral care also emphasised	(ii) *Girls'/Coed Schools:* Mercy Sisters, Presentation Sisters	Presentation Brothers, Holy Faith Sisters, Sisters of Charity	
Practical, pragmatic educational priorities	(iii) *Vocational Schools*		
B. Classical (Grammar school) education		Diocesan Colleges	
C. Academic, intellectual grammar school education (the development of individual ability, responsibility and personal development)			*Boys' Schools:* Jesuits, Holy Ghost Fathers, Most Protestant Schools, *Girls' Schools:* Loreto, St. Louis, Ursuline, Protestant Schools
D. Comprehensive curriculum	*Comprehensive/Community Schools:* all social groups and all ability groups		

the educational needs of the middle classes. Some religious orders like Loreto, Sacred Heart or the Religious of Christian Education were specifically asked in by members of the Catholic hierarchy to take care of the educational needs of their middle class church members. Others, like the Ursulines or St. Louis or the Jesuits, etc., because of their continental dedication to the education of the middle classes (indeed to an upper middle class clientele) came in and acquired equally exclusive clientele.

In all these latter cases the curricula and teaching/instructional approach emphasises the pursuit of academic excellence or intellectual goals, the development of individual judgement and responsibility and, in the case of girls' education, the development of accomplishments and social graces.

The above characteristics of the different religious orders and secular organisations involved in education is taken from the published literature on the subject and informal interviews with knowledgeables. (See Hannan, Breen et al., 1983, pp. 23-30.) We can, however, check the validity of that characterisation from the information gathered in our national surveys of Intermediate and Leaving Certificate pupils in post-primary schools, and from our extended interviews with Principals. In general, as we will see below, these independent data sources strongly supported the above conclusions. First the actual social class composition of the different pupil bodies within schools is described. And finally the explicit educational aims and objectives of school decisionmakers is explored.

Social Class Composition and Educational Disability Characteristics of Different School Authorities

The proportion of each authority's student body who are from working class backgrounds is taken as an index of the actual or "operative" social group orientation of that Order or sector. This information is from the extensive interviews which were carried out with pupils in Intermediate Certificate classes in a national survey of second-level schools in 1981. (See Hannan, Breen et al., 1983, pp. 27-29.) These estimates of the social class characteristics of pupils in the different schools are somewhat biassed in that almost 10 per cent of pupils had left schools before their Intermediate Certificate year. Such early dropouts, however, are highly selective of working class children and children in Vocational schools (see Breen, 1984). As a result, the figures, if anything, understate the extent of class differentiation that occurs amongst schools — mainly overstating the class characteristics of pupils in Vocational and working class Secondary schools. The results are given in Table 2.2 below.

It is very clear that Vocational schools and Community schools cater pre-

Table 2.2: *Proportion of Intermediate Certificate Pupils from Working Class Backgrounds by School Type/Order. Sample of Intermediate Certificate Pupils, 1981. (Working class = pupils whose fathers had skilled, semi-skilled or unskilled manual occupations)*

Vocational Schools	Community Schools	Christian Brothers Schools	Sisters of Mercy and Presentation Sisters	All High Status Religious Orders and Protestant Secondary Schools	Other* Status Male	Other* Status Female	Lay Catholic Schools
%							
54.7	50.6	27.1	41.2	9	28	47.6	25.8
N							
(310)	(715)	(970)	(1,346)	(334)	(279)	(768)	(231)

*Other status male (religious) orders = Presentation, De La Salle, Marist Brothers and Diocesan schools. Other status female (religious) orders = Holy Faith, Brigidine, Jesus and Mary orders. High status orders = Jesuit, Holy Ghost, Sacred Heart, etc., orders.

dominantly for a working class clientele with over half the pupils in both schools coming from working class backgrounds. Had pupils from poor farming backgrounds been included, the ratio would be close to two-thirds. Interestingly Secondary schools run by nuns whose orders are chartered to serve the interests of the poor have almost equally high levels of working class pupils — the Mercy, Presentation, Holy Faith, Brigidine, Charity, etc., Orders. Obviously the expansion of their educational role from the late 1960s onwards has meant that these schools incorporated more working class girls into their schools than did Vocational schools.

Amongst the male religious orders both the Christian Brothers' schools and other religious orders dedicated to the education of the poor had substantially lower proportions of working class pupils than have the relevant female orders. As was made clear in our previous study these schools did not expand their facilities and numbers after 1967 at the same pace or in the same way as did those schools run by nuns (Hannan, Breen *et al.*, 1983, pp. 53-59), and Vocational schools held their share of male post-primary school entrants. While the numbers of Secondary school girls more than doubled in the 10 years after 1967, the number of Secondary school boys went up only by around 60 per cent. Over time, in fact, while girls' Secondary schools expanded rapidly to include working class and lower ability pupils, boys' Secondary schools did not to the same extent and, in some schools, became increasingly selective in intake on ability grounds.

Many schools, on the other hand, which had historically directed their activities toward the upper middle class — most Protestant Secondary schools and schools run by certain religious orders like the Jesuits — quite clearly achieve their objectives. There is minimal working class representation in their schools. In our sample it is only in these few schools which, despite their original chartering objective, came into the "Free Scheme" after 1967 that one now finds such students.

The general view of the social class orientation of these different school authorities, therefore, which come from our review of their origins and charters is strongly supported by these findings and is further witnessed by the following results in the severity of numeracy and literacy problems prevalent within these different school types. These data are estimates given by school Principals and cross-checked against estimates given by the Career Guidance Teacher (see Questionnaire, Appendix I, Qs. 71 and 72).

Vocational schools particularly face very serious disability problems amongst their pupil intake — with over 2 out of 3 Principals reporting that over 15 per cent of their pupil intake — had serious numeracy and literacy problems. This is about ten times the proportion reported as present in Christian or Presentation Brothers' schools as well as in all high status Catholic and Protestant schools. Both Community schools and those operated by the Mercy and Presentation Orders have the next most serious disability problems; again indicating quite clearly the "open school" policy of both school types, as well as the openness or dedication of the latter two religious orders to poor or working class pupils' education. Many of the other religious orders dedicated to the education of the poor have equally serious educational problems in their school intake but the number of schools in our sample is too small to identify any of these.

Both sets of results, therefore, strongly support our earlier conclusions about the social class "bias" of the different school authorities. Vocational schools are clearly serving a highly residual class and educational clientele — dominantly working class pupils, a high proportion of whom have serious numeracy and literacy problems. Community schools are comprehensive in their class intake and in a higher than average educational problem intake. But those female religious orders who have oriented their apostolate to the education of the poor have almost equal levels of working class and educational disability rates. On the other hand boys' Secondary schools, particularly those run by male religious orders, are the most highly selective, even many of these orders which are directed toward the needs of the poor. And, finally, at the opposite end of the continuum to Vocational schools, are the small number of exclusive upper middle class Secondary schools with very few educational disability problems.

So, in their actual behaviour, those orders of nuns whose chartering objectives gave priority to the education of the poor and the deprived appear generally to have implemented their objectives — i.e., Mercy, Presentation,

Table 2.3: *Number and Percentage of Schools Principals who Estimate that Over 15 Per Cent of the Pupil Intake Have Serious Numeracy and Literacy Problems (N = 92, relevant information is unavailable from three schools. Source: Principals' Interviews.)*

No. (%) of Schools Who Have More Than 15% of Pupil Intake With	Vocational Schools	Community Schools	Mercy/ Presentation Nuns	CBS/ Presentation Brothers	High Status Catholic Orders and Protestant Schools	Other Secondary Schools
(i) Serious Literacy Problems	17 (71%)	5 (42%)	6 (40%)	1 (7%)	1 (10%)	3 (18%)
(ii) Serious Numeracy Problems	16 (67%)	6 (50%)	6 (40%)	1 (7%)	0 (0)	6 (35%)
Total Number of Schools	24	12	15	14	10	17

$p < .001$.

Charity, etc. That these outcomes were not chance or unplanned outcomes became very clear in the course of our interviews with their school Principals. Of 18 school Principals who were members of the Mercy, Presentation and Charity orders 12 explicitly emphasised that the main mission of the order was toward the poor, underprivileged or deprived and linked their school policy to providing for that goal. In addition to an original written charter many of these 12 emphasised the live nature of that commitment by emphasising the extent to which it had been discussed and emphasised at the local diocesan or regional chapters of the order as well as the recent updating of official documents which had emphasised this socially directed role.

Of the 14 interviews with the Principals of Christian Brothers' and Presentation Brothers' schools in only 3 cases was the current objective of "educating the poor" emphasised — as in "a bias toward educating the poor". But in 5 other interviews the Principals emphasised the original founding charter's bias toward the poor, but then explained that changes in circumstances occurred which had gradually shifted the bias toward the middle classes. In the remaining 5 cases no explicit mention was made of these foundation aims at all. It was clear, however, that in a majority of interviews these founding aims constituted a living and potentially delegitimising set of unrealised values, with 2 Principals saying that many Brothers believed that the order ought to go back to and serve its founding aims, while a number of others provided explicit rationalisations for allowing this departure from the founding aim: i.e., the extension of the value to cover "poverty of spirit", changes in the social class characteristics of local catchment areas after the school was established, the long-term effects of the academic curricular bias, etc. Clearly, therefore, although there has been a loss of commitment or ability to implement the founding goals or values of these orders they do constitute serious objectives for a minority, and a source of disquiet for a majority. Compared to the equivalent female orders, however, these chartering values cannot generally be regarded as actual or operative goals of school management and this is very clear in the pupil clientele catered for by the Brothers.

Ideological Orientations

Principals were also interviewed about their schools' educational objectives and means used for attaining objectives — 3 open ended questions with 2 supplementaries (i.e., 5 in all) being asked (Questions 9, 10, 11 in Principal's Interview Schedule, Appendix I). The responses to these questions were coded and statistically analysed and yielded 3 separate and very clearcut "factors" or scales which summarise the scored responses of Principals across the 5 separate questions. These 3 goal orientations and linked curricular arrangements gave priority to: (i) religious-moral education; (ii) instrumental-pragmatic education; (iii) pastoral-care or personal development goals and arrangements to achieve these goals. Other educational priorities or goals were mentioned but these were mentioned by small minorities, or conversely by pluralities in ways which did not yield reliable indices. For example, "intellectual development" goals were given priority by less than 10 per cent of Principals, and "socialisation" goals — which emphasised teaching/learning for participation in active citizenship roles — were emphasised by about a third of Principals. But in both cases their relationship to other related "goals" and to school type yielded no consistent patterns.

When the 8 separate categories of schools are collapsed to yield a sufficient number of respondents for statistical purposes these 3 dimensions of Principals', or school authorities', goal orientations exhibit quite distinct patterns. Vocational school Principals have different goals to Community/Comprehensive and Secondary school Principals, while schools run by female religious orders have equally distinct orientations to Principals in Christian Brothers' or other boys' schools (see Table 2.4).

"Christian Education"
The setting of "Christian Education" as a goal and the specific provision of formal courses of religious and moral instruction are given priority as a very important goal for most religious orders involved in education. It is emphasised or treated in different ways by different organisations, however.

Table 2.4: *Educational Ideologies* by School Type — Summary Table. Number of School Principals of Each School Type Who Emphasised (i) Christian/Moral Education; (ii) Personal Development/Pastoral Care Goals; (iii) Pragmatic-Instrumental Goals. (Score of 0 = Value Not Mentioned; 2 = Mentioned Twice at Least)*

Educational Ideologies (Score of 1 — mentioned at least once; Score of 2+ mentioned 2 or more times)		Voc. Schools	Comm. Schools	CBS/ Pres. Bros.	High Status Male Orders + Protestant Schools	Other (Lower Status) Male Orders + Lay Schools	Mercy/ Pres. Sisters	High Status Female Orders	Other (Lower Status) Female Order	(Tests of statistical significance)
		N	N	N	N	N	N	N	N	
	Scale Score									
(i) Christian/ Moral Education + Formal Religious Prorammes	0	25	11	2	2	6	8	1	0	$\chi^2 = 29$ df = 5 p <.001. (Scores 1+2 collapsed + smaller categories collapsed)
	1	1	1	4	3	2	4	3	4	
	2	0	0	8	0	3	4	0	3	
	Total	26	12	14	5	11	16	4	7	
(ii) Personal Development Goals + Pastoral Care Programmes	0	11	0	7	0	4	2	0	1	$\chi^2 = 16.5$ df = 5 p <.01 (Scores 1+2 collapsed + smaller categories collapsed)
	1	8	4	3	2	5	5	1	2	
	2	7	8	4	3	2	9	3	4	
	Total	26	12	14	5	11	16	4	7	
(iii) Pragmatic Goal + Explicit Curricular Provision	0	1	3	5	3	5	8	3	6	$\chi^2 = 32.4$ df = 8 p <.001 (4 of smaller categories collapsed)
	1	6	6	7	2	4	5	1	0	
	2	19	3	2	0	2	3	0	1	
	Total	26	12	14	5	11	16	4	7	
Number of Schools		26	12	14	5	11	16	4	7	N = 95 (Total)

**Scales:* Each scale is constructed from responses to 3 separate questions dealing with: (i) working objectives of the school "what are the 2 most important objectives, or important changes, which the school aims to bring about in its pupils?"; and (ii) "In what concrete ways does the school go about achieving these goals?" The number of times "Christian education" or "moral education", etc., is mentioned or explicit curricular/institutional, etc., means mentioned to achieve these or similar goals is counted: 0 = not mentioned at all; 1 = mentioned once; 2 = mentioned 2 or more times. The same procedure was employed for "Pragmatic Goals", and "Personal Development" programmes, etc. (See Questions 9, 10, 11, of Principals' Questionnaire, Appendix 1.)

Over 90 per cent of Vocational and Community school Principals did not mention it either as a goal or a curricular provision in response to any of the 3 relevant questions. This does not mean, obviously, that religious/moral education is not provided — it is in all schools; but it is not a burning issue or preoccupation with these Principals as it is in most Secondary schools (67 per cent of all Secondary school Principals mention it).

That the articulation of such goals is not an indication of whether a religious education of any kind is provided within schools becomes clear when we compare girls' Secondary schools with boys'. It is, in fact, in boys' schools that specifically formal religious/moral instruction is most emphasised, not in girls' schools. This is particularly so in Christian Brothers' schools where formal religious/moral instruction is emphasised in *all* schools — with formal provision emphasised in the curriculum and timetable. Only in some of the female religious orders dealing with working class or lower middle class pupils is there an equivalent emphasis on religious instruction. But, as we shall see, even here it is provided in a rather different context than in most boys' or CBS schools. The Mercy and Presentation Orders place much less emphasis on formal religious instruction *per se*, emphasising that religious/ moral development should take place within the context of personal development programmes. So, it is mainly male religious orders with lower middle or upper working class clientele that gives this goal highest priority. Schools run by female religious orders and schools catering for upper middle class clientele give it much less priority. The publicly-owned schools give it least priority. In the latter case, of course, formal religious instruction is often given by religious teachers from outside the school.

Personal Development and Pastoral Care

Personal development goals and pastoral care programmes are most developed in Community schools, girls' Secondary schools and indeed most Secondary schools run by female religious orders. Almost 2 out of 3 such schools place substantial emphasis (mentioned twice or more) on such objectives and attempt to provide relevant pastoral care programmes. They are least emphasised in Vocational schools and in boys' Secondary schools, particularly those oriented toward catering for working class or lower middle class pupils. The chartering objectives of specific religious orders — particularly female orders dealing with girls' education or coeducation — appear to emphasise personal development goals and link these in many cases to religious/moral development. Community schools as a group, on the other hand, being so recently established, have developed an explicit formal policy on pastoral care provision and such programmes are most developed in these schools. They are, on the other hand, of least significance in Vocational schools — except in the large ones, as well as in Christian Brothers' schools. In both cases pragmatic or instrumental goals, or goals which place priority on maximising educational achievement are most emphasised, and in these cases moral or religious education/development are not explicitly linked with personal development or pastoral care programmes. Such moral or religious education linkages with personal development programmes are clearly evident, however, in the few upper middle class boys' Secondary schools in our sample. In these respects, therefore, ideological differences between schools are quite marked.

Pragmatic/Instrumental Goals

Vocational school Principals in particular are highly instrumental and pragmatic in their goals and curricular planning: placement in jobs, a basic education for most pupils (who generally are not seen as "high fliers") is the main operative goal of these schools. Nineteen of the 26 Vocational schools clearly emphasised these goals. Community school Principals come closest to this level of priority on instrumental goals. But only 3 out of 12 such Principals accord it the highest priority. All Secondary school Principals place it at much lower priority and there is not much variation amongst Secondary schools in these respects. Schools run by religious orders with missions to educate the poor, and with objectively higher levels of educational disability in their pupil intake, do place higher priority on this goal but this difference is not very significant. Also male orders place slightly higher emphasis on it than female orders but again the differences are not very significant. Even dealing with the same social class intake and similar educational disability problems there appear to be, therefore, clearcut differences between the Secondary and the publicly-owned schools, between the male and female religious orders, and between orders with different chartering objectives.

To summarise, therefore, Vocational schools place a high priority on pragmatic-instrumental curricular and instructional goals, and significantly less emphasis than most other schools — particularly Community schools — on personal development goals. Like Community schools, however, Vocational school managements place less explicit emphasis on formal religious instruction. The main difference between the two publicly-owned school types thus relate to the much greater emphasis on formal programmes of pastoral care in Community schools and a much greater pragmatic-instrumented bias in Vocational schools. Peculiarly, providing a "Christian Education" is a much more salient goal for some male religious orders — particularly the Christian Brothers. And in their case it is less linked to personal development concerns than is true of female religious orders or religiously-run schools catering for upper middle class pupils. Equally a more instrumental bias is evident in their case. Schools catering for upper middle class pupils generally emphasise intellectual and personal development goals, and link religious/moral instruction to these. Their education also appears to be less directed toward immediate educational/occupational outcomes or the achievement of pragmatic/ instrumental goals than to long-term intellectual development, etc. The former goals are most emphasised in schools catering for working class pupils or pupils being sponsored for upward mobility.

Besides school type, therefore, there is an extremely clearcut correlation between the social class composition of the pupil body in a school and pragmatic curricular goals (Table 2.5). Almost 60 per cent of schools which are dominantly working class in composition (Categories 5 and 6) have pronounced pragmatic/instrumental goals, compared to around 10 per cent of schools which are dominantly middle class in composition (Categories 1 and 2). Equally working class schools are much *less* likely to emphasise formal religious instruction and somewhat less likely also to give priority to personal development goals and pastoral care programmes, the latter mainly a reflection of their predominantly vocational nature.

Table 2.5: *Summary Table of Relationships Between the Median Social Class of Schools' Pupil Body and the Principals' Curricular Objectives/Priorities. Proportion of Principals Not Mentioned, or Emphasising, Each Curricular Goal.*
(N = 94 schools total. Insufficient information to characterise 1 Principal.)

Relative Priorities Given to Different Educational Objectives/Goals	Median Social Class of Pupil Body					
	1 Upper Middle Class	2 Middle Class	3 Lower Middle Class	4 Upper Working Class	5 Working Class	6 Lower Working Class
(1) Christian Education and Formal Religious Instruction:						
(i) Not mentioned =	.29	.39	.41	.57	.90	1.00
(ii) Mentioned 2+ times =	.14	.39	.26	.17	.05	0
(2) Personal Development/ Pastoral Care Goals:						
(i) Not mentioned =	.14	.31	.26	.35	.21	.40
(ii) Mentioned 2+ times =	.51	.38	.56	.18	.47	.40
(3) Pragmatic Curricular Goals:						
(i) Not mentioned =	.57	.54	.48	.22	.26	0
(ii) Mentioned 2+ times =	.14	.08	.26	.35	.53	.80
Number of Schools:	7	13	27	23	19	5

While religious instruction is least emphasised in schools which have working class pupils — mostly Vocational schools, it is most emphasised in boys' lower middle or middle class schools — mainly Christian Brothers' schools as we have seen. There is no consistent linear relationship between the median social class of the pupil body and personal development or pastoral care programmes — unlike the other two goal correlations. These depend much more on the particular school authority, or the sex of pupils as we have seen —

mainly Community schools and girls' Convent schools.

Comparing schools, therefore, which cater mainly for upper middle class with those which cater for lower working class pupils we see that the former are mainly religious run and academically directed Secondary schools which emphasise academic, educational achievement goals; and which generally link personal development programmes to religious/moral education. The latter are predominantly public schools which emphasise highly instrumental or pragmatic educational (instructional) goals, and they usually separate formal religious instruction from pastoral care programmes. These latter programmes tend to be well developed for working class pupils only in the Community schools or in some Mercy/Presentation schools. The predominant goal or value orientations, therefore, of Irish post-primary schools provide quite distinct school environments for male and female pupils from different social classes.

Conclusions

There is a wide institutional diversity in Irish post-primary education, with three main sectors — Secondary, Vocational, Community. The latter two school types have charters that are quite distinct from those of the Secondary/grammar schools, in general tending to be both more vocational and more comprehensive in nature. Within the Secondary sector a wide range of organisations exist with distinct educational orientations and client characteristics. There appears, also, to be a close interrelationship between a school's "charter", its educational goals or ideology, its client selection characteristics and the educational and social placement role which these schools serve. Three main variables, however, appear to mainly determine how school organisations are likely to translate their objectives into school programmes: the gender and social class characteristics of the clientele, as well as the related principal "social placement" or social mobility role served by the school. A third factor, however, appears to be almost equally as important — the nature of the educational philosophy guiding the organisation: with the same sex and social class mix, Vocational schools and the Presentation Order, for instance, are likely to provide quite different types of education. Of course these latter institutional and ideological differences amongst schools to a large extent also influence the gender, social class, and ability selectivities of schools.

The founding charters and the rather particular histories of these different school authorities, combined with their diverse emergent roles, have resulted in quite divergent groups of schools with varying clienteles, educational objectives as well as operative goals. We can crudely summarise these school organisational differences in the following way, as well as indicate their consequences for educational differentiation (Chart 2.3).

Chart 2.3: *The Divergent Institutional Characteristics of Irish Second-Level Schools*

School Authorities	Founding Charter and Emergent Roles	Educational Philosophy or Ideology	Characteristics of Client Groups	Likely Effects on Educational Differentiation
Vocational Schools	Practical Vocational and Technical Education; with a recent acquisiton of an academic senior cycle function. *(Mainly Coed Schools)*	Highly pragmatic and instrumental.	Working class or small farm origins with a high proportion of educationally disadvantaged pupils.	Moderate to high probability of differentiation.
Community and Comprehensive Schools	Comprehensive in charter and role. *(Coed Schools)*	Moderately practical but Comprehensive. High attention to personal development and pastoral care goals. Ideal of mixed-ability teaching in original "charter".	Broad class clientele though with a low percentage of upper middle class pupils. Moderately high percentage of educationally deprived pupils, though less so than Vocational Schools.	Moderate probability of differentiation.
Christian Brothers and Presentation Brothers	Founded to educate the poor. General academic education however provided. Gradual emergence of sponsored mobility roles for able upper working class and lower middle class boys. *(Boys' Schools)*	Religious and moral formation and character development. Priority to academic goals.	Middle to lower middle class, and more able upper working class. Low percentage of seriously disadvantaged children.	High probability of differentiation so as to maximise the achievement of lower middle and working class pupils.
Mercy Sisters and Presentation Sisters	Founded to educate the poor. Girls' education at second level but have become progressively coed. General academic type general educational model with practical "vocational" orientation for girls. *(Girls' and Coed Schools)*	Personal development stressed. Pragmatic with strong community orientation.	Small farm, working class and lower middle to middle class. Moderate to high levels of intake of educationally disadvantaged pupils.	Low probability of differentiation.
Middle to Upper Middle Class Secondary Schools (various religious orders and most Protestant Schools	Classically grammar school in character and orientation. At its extreme concerned with the reproduction of upper middle class culture. *(Boys', Girls' and Coed Schools)*	Highly academic individualism and individual achievement stressed. Personal development also emphasised.	Upper middle class, and aspiring upper middle class.	Low to very low probability of differentiation.

These quite distinctive types of schools with their diverse origins and distinct objectives strengthen the argument put forward in Chapter 1 for institutional or cultural rather than "technical-rational" factors explaining why individual schools vary in their differentiation strategies. On purely technical grounds we would expect that the greatest differentiation would occur in schools showing greatest variation in their intake on social class, ability and educational disability grounds, as well as in schools with greatest variation in their "planned outputs" — i.e., in Group Certificate classes being prepared for entry to apprenticeships, etc., Intermediate classes being prepared for entry to clerical training courses, and Leaving Certificate classes being prepared for University entry, etc. In this sense Comprehensive/Community schools, or the larger Vocational schools should show greatest variation in the schooling process. For institutional and ideological reasons, however, we have hypothesised that differentiation will in fact be greater in schools whose main aim or acquired objective is to select and sponsor an elite of pupils — particularly male pupils — from their intake for upward social mobility, who are assigned "favoured treatment" so to speak. These schools, therefore, are not necessarily more diverse in the origins or abilities of their pupil intake, indeed they are likely to be less diverse in social class and pupil intake than most Vocational, Comprehensive or Convent schools. Obviously, variation in "technical characteristics" of pupil intake as well as variation in projected or planned output will have an effect on "differential treatment" strategies; but the quite diverse origins, roles and functions of our second-level school system, described in this chapter, clearly indicate that such institutional differences are likely to have even greater effect on strategies of schooling differentiation. In the following chapter we examine the extent to which different elements of the schooling differentiation process fit together to form a coherent set, and in Chapter 4 we return to examine the extent to which our hypothesised relationship between institutional factors and greater differentiation actually holds.

Chapter 3

THE STRUCTURE OF THE SCHOOLING PROCESS

The first objective of this chapter is to derive a valid and reliable typology of the schooling process: to find out what the underlying similarities are amongst the different variables involved in the schooling process, and to "fit" them to a limited set of types. A similarity or "affinity of form" is postulated as existing amongst a set of variables which define schooling: the way the pupil "raw material" is categorised, the packaging and allocation of the curriculum, the nature of the "search process" employed by teachers and pupils in fitting the curriculum to individual pupil's needs, etc. Once we have derived a valid and reliable typology we can then examine its antecedents ("causes") and its consequences.

Initially three sets of variables defining the "classes of action" taken by schools appear most relevant: (i) the nature and extent of categorisation ("streaming") of the pupil intake; (ii) the nature and extent of curricular differentiation — the different "treatments" allocated to different categories of pupils; and (iii) the extent of openness of the "search process" amongst pupils, teachers and parents in deciding on subject and level choices as well as in final occupational choices. Before proceeding to examine the nature of the relationship between these three sets of variables we first describe the way in which we measured each variable as well as the quite wide variation that exists amongst our sample of schools in all of these respects.

Variation in the "Schooling Process"

The detailed study of schools carried out for our earlier paper (Hannan, Breen *et al.*, 1983) provides the basic data for this report. In that project a national sample of 95 schools was studied in detail — and it is the data taken from the extensive interviews with school Principals and Career Guidance Teachers that provide the evidence for this report. A copy of the main interview schedule concerned is provided in Appendix I. In the following we provide a brief outline of the kind of data available which will be used to devise measures of the overall schooling process, so as to derive a valid and reliable typology of the work processes actually used by schools.

As we have already indicated three "schooling process" variables are of interest — (i) the nature and rigidity of categorisation of pupils; (ii) the extent of differentiation of the curriculum as it is applied to different categories of pupils; and (iii) the extent of subject/level choice left to individual pupils, their parents and individual subject teachers.

Pupil Categorisations

Initially, in applying Perrow's "materials technology" theory to an analysis of second-level schools, the main variable of concern is the way in which the "raw materials", (i.e., the pupils), are defined: whether the pupil is seen as unique, as a little understood entity, as an "exceptional case"; or whether the pupil is defined in narrow "educable" terms (in terms of some notions of "general ability" usually), and as easily categorisable into a limited number of types with few exceptions presenting themselves. Where each pupil's individuality is emphasised and where the many exceptions to an "average type" are not easily analysable or predictable, thereby rendering a formal and routinisable "search process" difficult, we might expect to find a much more open "search process"; i.e., mixed ability classes with subject level choices. On the other hand, if the work is to be carried out on what are perceived as "well understood", easily analysable "raw materials" (pupils), we may expect to find a highly formal and routinised "search process", i.e., a highly streamed class with little choice of subjects/levels, etc.

These two extreme situations are somewhat analogous to the extremities of the mass-production/hand-crafting continuum. In one instance, we have a school where pupils are perceived as well understood and easily categorisable and where the schooling process has been highly routinised. Here, rigid streaming, clear curricular and instructional differentiation by stream, with limited individual choice by pupil and teacher, is often characteristic. A major goal of this study is to explicate the way these routinised procedures of pupil categorisation are constructed and related to differential curriculum delivery, rigidity of class boundaries and the organisation and allocation of subject teachers.

At the other extreme, pupils may be perceived as unique or highly individualistic units, with numerous exceptional cases, not easily placed into a limited set of categories. Here, we may expect to find a much more open and flexible schooling process which is responsive to individual student's needs, and teachers' and parents' demands. This distinction in the schooling process is somewhat analogous to that offered by Bernstein (1971). The rigidly rationalised educational system with its separate highly differentiated subject-based curriculum is akin to what Bernstein describes as "the collection code", which is associated with strong classification — i.e., rigid boundaries between curricular contents — and strong "framing" or little control by pupils over the selection, organisation and pacing of knowledge transmitted and received in the pedagogical relationship. The less rationalised system, however, is only roughly analogous with Bernstein's "integrated code", which stands at the opposite end of the continuum.

However, even schools of the latter type will experience the pressures which constrain all organisations to rationalise their activities. Indeed Perrow (1967) saw it as the aim of most organisations to increase their technical knowledge and thus increase the reliability and efficiency of their "search" and processing procedures. Schools then will tend to, in time, succumb to the considerable pressures upon them to simplify and reduce the uncertainties and ambiguities of the work process.

Of course schools vary widely in their intakes — as we have already seen. The most selective of schools — those who select their intake and reject many applicants — are a minority. Yet 26 of the 95 schools surveyed rejected or actively discouraged some applicants — less than a third of these being fee paying. Even these figures, however, considerably understate the amount of local between-school selection and discrimination that occurs. For example, the median number of male applicants to our sample of schools was 52, but the median number of entrants was 33 in 1981. A substantial amount of sorting obviously occurs, therefore, before boys enter second-level schools at all. For girls the difference between the numbers of initial applicants and final entrants was somewhat less pronounced but an equally obvious sorting process occurs. The "search process" as to choice of school is, therefore, almost as important as the choice of schooling applied once pupils enter schools. The main basis of rejection of applicants appeared to be on particularistic rather than achievement grounds, that is on the basis of sibling or parental connections with the school, or belonging to a catchment area, or attendance at an attached primary school. But in 10 schools the main criterion used was performance in an entrance examination.

Over 40 per cent of schools, however, use some kind of assessment or performance test *before* pupils enter the school although only 10 schools use this for screening entrants. An additional 34 per cent of schools apply an assessment test relatively soon after pupils enter the school — a small number (11) using both types of assessment tests or examinations. The great majority of schools, therefore, apply an assessment test or examination to their pupil intake before or very soon after they enter the school, and about two-thirds of these (66%) use the results of these tests or examinations to allocate pupils to different classes in first year, or to determine whether to put pupils into honours classes in Irish, English or Mathematics.

As we can clearly see from the following summary of results from our sample of 95 schools, schools vary widely also in the extent and nature of "streaming" of their pupil intake.

Table 3.1: *The Extent and Nature of Categorisation/Differentiation of Pupils at Point of Entry, at the Intermediate Certificate and Leaving Certificate Levels*

Extent of Streaming of Classes	Entry Classes 1980/81	Intermediate Certificate Classes 1980/81	Leaving Certificate Classes 1980/81
		%	
(1) Only 1 class	9.5	14.0	30.0
(2) Purely mixed ability classes (with	34.7	23.2	34.4
remedial or low ability classes)	(3.2)	(3.2)	—
(3) 2 broad bands	6.4	11.7	8.9
(4) 3 broad bands	10.6	6.4	3.3
(5) Streamed (streamed boys with	34.7	40.4	22.4
separate girls' class)	(6.3)	(4.3)	(0)
(6) Boys and girls in separate classes	4.2	4.3	1.1
Total %	100	100	100
No.	95	94	90

Almost 10 per cent of our sample of schools had only 1 class at entry. In addition 4 per cent of schools set up separate boys' and girls' classes at entry. The remaining schools varied from one extreme where one-third "streamed" their pupil intake very rigidly, to another extreme of one-third with mixed ability classes. Rigidly streamed classes, in this sense, refer to schools which allocated pupils to relatively homogeneous ability groupings and ranked their entry classes from high to low in terms of the average assessed ability of the pupils concerned. This hierarchical organisation of classes was seldom made so explicit, however, most school decisionmakers attempted to avoid the explicit labelling of classes of pupils in an obvious hierarchical order. A minority of streamed schools was quite open, however, making quite explicit the hierarchical grading. Mixed ability classes, on the other hand, were usually set up by allocating pupils randomly to classes or in some general order such as the first or last name of the pupil.

Between these two extremes are 1 in 6 of all schools which "Broad Band". These are generally larger schools — usually the Community schools — with over 4 entry classes, where the school decisionmakers either dichotomise or trichotomise the ability distribution of pupils and usually allocate pupils on a random basis to classes within each of these relatively more homogeneous

ability "bands". Between class boundaries are, therefore, much less pronounced within these schools, but a clear ordering of either 2 or 3 "bands"
of such classes does exist.

As can be seen from Table 3.1 as one moves from entry to Intermediate
Certificate classes the extent of streaming increases. This is partly because
a number of schools do not stream until late in first year or at the beginning
of second year. But it is also the result of a slight decline in recent years in
the extent of streaming or banding present in junior cycle classes. In the 3
years preceding the study 15 per cent of schools (N = 14) had changed from
having banded/streamed to mixed ability classes, and another 5 per cent had
changed from rigid streaming to "broad banding". This was counterbalanced
to some extent by 11 per cent of schools which had gone in the opposite
direction — changing from being mixed ability to being banded or streamed.
The general trend, however, was in the opposite direction.

As dropout levels increase with years in school the proportion of schools
with only 1 class increases from less than 10 per cent at entry, to 14 per cent
at the Intermediate Certificate level to 30 per cent at Leaving Certificate
level. In the transition to senior cycle, however, almost half the larger schools
changed their streaming practices. One in 5 of the schools changed from rigid
streaming or banding in the junior cycle to mixed ability classes or to no set
classes as such in the senior cycle. An additional 10 per cent of schools had
to change from streaming/banding of classes because of declining numbers
and were left with only 1 class. Four schools out of the 90 with senior cycle
programmes had, however, gone in the opposite direction with the recent
introduction of "banding" into the whole school.

At Intermediate Certificate level almost 40 per cent of schools have either
only 1 class or completely mixed ability classes. This is nearly balanced by
an almost equal proportion of schools who "stream" their classes very rigidly;
the proportion who "band" remaining roughly the same as in the first year.
These figures, however, somewhat understate the extent of this ability/
aptitude differentiation. A high proportion of the larger Vocational and
Community schools also differentiate their entry classes by the terminal
examination to which they direct their pupils. Almost a quarter (24%) of
schools, mostly Vocational and Community schools, had terminal Group
Cert. classes, for instance, for their lowest ability pupils. These were perceived
as having such serious literacy and numeracy problems that special 2 or even
3 year Group Cert. programmes had been set up for them. In addition a
small number of schools maintained separate 4 and 3 year Intermediate
Cert. streams for "fast" and "slow learning" categories of pupils. So the
above figures understate the extent of ability/aptitude differentiation or
categorisation that occurs in post-primary schools.

In constructing these different "treatment groups" — mostly on the basis of assessed ability, aptitude or performance — either formal standardised tests are used (usually the Drumcondra tests) or else, in a minority of cases, standard I.Q. or aptitude tests. In addition some schools used their own "entrance examinations" — usually based on the Primary school curriculum. But in almost all cases school decisionmakers appeared to use such, widely varying, assessment tests unquestioningly. There also appeared to be little movement between classes/categories as one moved from first to the Intermediate Certificate year. In other words the underlying ideological and psychological rationales for the use of such "tests" — although varying widely in content across schools — appeared to be largely taken for granted and remained largely unquestioned. A small minority of school decisionmakers, however, had recently changed their sorting/categorising behaviour, mainly because they had become worried by the effects of rigid streaming on the lower ranked classes; particularly effects on the morale, behaviour and, in some cases, alienation of pupils in these classes.

Overall, however, the impression is of a very high degree of enforced standardisation of the intake "raw material" by schools — particularly in the junior cycle. Some relaxation of the strictly hierarchical class assignment on the basis of ability occurs after the Intermediate Certificate — partly due to a reduction in numbers and a decline in the resultant variance in performance as low performers dropped out. But this partly occurs also because there appeared to be a general belief that the increasing age and maturity of pupils allowed them to make more rational and productive choices at this stage.

As a corollary of such "ability" segregation of pupils there is an associated social or interactional segregation — that between groups of pupils allocated to different classes. The greater the extent to which homogeneous groups of pupils are educated together — by taking the same subject classes together, for instance — the greater the constraint on inter-pupil interaction across such class boundaries and the greater the encouragement of "within class" networks of supportive peer group relationships (see Lacey, 1970, pp. 74-95). Combined with the hierarchical ordering of classes on the basis of ability grouping, and associated curricular-academic ranking, such an hierarchical and socially segregated set of pupil peer groups creates a particularly intimidating set of social and cultural boundaries to pupil achievement in the lower classes (see Hargreaves, 1967; Lacey, 1970; Rosenbaum, 1976; Oakes, 1985).

The relationship between such class boundaries and streaming will be examined later. Here, as we can see from the results in Table 3.2, high between-class boundaries are pretty universal in the junior cycle with only 10 per cent of schools teaching classes of pupils in such a way that most subjects are not taken together — thus opening up to a large extent both subject and inter-personal friendship choice across class boundaries or loyalties. At the other extreme were about half of all schools (46.3%) where such between-class boundaries were maximised.

Table 3.2: *Distribution of Sample of Schools in Terms of the Average Number of Subjects that Classes of Pupils Take Together in the Junior and Senior Cycle*

Boundaries between Classes of Pupils	Junior Cycle Classes	Senior Cycle Classes
	%	%
(1) No "classes" as such: No required subject that all pupils in class take together	1.1	14.4
(2) Only non-exam subject (PE and RE) taken together as a class	1.1	15.6
(3) (2) + 1 or 2 other subjects	7.4	15.6
(4) (2) + 3 – 6 other subjects	44.2	45.6
(5) (2) + >6 other subjects	22.1	5.6
(6) All subjects taken together	24.2	2.2
Total %	100	100
No.	95	90

Such organised social segregation of pupils is much less pronounced at the senior cycle, however. Here 30 per cent of schools do not have rigid class boundaries as such. Of course some of these are the small single class schools which maintain wide choice of subjects. But more than half have 2 or more "classes" where, however, there is a minimal consolidation of "within class" interaction. And, through mixing with pupils from other classes in their optional subject choices, maximum encouragement is given to "between class" interaction. Of course many of these schools are ones where rigid class segregation occurs in the junior cycle so that friendship networks and peer group loyalties, or inter group jealousies, had already been solidly laid.

As we shall see later the combination of streaming with such between-class boundaries creates a quite hierarchical structure of closed, ranked classes at one extreme and at the other extreme a very open mixing of pupils of different ability levels. A consolidation of peer membership and reference group influences are likely to be maximised in the former case and to be minimised in the latter.

Subject and Level Distinctions Amongst Classes of Pupils

Once pupils are categorised and segregated by their presumed ability or performance levels most schools use rules which allocate different subjects or levels (Pass or Honours) to different classes, or which exclude certain classes of pupils from particular subjects or levels. The level (Pass or Honours) at which a subject is taken is the most obvious distinction in these respects. However, even in highly streamed schools some flexibility is allowed in subject and level choice in these respects.

The bases on which such decisions are taken, the extent to which distinctions are made between classes of pupils in these respects, and the timing of those decisions varies considerably across schools as we can see below in the results given in Table 3.3.

Table 3.3: *The Provision of Honours Level Courses and the Timing of Decisions on Level (Pass or Honours) for Intermediate and Leaving Certificate Courses, and Examination*

	Intermediate Certificate	*Schools (N=95)*	*Leaving Certificate*	*Schools (N=90)*
		%		%
(i)	Percentage of schools providing separate Honours level courses in Irish, English and/or Maths for Inter Cert. (2 or more):	64	Percentage of schools providing separate Honours level courses for *most* subjects in the Leaving Cert: (3 + separate honours)	31 (51)
(ii)	Allocation to Honours level courses depends on allocation to top streamed classes:*	39	Allocation to Honours level courses depends on allocation to top streamed classes:	18
(iii)	All Honours level courses provided are "set" with pupils from all classes being allowed to take them if able:*	40	Most Honours level courses are "set" and pupils from all classes may take them if able:	44
	Timing of Honours Decisions		*Timing of Honours Decisions*	
(iv)	During 1st year.	18	Immediately after Inter Cert. results:	34
(v)	During 2nd year:	35	End of pre-Leaving Cert. year:	27
(vi)	During 3rd year:	46	After "mock" Leaving Cert. in Leaving Cert. year	20

*(ii) and (iii) do not add up to (i) because they refer to all schools where even 1 separate Honours level subject is provided.

Two-thirds of these schools provide separate Honours courses (classes) in Irish, English and/or Maths at junior cycle level. But in a high proportion of these cases these courses are reserved for the top streamed classes. This elitist provision is must less pronounced in the senior cycle — even discounting the smaller number of pupils and classes involved. At the other extreme are the mainly "mixed ability" schools, or schools which "broad band", and which "set" their separate Honours/Pass level courses. In these schools pupils from all classes are free to take or compete for Honours level courses. Schools, therefore, which are large enough — with at least 2 classes — to provide such separate Honours courses in most subjects, are roughly evenly divided in their behaviour between those who: (a) "set" Honours classes, allowing pupils from different "classes" to take them; and (b) schools which rigidly differentiate their pupil intake into higher and lower ability classes and rigidly differentiate between these in the allocation of levels and subjects.

The timing of these decisions also varies widely. About 1 in 5 schools make such level/subject decisions on entry to first year. An additional 1 in 3 schools make such decisions during the second year, the remainder at the end of the second and beginning of the third year. Most such decisions are taken by school Principals or Career Guidance Teachers or, more rarely, subject teachers; mostly on the basis of either ability or examination performance tests. Only in a small proportion of cases (11%) is it left formally open to negotiation between pupils/parents, and teachers — although informally, of course, intervention by middle class parents particularly, are likely to be more frequent and more "successful" than by working class parents (see Lacey, 1970, pp. 125-154). Rigidly streamed schools which use "broad banding", and most unstreamed schools, "set" Honours courses in Irish, English and Maths — i.e., set up separate Pass and Honours classes in each subject, to which pupils from each "class" move. In the latter case final "levels" choices are usually left later in the cycle and are usually more open to negotiation between pupils, parents and subject teachers.

At senior cycle level almost 80 per cent of such decisions are taken at the beginning of the Leaving Certificate course or by the end of the first year of that course. But in 1 in 5 schools, decisions on which level will be taken in the final Leaving Certificate (LC) examination are only made after the results of the "Mock" LC have come out. At that stage a minority of poorer candidates who had taken the Honours level courses are discouraged from taking the final examination at Honours level.

The average school in our sample teaches 12.5 examination subjects in the senior cycle and around 2 more in the junior cycle, with very wide school variances in both cases. Less than half of this variance is explained by size of school, however (Hannan, Breen et al., 1983, pp. 156-224). Most of the remainder appears to be explainable by the nature and effectiveness of school-level decisionmaking. Also the provision of separate Honours level courses, or of specialist groups of subjects — like Science or Technical subjects, for instance, although equally related to size of school and highly correlated with the size of the curriculum, left very wide leeway for management initiative.

As we have seen there is remarkable variation in the way Honours and Pass level courses or subjects are applied within schools at junior cycle. At one extreme are about a third of schools where an extremely rigid curricular differentiation occurs — with very little choice left to the individual pupil. In these schools substantial differences exist amongst classes of pupils in both the level and identity of subjects they are allowed to take; i.e., upper streams being allocated academic subjects and Honours levels, and bottom streams Pass levels and technical subjects, etc. In about 40 per cent of schools (Table 3.3) Honours/Pass level distinctions are made purely on the basis of streaming — if in top streams pupils are allocated Honours levels, and if in bottom streams Pass levels only. Even within Honours levels, Maths is often treated differently to Irish and English — being allocated completely to the top stream, with the other 2 subjects being assigned to the top 2 or 3 classes. Therefore, although two-thirds of all schools provided separate Honours/Pass courses in Irish, English or Maths, more than half of these schools had introduced very rigid allocation rules as to which classes of, usually highly streamed, pupils can take these subjects.

At senior cycle level the overall provision of Honours level courses is equally pronounced — with just over half the sample of schools providing separate Honours level courses in at least 3 subjects, and around a third of schools providing separate Honours courses for more than 5 subjects. Although generally subject choice is wider in the senior cycle about one-third of schools providing the Leaving Certificate course make rigid distinctions in the allocation of subjects to different streamed/banded classes, with even 1 in 6 schools providing Honours level courses only to the top 1 or 2 classes.

As we shall see, these subject and level distinctions are not determined by school size constraints; nor indeed are the correlations amongst those variables sufficiently pronounced to indicate that we are dealing with a simple and straightforward "streaming" phenomenon. Although clearly correlated with streaming, schools still varied widely in the extent to which they used such pupil "ability" distinctions in allocating subjects or levels, or in the extent to which such choices were allowed at the individual pupil and subject/teacher level. The interrelationship of choice, streaming, and curricular differentiation in the overall schooling process is more complex and needs more analysis before a satisfactory typology can be determined.

The "Search Process": The Extent of Choice and the Level of Involvement
of Pupils and Subject Teachers in Educational Decisions

If there are rigid schooling practices which act to minimise the degrees of freedom pupils and individual subject teachers have in fitting pupils to the curriculum available in the school, then a number of obvious consequences follow for pupil-teacher-parent autonomy at the classroom level:

(1)   Decreased involvement of teachers in pupil-choice of subjects and related aspects of schooling. Little autonomy left to pupils, parents, teachers in curricular choice.

(2)   Little improvisation or spontaneous choice making of subjects, teachers or levels is allowed. This suggests limited adaptability to individual pupil needs or change in pupil needs. At the extreme classes of pupils are rigidly categorised, their "destiny" centrally determined.

(3)   Restrained and more formalised pupil-teacher interaction. The roles of teachers and pupils are much more rigidly and formally defined and the boundaries between them are made much clearer.

The use of the more formalised "collective code", as Bernstein (1977, pp. 79-115) pointed out, has, therefore, a number of organisational consequences for schools. At this stage we are not interested, however, in these wider organisational implications, but in the way the overall process is organised at the classroom level. In regard to the "search process", therefore, the main variables we are interested in are the extent of choice allowed to pupils, or the range of educational options open to them, and the extent to which teachers and parents are involved actively in that choice making. In the following two tables we provide some idea of the amount of school variance involved at both junior and senior cycle levels.

Again we can see a lot of variance between schools in all of these respects. In almost half the schools at junior cycle level there is very little choice and very little involvement of pupils, teachers or parents in choice making. None of this is necessarily due to restrictions in the number of subjects actually available in the school for junior pupils. As often as not it is due to discriminations made by school decisionmakers about what kinds of "classes" of pupils are to be taught which kinds of subjects. At the other extreme there is somewhat over a quarter of schools with very wide choice of subjects and relatively high subject teacher and parental involvement. Much wider choices exist, however, at the senior cycle level as can be seen in Table 3.5.

Choice, as we have already seen, is a lot freer at the senior level. Almost all but the smallest of schools have some choice and up to two-thirds have substantial choice — as can be seen from Table 3.5. On the other hand, most of this choice making is carried out in the context of organised meetings

Table 3.4: *Extent of Subject Choice and Extent to Which Parents and Teachers are Involved in Pupil Choice Making. Number of Schools with Various Levels of, and Participation in, Choices*

No. of Optional Subjects Offered to all *Pupils at Intermediate Certificate Level*		*Extent of Individual Subject Teacher Involvement in Choice Making for Intermediate Certificate Year*		*Extent of Parental Involvement in Choice of Intermediate Certificate Subject*	
No. of subjects	*No. of schools*	*Teacher involvement in choice making*	*No. of schools*		*No. of schools*
1. None*	42	1. No or little choice or little teacher involvement in choice	44	1. No choice or parents not involved	35
2. 1 to 2:	13	2. School organised central (official) "help" with choice	25	2. Parents are involved: but meetings with school staff not generally organised	28
3. 3 to 4:	15	3. Moderate to high level of teacher involvement with choice	26	3. School organised meetings with parents re choices	32
4. > 4:	25				
Total No.	95	Total No.	95	Total No.	95

*Optional subjects may still be offered within streamed or banded classes of pupils.

between individual pupils (or a class of pupils) and the central school decision-makers — the Principal, Vice Principal or Career Guidance Teacher. Only in 1 in 4 schools are the subject teachers explicitly and formally included in this decisionmaking process. And only in 12 schools are formally organised meetings arranged between parents and individual subject teachers in these respects. Most of the officially organised school negotiation/advisory sessions with pupils/parents are with the schools' officials (Principals, Vice Principals or Career Guidance Teachers), not with individual subject teachers.

The three sets of variables we have examined — extent of streaming/categorisation of pupils, the extent of subject/level distinctions amongst categories of pupils, the extent of "choice" left to pupils and subject teachers as to what kind of education to apply to each pupil — as we shall see are moderately inter-correlated, particularly in larger schools. But the inter-relationships involved are not very straightforward. And neither individually nor collectively are they explainable simply as straightforward technically

Table 3.5: *Extent of Subject Choice and of Subject-Teacher and Parental Involvement in Subject Choice at Senior Cycle Level*

No. of Optional Subjects Made Available to All Pupils in Senior Cycle		Extent of Individual Subject Teacher Involvement in Subject Choice for Leaving Certificate		Extent and Nature of Parental Involvement in Choice	
	No. of schools		No. of schools	Extent of Involvement	No. of schools
1. No choice:	6	1. No or very little choice or little school/teacher involvement in choice:	11	1. Parents not involved formally by schools; or individual arrangement:	26
2. 1-3 subjects:	13	2. Only school officials involved directly:	49	2. Parental involvement organised/facilitated by school:	64
3. 4-6 subjects:	14	3. Subject teachers involved and other school officials:	24	Total	90
4. >6 subjects:	55	4. Only subject teachers involved:	6	*Type of Arrangement*	
(Missing Data)	(2)			1. Organised meeting with individual subject teachers arranged for parents:	12
				2. Organised meeting arranged with school officials - Principal/ Vice-Principal or Career Guidance Teacher for parents:	48*
				3. Other arrangements:	26
Total No. schools	90	Total No.	90	Total	90

*Information unavailable for 4 schools as to type of parent-school arrangements made.

determined responses to increasing pupil numbers or increasing variance in pupil characteristics. In the following section we propose a conceptual approach to examining these interrelationships.

The Structuring of the Schooling Process

To simplify our discussion, if we take the three sets of school processing variables we have used so far and dichotomise each variable, we get the following:

Variable 1:   *Pupil Conceptualisation/Categorisation:*

Categories A_1: Streamed classes (by ability of pupil).
         A_2: Mixed Ability classes of pupils

Variable 2: *Curriculum Packaging:*

Categories B_1: Differentiation in applying the curriculum to different categories of pupils.

B_2: No differentiation in application of curriculum.

Variable 3: *Search Process* (Pupil-teacher interaction in the search for schooling "solutions"):

Categories C_1: Not Elaborated/Closed – decision made centrally, little pupil-teacher choice.

C_2: Elaborate/Open – high choice and high level of pupil-teacher interaction in choosing.

Taking the dichotomised variables 1, 2 and 3 together there are eight possible combinations of the categories as can be seen below in Figure 3.1.

Figure 3.1: *The Limits of Covariation Amongst the 3 Sets of Schooling Variables: Eight "Types". (2 x 2 x 2)*

Search Process	Streamed Schools (A1)		Unstreamed Schools (A2)	
	Curriculum	*Differentiated (B)*	*Curriculum*	*Differentiated (B)*
(C)	Yes$_{(1)}$	No$_{(2)}$	Yes$_{(1)}$	No$_{(2)}$
Closed$_{(1)}$	$A_1 B_1 C_1$	$A_1 B_2 C_1$	$A_2 B_1 C_1$	$A_2 B_2 C_1$
	(Most Likely)	(Not Feasible)	(Not Feasible)	(Possible)
Open$_{(2)}$	$A_1 B_1 C_2$	$A_1 B_2 C_2$	$A_2 B_1 C_2$	$A_2 B_2 C_2$
	(Possible)	(Not Feasible)	(Not Feasible)	(Most Likely)

Of the eight possible combinations a small number of categories could not logically or realistically occur. Rigid streaming with no curricular differentiation by stream makes no sense – either in logic or practice. Schools stream pupils to create homogeneous ability groupings so that they can apply a separate curricular/teaching process to each ability category that is thought to be suitable to their capabilities and likely careers (Hargreaves, 1967; Lacey, 1970; Rosenbaum, 1976; Oakes, 1985). It makes no sense to stream pupils by their assessed or assumed ability levels unless with the explicit intention of applying a differentiated curricular and teaching process to each stream. And if both of these conditions hold, then, almost by definition, one cannot have a highly elaborated "search process" by pupils, parents and teachers, in an attempt to find unique teaching/curricular solutions to fit each individual pupil's needs. So, according to our logic, types $A_1 B_2 C_2$, $A_1 B_2 C_1$ are extremely unlikely to occur — streamed schools with no curricular differentiation. If one has a streamed pupil body, with clear curricular differentiation ($A_1 B_1$), however, it is still possible to have an elaborate and highly involved pupil-teacher "search process": by having a large number of optional subjects, although empirically less likely to occur than type $A_1 B_1 C_1$. Schools which so centrally control pupil categorisation and curricular differentiation are much less likely to allow wide freedom of subject/level choices to teachers and pupils. Still it is possible to leave open a moderate level of optional subject choice, depending on the number of subjects taught.

The contrasting argument that the use of mixed ability classes is unlikely to coincide with clear curricular differentiation or a minimal "search process" appears equally logical. If schools have genuinely mixed ability classes then they do not or should not distinguish between such classes by curricular or teaching practice; i.e., $A_2 B_2 C_2$ is the most likely combination. However, if schools do not have many "extra" or optional subjects available, subject choice may be very limited, so that type $A_2 B_2 C_1$ is possible in these circumstances. Mixed ability classes with curricular differentiation make no sense, however, and is extremely unlikely to occur (i.e., $A_2 B_1 C_1$ or $A_2 B_1 C_2$). However, schools which are in process of changing their teaching strategies from "streaming" towards "mixed ability" teaching may retain some such mixtures of types for a short time. Or schools with poor teacher participatory characteristics may have very limited teacher involvement in the "search process" — irrespective of the number of optional subjects available to pupils.

The two "ideal types" of $A_1 B_1 C_1$ and $A_2 B_2 C_2$, at both extremes of the continuum, are the most logically consistent schooling process outcomes — at one extreme with rigid streaming, high levels of curriculum differentiation and a "search process" which is mainly organisationally, not interpersonally, determined; and at the other end schools which have mixed ability classes, minimal curricular distinctions applied to classes, and a highly elaborated "search process" operating at the individual pupil level.

As we have pointed out, however, other outcomes (profiles) are likely to occur, though less logically determined, particularly outcomes like $A_2 B_2 C_1$. Here with mixed ability classes and a curriculum which is applied without constraints across the different classes of pupils the school may not achieve even a moderate level of teacher involvement in the "search process". This may be due either to very few optional subjects being made available by the school or the failure of school management and teacher commitment to getting involved in a "search process". And at the other extreme, of course, it is possible to have streamed classes which are, however, only differentiated by curricular type and level to a minimal extreme, and with high teacher involvement $(A_1 B_1 C_2)$ in a relatively unrestricted "search process" amongst a set of optional subject choices made available to individual pupils.

It is apparent in discussing the makeup of these profiles that the three variables — pupil categorisation, curricular differentiation, choice or "search process" — have different organisational sources and characteristics. The first two result from school management decisions: to stream or not, to develop and apply a curriculum in a differentiated way or not. And the implementation of these decisions is usually handled through formal administrative procedures within the school. Although individual teachers' role expectations, motivational commitments and basic interests are closely linked to implementing these schooling process decisions, and they may have been highly involved in, or consulted about, the relevant decisions, the working out of these decisions in practice — particularly where rigid streaming occurs or where an elaborate curricular differentiation occurs — is usually a product of a centralised and routinised arrangement within the school. The same cannot be said, however, about the "search process". This demands direct teacher involvement and commitment — irrespective of whether it occurs in the constrained subject/level choices available in a highly streamed/differentiated school or the much wider and freer choices available in a mixed ability and undifferentiated curriculum school.

Underlying Principles which Structure these Relationships

Implicit in the above discussion is a belief that underlying these schooling decisions there are certain structuring principles. An obvious one is the extent to which schooling has become a routinised, organisationally unproblematic process in which almost everybody involved knows their place and their tasks well and carries them out in a routine and unquestioned way. This was obvious in the relatively high proportion of schools which had not changed their streaming or curricular allocation practices for at least 10 years preceding our survey and in addition had not even changed their pattern of core/optional subject sets in either their junior or senior cycle programme. Over 40 per cent of all schools, for instance, had made no change in their junior cycle "optional package" of subjects in the 5 years preceding the survey: and about 30 per cent of schools had been equally conservative in regard to senior cycle "optional subject packages" offered to pupils. Although this conservative tendency is related to purely circumstantial factors — like growth or decline in pupil/teacher numbers and so on — the routinisation and the taken for granted nature of the schooling process in a large number of schools could not be so easily explained away.

Organisationally, there is pressure on any school to simplify and routinise both its work process and its "search process". "Organisations uniformly seek to standardise their raw material in order to minimise exceptional cases" (Perrow, 1967, p. 197). This, in turn, allows for a more routinised "search process" and "work process". Thus, the three variables — streaming, curriculum differentiation and a minimal search process — are individual aspects of an overall process of greater routinisation and rationalisation of the schooling process. In this kind of school a lot of what is problematic in the schooling process has been organisationally resolved in favour of one "solution" which minimises work effort — at least in the formally defined teaching/learning tasks to be carried out within the classroom. The "what", "how", "who" and even "why" have been formally preordained. Other work tasks, of course, have not and cannot be foreordained — control within the classroom, motivating pupils to learn, the dynamics of pupil-teacher interaction within the constrained classroom environment, etc.

In the above set of profiles, therefore, one might say that the more *1s* that turn up in a school profile the more bureaucratically or organisationally resolved are the problems — rather than interpersonally negotiated. And, at the other extreme, the more *2s* that appear in a school profile the more "active" all the individual workers are within the school in the process of constructing the schooling experience.

In terms of our theoretical framework, therefore, as we have already noted, it is, in fact, those schools which do not stream (A_2), which do not differentiate curricula (B_2) and which have elaborated search process (C_2), which might be deemed to be the most active in the construction of the schooling process. There is more sustained effort required on the part of the school, and on the part of individual teachers, if they:

(1)   teach individuals as unique persons and do not categorise them by "type" (i.e., do not stream);
(2)   treat the curriculum openly, with fluid boundaries and wide choice (i.e., do not differentiate the curriculum);
(3)   maximise the energy and effectiveness of the search process.

However, we cannot simply add scores together as in the normal Likert scale or as in most indices. If we simply add all three scores together it would be possible to get the same outcome "score" for 2 schools which had quite different schooling processes. For example, the following two profiles have exactly the same "score" if we add up the values across:

$$\text{Profile } A_1 B_2 C_2 = \text{Profile } A_2 B_2 C_1 = 5$$

However, the profiles have quite different meanings: the first school, though streamed, has little curricular differentiation and wide choice, the second though "unstreamed" as such, and with little curricular differentiation, has little choice. Since the 8 profiles represent qualitatively different solutions from one another, they cannot, in fact, be quantitatively compared to one another (Shye, 1978, p. 265). The Guttman-Lingoes "implicative" approach, which takes such "meanings" into consideration, is a much more useful model to use (ibid.).

The assumption implicit in our discussion of the likely relationship amongst these "schooling process" variables could be summed up in terms of a "closed" versus "open" system model (using these terms in a slightly different sense from that normally used in the organisational literature). On the one hand we have organisations where decisionmaking is centralised and where roles/tasks are highly differentiated and routinised. At the other extreme are organisations where decisions are diffused, and where relationships are open to negotiation, and the work process demands an elaborate "search process". For example, at one pole one could posit streamed schools whose "organisational solutions" to their schooling processes have remained unchanged for a long time, and at the other pole mixed ability schools with wide subject choice, high teacher involvement and a continuous process of negotiated change and adjustment to schooling arrangements.

This conclusion may suggest a simple unilinear and additive set of relationships amongst the variables and this as we have seen is not, indeed cannot be, so. There are both logical and empirical constraints on the way these variables may be related to each other. The "search process", for instance, could be regarded very much as an outcome of pupil categorisation and curriculum differentiation decisions. If changes are made in pupil categorisation then changes have to follow in curricular differentiation, and subsequently in the search process. Changes towards less rigid streaming make no sense unless schools also release the constraints on what subjects or levels the new classes of pupils can take — whether these are loosely "banded" or "mixed ability" classes. Changing the criteria on how pupils are allocated to classes as well as the rigidity of between-class boundaries would have very little impact on pupil learning or subject teaching without also changing the content and nature of the subjects and levels allocated to these classes and the rigidity of rules which constrain pupil choices of subjects' levels. On the other hand, changes could quite conceivably occur in the latter two variables without any change having been made in pupil categorisation: subject option choices could be widened for all streamed classes and access to Honours and Pass level courses would be widened by "setting", etc.

Thus, there is a highly interactive relationship between the variables — particularly between pupil categorisation and curriculum differentiation —

and the flow of influence would seem to be as follows: Changes in Pupil Categorisation → Changes in Curriculum Differentiation → Changes in the Search Process.

Thus, from a school's definition or categorisation of its "raw materials", it follows that a certain mode of treating that raw material is largely determined, and this in turn affects the "search process". This, however, assumes a simple unidimensional model of change — from an "open" to a "closed", and organisationally determined, teaching process; or from an organisational solution which had become centralised, highly routinised and organisationally differentiated to one where there is a very high level of pupil-teacher-parent involvement at an interpersonal level in the schooling process. In the following analysis we first examine the extent to which our data fit such a unidimensional model.

The Relationship Amongst the "Schooling Process" Variables: Is it Unidimensional?

In our attempt to see whether these various measures of schooling process fall into a unidimensional pattern, 6 measures of pupil/curricular categorisation or allocation and of the pupil-teacher "search process" were used. All scales were scored from low to high in terms of the "closedness" or "openness" of their teaching/schooling effects — of the school's adaptiveness to individual differences. At one extreme are schools, which stream pupils into rigid ability categories, which make many subject type and level distinctions in adapting the teaching process to individual needs of pupils, and have low pupil and teaching autonomy in fitting pupils to the choices that exist. At the other extreme are schools which have mixed ability classes, which have fluid boundaries between classes, which use a completely open curriculum with all subjects/levels available to all "classes" of pupils, which have many subject options open, and which have high teacher involvement in the "search process", etc.

The following 6 variables were first chosen to represent the range of schooling process "solutions" adopted by schools in both the junior and senior cycle. They are constructed from responses to detailed questions asked to Principals of schools in the survey.

1. *Streaming of Classes*[1] (i)

   4 = completely streamed in junior and senior cycle.
   ↓
   1 = completely mixed ability in junior and senior cycle.

2. *Subject Distinctions*[1] (ii)

Extent of subject and level distinctions used by school in allocating subjects/teachers to different classes of pupils.

4 = very high level of distinction amongst classes of pupils in allocating
↓   subjects/levels.
1 = very low level of distinction or none.

3. *Class Boundaries*[1] (iii)

The number of subjects taken together by the typical class of pupils within the school in junior and senior cycle. (The boundaries, or flows between classes, are measured by this variable.)

3 = almost all subjects taken together as a class in junior and senior
↓   cycle.
1 = very few or none taken together as a class.

4. *Choice of Subjects*[1] (iv)

Extent of pupil choice of subjects at the Intermediate and Leaving Certificate.

3 = low or none.
↓
1 = high number (> 10 at Leaving Certificate).

5. *Teachers' Involvement in choice*[1] (v)

Extent to which teachers are involved in pupil choice making for subjects and occupations and guidance, etc.

4 = low involvement of teacher or none.
↓
1 = high involvement of teachers.

6. *Parents' Involvement in choice*[1] (vi)

Extent of parents' involvement in pupil choice in school and their interaction with teachers.

3 = low or absent.
↓
1 = high.

---

1. (i) *"Stream"* -- has 4 values; 4 = completely streamed classes on basis of assessed ability, 3/2 = 2 or 3 rigid bands of classes; 1.0 = completely mixed ability classes. (ii) *"Subject distinction"* is a scale constructed from 6 items each scored 1.0 if subject/level distinctions are made, or 0 — if not. These are summed and divided by no. of applicable items. Three questions refer to junior cycle and 3 to senior

For each variable the values are rank ordered from the most organisationally "closed" or most restrictive (3 or 4) to the most "open" or most participative (1). The values of all of the scales, therefore, are ordered so as to consistently index degrees of schooling differentiation, or degrees of centralisation of schooling decisions. The highest value in all cases is the most "closed" one, or the one having the highest degree of differentiation of pupils and curricula as well as of centralisation of schooling decisions.

In the following table we provide the correlation amongst these 6 variables for those schools with at least 2 separate classes of pupils at Leaving Certificate level. Details on the construction of these scales are given in footnote 1. Our hypothesis was that they would be all positively though moderately correlated.

We restricted consideration to schools where there was at least a necessity to have more than 1 class in Leaving Certificate to allow the decisions to be relevant and meaningful at that level. Restricted in this way it is obvious that all relationships amongst the 6 variables are positive, with the strongest set of relationships found amongst 5 variables — "Streaming", "Subject Distinction", "Class Boundaries", "Teacher Involvement" and "Choice" (Table 3.6). Parental involvement in choice making, although positively correlated with all of the other variables, has a low overall level of association. This suggests that, while teachers' level of involvement is to a substantial extent predicated on the school's organisational "openness", in the above sense, this is not equally true of parental involvement. Different social and organisational factors are obviously involved in the latter case.

Further analysis of these relationships showed that the larger the school the greater the level of intercorrelation involved amongst the 5 variables mentioned above. In other words the greater the size and associated complexity of the organisational tasks involved the greater the extent of coincidence of decision outcomes across all variables. The following table shows this very clearly.

In very small schools (<200 pupils) there is no consistent relationship amongst the 5 items — as one might expect when there is only 1 to 2 classes.

cycle distinctions by schools between streamed classes of pupils in being allowed to take Honours courses or not, and distinctions in the "packages of subjects" allocated to such distinctive classes. (iii) *"Class Boundaries"* = 2 items, 1 for junior and 1 for senior cycle, measuring extent to which "classes" of pupils take all/some subjects together as a class, or separately as individuals from different classes: 3 = classes where pupils take 6 or more subjects together, 1 = only non-exam subjects taken together. (iv) *"Choice"* is a scale made up of more than 10 items indexing number of optional subjects made available to *all* pupils/classes in the junior and senior cycle: 2 = No optional subjects, 1 = 1-4 optional subjects, 0 = 5 or more optional subjects. (v) *"Teachers' Involvement"* is a scale constructed from 4 items measuring teachers' involvement in pupils' choice of subjects and in their occupational choices: 3 = No choice or subject teachers not involved in choice → 1 = high subject teacher involvement in choice. (vi) *"Parents' Involvement"* scale is exactly equivalent to "Teachers' Involvement" scale.

Table 3.6: *Intercorrelations Amongst 6 Scales Measuring Aspects of the "Schooling Process" (N = 63)*

Scale	Stream	Subject Distinction	Class Boundaries	Choice	Teacher Involvement
Streaming	1.00				
Subject Distinction	.50*	1.00			
Class Boundaries	.40*	.45*	1.00		
Choice of Subjects	.34*	.25*	.27*	1.00	
Teacher Involvement	.39*	.20*	.27*	.54*	1.00
Parents' Involvement	.16	.10	.31*	.19	.17

*Correlations significant at the .05 level, one tailed.

Indeed there is a slight though consistent negative set of relationships between the extent of subject distinctions present, and the 4 other variables involved. However, the sample of such small schools is so low that only one of these correlations is significant; though the overall average intercorrelation is negative. This average intercorrelation increases consistently and positively with school size. This is particularly true for the correlations between streaming, subject/level distinctions and all other variables. The average inter-correlation and "alpha" increases consistently with size.

Our main hypothesis on "structuring", therefore, is strongly supported in these respects. These variables are clearly unidimensionally related, the extent of covariation in decisionmaking increasing consistently as size of school increases. Increasing size appears to constrain or force organisations' choices or strategies to be consistent with each other. As we have already stated we do not wish to treat these variables as simply additive, however, and, there-fore, construct a straightforward Likert scale — although it would yield a highly reliable one. The relationships are highly interactive or "implicative" and Guttman ordinal scaling procedures are much more revealing in these cases.

Scaling the "Schooling Process" Variables

We first attempted a simple unidimensional scaling approach using the ordinary Guttman scalogram procedure. If there is only one dimension involved in either the total set of variables isolated or amongst an identi-fiable subset this will become apparent.

A unidimensional Guttman scale is also a "reproducible" one: in that it allows us to know precisely from the score assigned to some person, or school, which items were true for that person. It is, therefore, more meaning-

Table 3.7: *Intercorrelations Amongst the 5 Main Scale Items for 4 Different School Sizes*

Scale Variables	School Size < 200 Pupils (N = 19 schools)				School Size 200-400 Pupils (N = 36 schools)				School Size 400-600 Pupils (N = 24 schools)				School Size > 600 Pupils (N = 16 schools)			
	(i)	(ii)	(iii)	(iv)	(i)	(ii)	(iii)	(iv)	(i)	(ii)	(iii)	(iv)	(i)	(ii)	(iii)	(iv)
(i) Stream	1.00				1.00				1.00				1.00			
(ii) Sub. Distinction	-.08	1.00			.46[1]	1.00			.25	1.00			.39	1.00		
(iii) Class Boundaries	-.33[2]	-.50[1]	1.00		.27[2]	-.05	1.00		.31[2]	.53[1]	1.00		.41[1]	.70[1]	1.00	
(iv) Choice	.02	-.33[2]	.17	1.00	.16	-.21	.24[2]	1.00	.34[1]	.11	.59[1]	1.00	.64[1]	.35[2]	.34[2]	1.00
(v) Teacher Involvement	.04	-.24	.01	.18	.04	-.19	.31[1]	.65[1]	.39[1]	.04	.18	.41[1]	.63[1]	.10	.39[2]	.29
Average Intercorrelation	$\bar{R} = -.14$				$\bar{R} = .17$				$\bar{R} = .32$				$\bar{R} = .42$			
Cronbach's Alpha	a = negative				a = .51				a = .70				a = .79			

[1] Statistically significant at the .05 level, one tailed.
[2] Statistically significant at the .10 level, one tailed.

ful than a simple index or a Likert scale, for instance. The overall score of a Likert scale — which is the sum of scores from a large intercorrelated set of individual item responses — can be arrived at in a number of different ways, not allowing one to know how particular individuals responded to any single item or identifiable combination of items. Each Guttman scale, however, has a fully identifiable set of responses — allowing for a minimal level of error (Torgerson, 1958, pp. 298-350; Oppenheim, 1966, pp. 143-151). From each individual's score we can tell — within certain allowable error limits — which items were positive and which negative.

All items in a Guttman scale, therefore, are ordinal, "cumulative" and "reproducible" — they are ordered in an increasing or cumulative degree of "difficulty". Those who answer or are in agreement with higher order questions, etc., will have agreed with lower order ones. Like lead, glass and diamonds, they are ordered in an increasing degree of "hardness" or "difficulty". It is hypothesised that certain aspects of the schooling process occur in the same way — in terms of clearly linked and cumulative decisions. For example, only large schools can stream their intake — one has to have at least 2 classes. But such schools need not do so. However, (i) if they stream their pupil intake in terms of their assessed "ability" or performance levels, (ii) they can make very clear distinctions between such ranked classes in terms of the level of subjects and type of curriculum assigned to them, even the quality of teachers applied. Clearly such curricular/teaching distinctions presume streaming — but streaming does not necessarily lead to rigid curricular/teaching distinctions. (iii) If both the above conditions are met then very clearcut boundaries can come to exist between different classes of pupils within the same year group — with pupils sharing few subjects or teachers. Pupils within such classes will tend to increasingly restrict interaction to pupils within their own class. However, this need not occur. Many subject levels/types can be "set", such that pupils from the lower classes might be allowed to take Honours English, or Mathematics, for instance; while students from higher classes may be allowed to "drop down" to take Spanish, or Pass Irish or Technical Drawing and so on. Such schooling process decisions almost necessarily cumulate in an ordinal, implicative, fashion. (iv) If, however, schools do stream and there is little such "setting" or movement between classes, with very clear between-class boundaries, then other consequences almost necessarily follow — unless the school intervenes to prevent it occurring. If subject/level decisionmaking has been so reserved to central school decisionmaking, then interactive decisionmaking amongst pupils-teachers-parents over what subject/levels individual pupils should or should not take has been very severely curtailed. However, some school authorities may decide to leave as many decisions as possible at this level —

through maximising optional subject arrangements and good timetabling procedures, etc. Whichever choice is taken has considerable consequence for the interactive nature of the "search process" amongst pupils, their parents and teachers.

So these cumulative schooling decisions have clear "implicative" relationships for each other. They proceed from "lower level" decisions, which still leave many options open, to increasingly more constrained choices as options become reduced. As one organisational decision follows another, in something like the above sequence, "later" options are cumulatively and progressively reduced.

The procedure of Scalogram Analysis allow us, therefore, to test whether a set of items are: (i) unidimensional (unmasking an underlying single dimension), (ii) ordinal and "reproducible" — arranged according to their cumulative degree of "difficulty". A "Coefficient of Reproducibility" is computed to test the extent to which such item scores fall into such an ordinal, cumulative arrangement. An error level of 10 per cent is normally accepted in the above sense — or a "Coefficient of Reproducibility" of .90 or higher.

When we restrict the scale analysis to schools where there are 2 or more Intermediate Certificate classes in the school and use the most strict definition of what is: (a) rigid streaming; (b) rigid subject and (Pass/Honours) level distinctions between classes of pupils; (c) rigid distinctions between classes of pupils — with most/all subjects taken together as a class; (d) no or very little choice amongst subjects/levels by pupils; and (e) little pupil/teacher interaction over such choice making in general, a number of almost perfect Guttman scales emerge depending on the "cutting points"[2] used for each item. Parents' involvement in subject choice making did not fit into this pattern to the same extent, so it was dropped. Apparently such "external" parental involvement in the school is not explainable by the same logic as that determining "internal" school decisionmaking.

The following table provides the best solution — the one with the least number of errors. All of the following "solutions" are achieved by hand, the SPSS Guttman scaling procedure does not minimise either subject or item errors.

The Guttman scale emerging from the analysis of the 80 schools with 2 or more Intermediate Certificate classes is an almost perfect unidimensional scale, with a Coefficient of Reproducibility of .93 and a Coefficient of

2. Guttman scales are based on dichotomous items, e.g., Yes/No, True/False, Present/Absent, etc. Where there are items with multiple responses, as in the 5 items above, these are collapsed into 2 categories. However, there are 4 possible points at which one can dichotomise a 5 category response scale — i.e., from rigid streaming (=4) to complete mixed ability classes (=1). A certain amount of trial and error will reveal which cut-off point yields a scale with the least error. The "cutting point" then is the point in an item scale at which one dichotomises such responses.

Table 3.8: *The Guttman Scaling of Five Schooling Process Variables, Some "Cutting Points" which Indicate Very Rigid Differentiation***

Scale Type	Variables**					Distribution of Schools on Guttman Scale Based on Schools with at Least 2 Inter Cert. Classes (N = 80)	Distribution of Schools on Guttman Scale Based on all Schools (N = 95)
	A Extent of Subject/Level Distinction Amongst Classes of Pupils ("Subdist")	*B* Extent of Choice of Subjects by Pupils in Junior and Senior Cycle ("Choice")	*C* Extent of Involvement of Teachers in Pupils' Choice ("Teachinv")	*D* Extent of "Streaming" Hierarchical Ordering of Classes of Pupils ("Stream")	*E* Extent of Boundary Between Classes of Pupils ("Clascore")		
	X = extensive subject/level distinctions	X = almost no subject choice	X = very little or no teacher involvement in pupils' choice making	X = rigid streaming or banding of classes of pupils	X = rigid boundaries between classes (more) than 5 subjects taken together		
	(Score >.60) (Range 0-1.0)	(Score >1.5) (Range 0-2)	(Score >2) (Range 1-3)	(Score >2.5) (Range 1-4)	(Score >2) (Range 1-3)		
5	X	X	X	X	X	9	9
4	0	X	X	X	X	18	22
3	0	0	X	X	X	13	13
2	0	0	0	X	X	16	16
1	0	0	0	0	X	12	22
0	0	0	0	0	0	12	13
No. of "X"s	10	26	43	48	61	80	95
No. of errors	1	3	9	8	6	27	39
No. of "X"s	10	30	53	49	75	0	0
No. of errors	1	3	17*	12*	6	0	0

*These errors are particularly large partly because of distinctions between classes based on sex rather than ability.

**(A) "Subdist" is a scale constructed from 6 items scored 1.0 or 0 which measures the presence or absence of different subject and level distinctions amongst classes. These are summed and divided by No. of applicable items. A score of .60 means that half of items were positive indicating a high level of subject/level distinctions between classes. (D) "Stream" — has 4 values = completely streamed classes on basis of assessed ability, 3/2-2 or 3 rigid bands of classes; 1.0 = completely mixed ability classes. (B) "Choice" is a scale made up of more than 10 items indexing number of optional subjects made available to all pupils/classes in the junior and senior cycle: 2 = no optional subjects; 1 = 1-4 optional subjects; 0 = 5 or more optional subjects. (C) "Teachinv" is a scale constructed from 4 items measuring teachers' involvement in pupils' choice of subjects and in their occupational choices; 3 = no choice or subject teachers not involved in choice → 1 = high subject teacher involvement in choice. (E) "Clascore" — 2 item scale measuring extent to which "classes" of pupils take all/some subjects together as a class, or separately as individuals from different classes: 3 = classes where pupils take 6 or more subjects together → 1 = only non-exam subjects taken together.

Scalibility of .77. In other words in reproducing any set of individuals' exact responses from the score assigned one, would be correct 93 times out of 100.

A Guttman scale is both implicative and "reproducible". Thus for any school once we know its "score" or scale type, we can reproduce (with 93 per cent accuracy) its pattern of responses on each variable. Thus schools with a "scale type" or score of 5 had as its most "difficult" item (or one least likely to occur) substantial subject and Honours/Pass level distinctions being made between classes of pupils. Here the 9 schools involved generally allocated Honours level courses to the top streamed classes, and Pass courses and some subjects — usually technical or vocational subjects — to the bottom 1/2 classes. If schools were so characterised then this "implied" that such schools also had: (a) almost no choice of subjects — almost all were allocated; (b) little consequent involvement of teachers and pupils in choice making; (c) rigid streaming or "banding" of pupils, and (d) had relatively rigid boundaries between classes of pupils. In other words such subject/level distinctions occurring in highly streamed schools have clear "implications" for subject choice, teacher involvement in choice, and distinctions or clear boundaries between classes of pupils. The reverse is not the case — as is obvious from Scale Types 4 and 3. If schools have rigid streaming and little teacher involvement in the little subject choice that is available, this does not necessarily imply that there are high levels of subject/level distinctions: it may only mean the presence of few subjects or levels. The relationships between items here tend to be unidirectional — i.e., if A then B, C, D, E; but if E, D, C and B occur then A need not occur. So schools which stream rigidly, and have limited choice making at an individual pupil-teacher level, can still leave some leeway in the allocation of subjects/levels to classes.

The most "difficult" and the most predictive items, therefore, deal with curricular differentiation and the "search process" not with pupil differentiation. If such rigid curricular distinctions are present and the "search process" is highly routinised and rigidly interpersonally constrained within schools, it almost universally predicts a schooling process which also uses administrative procedures or rules to categorise and segregate pupils into distinct and hierarchically organised groupings who receive quite distinct "schooling treatments"

Nine of our sample of larger schools have these very rigidly controlled characteristics (Scale Type 5). An additional 18 schools (Scale Type 4), with 2 or more Intermediate Certificate classes, have less rigid subject/level distinctions but have very little subject choice — in most cases having fewer subjects overall. They have as a consequence low teacher involvement in choice, high levels of streaming/banding and rigid hierarchically organised "closed" classes of pupils with little between class mobility. These 18 schools, with less rigid "treatment differences" between classes of pupils, do however allow some "setting" for Honours level courses. Some choice of Honours/ Pass levels is left at the pupil level as are certain subjects like French, Spanish or Technical Drawing which are "ability differentiated" in the former Type 5 schools.

Absence or scarcity of choice necessarily constrains teacher involvement in choice, but low teacher involvement can occur even with considerable choice (Scale Type 3). Obviously whether subject teachers get involved to a moderate or high extent with pupils' subject decisions depends also on the school ethos and management encouragement. Even where there is a considerable choice, and less rigid subject/level distinctions between streamed classes, teachers may still not get involved in the choice process (Scale Type 3). An additional 13 of the larger schools fall into this scale type.

That rigid streaming/banding can occur in schools where there is at least a moderate level of subject choice and teacher involvement in that choice is obvious from the 16 schools which fall into Scale Type 2. Streaming or banding of pupils, therefore, can take place in schools which make very rigid and major distinctions in the type of schooling process they apply to different streams or bands, or in schools which make minor distinctions in these respects. Considerable choice and substantial teacher-pupil interaction around that choice can still occur in schools which organise the pupil intake into rigidly streamed classes.

And even where one has either truly "mixed ability" classes or minor banding/streaming distinction, as in Scale Types 1 and 0, one can do so where there are rigid between-class boundaries or where there are not. Almost a third of all larger schools fall into these 2 scale types — equally distributed between the 2 types. Some mixed ability schools allow their pupils a very wide choice of subjects so that there are no clear class boundaries. Others, partly mixed ability because they have few optional subjects or levels anyway, allow little choice and pupils take most/all of their subjects within the same class of pupils.

This scale, therefore, allows us to categorise the larger schools in our sample into a highly reliable and hierarchically ordered set of schooling types. One-third of schools have very clearly defined, rigid and hierarchically ordered sets of classes with little subject choice and little teacher involvement in choice and usually clear subject/level distinctions being made in the kind of curricula applied to these different categories of pupils. These schools, therefore, have highly differentiated schooling processes in which central administrative decisions structure the schooling process. At the other extreme are almost an equally large proportion of schools which have either mixed ability or very low "banding" amongst their pupils and low between-class boundaries. These schools generally have wide subject choice and high teacher involvement in that choice. Here the decisions on schooling practice are being left to a large extent to emerge from individual pupil-teacher-parent discussions. The remaining schools fell somewhere between these two polar extremes.

But what was even more confirmatory of the surprising degree of uni-dimensionality of the scale was that many of the "errors" occurring in the higher scale types — particularly Scale Type 4 — occurred in Vocational schools where there were 2 classes rigidly segregated by sex. In these schools equally rigid subject distinctions occur as in ability streamed schools and equal restrictions on individual pupil choice and in teacher involvement in the pupil "search process" but they are based on sex not ability. If we recode these "errors" to being equivalent to rigidly streamed schools the scale gains considerable reliability (CR = .94 and CS = .82). These are very high co-efficients for any such set of relationships.

There is, therefore, a quite extraordinary degree of cohesion in the management of the "schooling process" in Irish second-level schools and a substantial degree of variation amongst schools in these respects.

When we include those schools which have only 1 Intermediate Certificate Class this conclusion becomes even more strengthened. Although the "error" level jumps slightly — as can be seen from the (extreme) marginal row and column of Table 3.8 — we still get an extremely reliable scale with CR = .92 and CS = .74. As we can see also from Table 3.8 the relative order of the items on "streaming" (D), and the extent of teacher involvement (C), becomes reversed — although both items are left as they were to maintain the correspondence with the original scale order derived.

Of the 15 schools which were originally excluded because they had only 1 class and therefore were not in a position to stream, most fell into Scale Types 1 or 4. Although they usually do not or cannot stream they have very little choice and little consequent involvement of teachers in such subject decisions. Eight of these schools were Vocational schools and 7 Secondary schools. Of course we do not know what these schools would do if their pupil numbers were to increase substantially but their subject provision and choice-making behaviour would suggest they would tend to rigidly differentiate pupils and curricula.

The above set of scales provided the best "solution" — the ones with the least number of "errors" in the Guttman scale. Of course a number of other cutting points could have been used and some of these give only slightly higher levels of error. Almost all "solutions", however, gave almost equivalent scale forms, the rank order of "difficulty" of most items retaining their relative position in most solutions. We can, therefore, regard most of these scales as being almost equivalent in form, indicating a dominant unidimensional structuring of the schooling process variables involved. Such schooling process decisions "fit together" as if decisions on one schooling variable were systematically related to decisions on other ones in terms of our hypothesised dimension — from an increasingly "open" to an increasingly "closed" system of schooling: from rigid pupil categorisation/streaming, to little pupil choice and an increasingly bureaucratic "search process", and consequently ever greater subject/level distinctions between classes of pupils.

Variants of the "Schooling Process" Scale at Junior Cycle Level

As we have already seen the Guttman scale already derived is based on measures of streaming, subject distinction and choice, etc., which are averaged over both the junior and senior cycle. But as we also have seen the schooling process in the senior cycle is substantially less rigid than in junior cycle. For this reason and because we shall be using the scale to examine the effects of such schooling variation on pupils' progress and behaviour, etc., for our separate samples of Intermediate Certificate and Leaving Certificate pupils we decided to do a separate scaling exercise for junior and senior cycle levels.

In the table overleaf we give the results of the junior cycle scaling exercise.

Using the 5 previous variables and using the cutting points as indicated in Table 3.9 we derived an almost perfect scale again with an overall CR = .93. As can be seen from the results presented in Table 3.9, however, 2 of the variables — "Choice" and "Teachinv" — are almost perfectly correlated. So, with "Teachinv" giving much higher levels of "error" and, since it does not give us any further significant discrimination over and above that provided by "Choice" we can drop it from the scale. If we do so the error levels drop considerably and the CR increases to .97, an almost perfect Guttman scale. In other words by taking "purer" measures of the schooling process at junior cycle level the scale reliabilities increase considerably.

Its "face validity", of course, has also improved considerably since the ordinal position of one of the crucial variables has changed. Now "Subdist" and "Streaming" are almost exactly collinear — the most "difficult" (or least frequently occurring) condition is very rigid subject/level distinctions. This occurs only in conditions where there is very rigid streaming. It is possible here to derive two "cutting points" for "Subdist" — rigid streaming with extremely rigid (4) subject and level distinctions (i.e., Scale Type 7), and less rigid subject and level distinctions with rigid streaming or "banding" (Scale Type 6). Where both of these conditions are met there is very little subject choice left at the individual pupil level, and there is *no* subject-teacher involvement in any such choice making that does occur. Consequently, very high interactional boundaries occur between the different streamed classes of pupils. These "boundaries" between ranked classes of pupils are

Table 3.9: *The Guttman Scaling of Junior Cycle Schooling Process Variables (*"Cutting Points" of Variables are Provided at Base of Table)*

Scale Type	Extent of Subject/Level Distinctions Between Classes of Pupils (Subdist)	Extent of Streaming of Classes of Pupils (Stream)	Extent of Choice of Optional Subjects by Pupils (Choice)	Extent of Teacher Involvement in Pupil Choice Making (Teachinv)	Extent to which Pupils Take Subjects Together as a Class (Class Bound)	Total Number of Schools (N = 95)	Number of Schools with > 1 Class of Pupils at Inter Cert. (N = 80)
						No.	No.
7	⌐3	4	3	3	3	7	7
6	2	⌐3/4	3	2	2	25	25
5	1/0	2/3	⌐2/1	2	2	25	25
4	0	0	2/1	⌐2	2	22	11
3	0	0	0	2	⌐2	3	1
2	0	0	0	0	2/1	8	6
1	0	0	0	0	0	5	5
No. of "X"s	7/40	58	70	66	9	95	80
No. of errors	0	1	11	17	4	33	32

*"Subdist" has 4 values (0-3). It was possible to derive 2 cutting points: at 3, with very high levels of subject/level distinctions, gave a perfect scale type "predicting", very rigid streaming, almost no choice, no teacher involvement in choice, and high boundaries between classes. If "cut" at 2, slightly lower level of subject distinction, it gave an almost equally perfect scale type but with slightly less rigid streaming/choice restriction practices. "Streaming" has 4 values (1-4): 1 being completely mixed ability or a single class, to 4 which is a completely streamed set of classes. "Choice" of subject has 4 values (0-3): 3 with none or just 1 optional choice of subject available to all classes; to 0 where there is a very high degree of choice of subjects. "Teachinv" equally has 3 values (1-3); 3 with no subject teacher involvement in choice making, to 1 with very high levels of involvement. "Class Bound" has 4 values (1-4), 4 where almost all subjects are taken as a class, to 1 where almost none are.

maximised in Scale Type 7 schools — where a rigid hierarchy of streamed classes exists with little or no leeway to give expression to individual pupil differences which are not very highly correlated with class rankings. The central school authorities decide who is to go where and what they are to do, constructing a very tightly constrained educational achievement process.

In total there are 7 schools with extremely rigid streaming and equally pronounced subject/level distinctions imposed between classes of pupils. There are 25 schools with slightly less rigid streaming or banding and less rigid curricular distinctions amongst classes of pupils (Scale Type 6 — the second row of Table 3.9). Here partly as a result perhaps of such lower rigidities and somewhat more choice of subjects, with more sophisticated timetabling in some cases, there is higher teacher involvement in choice making and more open boundaries between classes of pupils — more movement up and down to take Honours levels, for instance, or technical and vocational subjects, etc.

It is possible, however, to get "banding", particularly the less rigid banding, without subject/level distinctions being made on the basis of which class pupils belong to — though some minor distinctions are, of course, present (i.e., Scale Type 5 — Row 3 of Table 3.9). If this occurs then subject choice and teacher involvement in choice making is much less restricted. This greater openness in choice of subjects/levels may be brought about by having greater provision or by better timetabling and more open options being made overall. The boundaries between such "banded" classes, though still present, are not as rigid as in higher scale types. Widening the choice of options and releasing the constraints on who can take particular subjects and levels has positive consequences on pupil-teacher and pupil-pupil interaction across class boundaries. There are 25 schools in this scale type. In total there are over 70 per cent (57) of schools, therefore, with either rigid streaming or "broad bandings" at junior cycle level; with varying degrees, however, of subject/level distinctions between streams/classes and associated variation in subject choice and teacher involvement in such choice making, and with a small minority of schools (7) being very highly differentiated.

There are, in addition, 22 schools which have no such streaming or banding arrangements but have severe restrictions on pupils' subject choices and little involvement of teachers in these choices (Scale Type 4). Half of these have only 1 class (11); the others usually having very limited subject or level offerings or poor timetabling of those they have, though being large enough to have many offerings.

As can be seen only 3 schools fall into Scale Type 3 — schools which do not stream or band and with some subject choices, but with limited or no teacher involvement in that choice. Two of these schools have only 1 class — the other school having many subject/level offerings but where pupil/parent choice making does not incorporate subject teachers as advisors, etc. For most purposes however, the scale type can be amalgamated with Scale Type 4.

An additional 8 schools fall into Scale Type 2 — schools where, despite being mixed ability and with some subject choice and teacher involvement in these choices, there are still substantial boundaries between classes of pupils. Each class takes a moderate to large number of subjects together and very few subjects/levels are "set". Timetabling also appears to be particularly underdeveloped. Only 2 of these schools have only 1 class — so the other 6 are not too small to allow greater mixing amongst classes of pupils.

At the mixed ability extreme are 5 schools which do not "stream" or "band", which have wide choices, high teacher involvement in such choice making and relatively fluid or permeable boundaries between classes of pupils (Scale Type 1). These are the truly mixed ability schools — but, as can be seen, they are extremely few in number.

As can be seen from these results, when we restricted consideration to the junior cycle we found not only a slightly more reliable and valid (on face value) scale but also one which gives us a slightly different distribution of schools. Thirty-two schools are highly streamed or banded with substantial subject/level distinctions amongst classes of pupils, with little individual choice left, limited pupil-teacher interaction over choice-making, and rigid boundaries between classes of pupils. The earlier results, given in Table 3.8, provide a slightly different number (31) but with somewhat different and less clearcut distinction between Scale Types 5 and 4 (Table 3.8), than amongst Scale Types 7 and 6 in Table 3.9. The latter provides a "cleaner" and more meaningful distinction between the two scale types.

But it is at the other extreme of the scale where the differences are most marked: there are only 11 unstreamed or non-banded schools with 2 or more classes which have substantial subject choice and teacher involvement in the junior cycle; whereas the equivalent for Table 3.8 — based on averaging the junior and senior cycle results — was 24. It is apparent, therefore, that although Scale 1 (Table 3.8) does give us an overall or average view of the schooling process it would be much better to use more specific measures when we are examining either the correlates or consequences of such arrangements at either the junior or senior cycle levels.

Interestingly also there are clearer interpretations possible of the organisational basis of the junior cycle scale. The three most discriminating items — "streaming", subject/level distinctions and extent of choice — result from organisationally imposed decisions. And 3 of the Scale Types (7, 6, 5) result from differences in the type and level of sophistication of these decisions and actions. The other two items — the level of teacher involvement and the "permeability" of class boundaries — are by and large, outcomes or consequences of such organisationally imposed practices — which may or may not be planned for or taken into consideration when decisions to "stream" or not, or to make rigid subject/level distinctions amongst streamed classes, were being taken. To a large extent one would suspect that these are social organisational consequences which are not initially considered. They may, however, be as important in their educational consequences as the original decision to stream or not.

School Size and Rigidity of the Schooling Process

As we have already seen the intercorrelations amongst the various items of these scales increase with size of schools — all of them apparently relating to size constraints in the same way. As one can see, however, from the following table this is clearly not the case.

Table 3.10: *Correlation Between Number of Subjects and Number of Pupils in Schools, and "Schooling Process" Variables*

	Streaming	Subject Distinction	Class Boundaries	Choice	Teacher Involvement	Overall Scale
Number of Pupils Total (N = 95)	.30	.10	−.31*	−.23*	−.36*	−.16
(>1 Class at Inter Cert. N = 80)	(.11)	(−.04)	(−.24)*	(−.27)*	(−.29)*	(−.11)
No. of Inter Cert. Classes (N = 95)	.15	.06	−.14	−.23*	−.18	−.13

*Statistically significant at p < .05, two tailed test. It should be remembered that "Choice", "Teachinv" and "Class Boundaries" are scored from high = 0/1 to low = 3/4 (see Table 3.9 footnote).

Obviously there is no consistent relationship between the overall scale, or its constituent variables, to size of school. Some of the component scaled items have clearly negative relationships to size of school: "Class Bound", "Choice" and "Teachinv". The greater the size of school the greater the extent of subject choice and teacher involvement in such choice, as well as the lower the extent to which pupils take all or most of their subjects together. But, as one might expect, the larger the school the greater the extent to which schools stream and, to a limited extent, the greater the extent of subject allocation differences amongst such streams. The constituent item relationships are going in different directions. But in all cases this "size constraint" explains very little of the overall variance — a maximum of 9 per cent in "streaming" propensity and of 13 per cent in the case of "teachinv", for instance. Given these findings it is obvious that our scale on "schooling process" does not measure a simple technical-organisational response to increase size. It is rather, we would argue, based on strategic decisions (Child, 1972) by school authorities — on the basis of their underlying assessment of the "basic long term goals and objectives of the enterprise" (Chandler, 1962). These are based on their underlying values and conceptions about how best to handle their individual schooling project. It is also, however, obviously affected substantially by administrative or organisational constraints not indexed by size of school. It may well be that larger schools with greater bureaucratic and administrative rules and procedures, and greater co-ordinative imperatives — the division of labour being much more easily interpersonally co-ordinated in small schools — require much higher levels of formal co-ordination amongst different administrative arrangements. Whatever the reason it is clear that despite these contrasting individual correlations with school size, increasing school size clearly imposes consistencies on organisational decisionmaking, whether those strategic decisions are to stream or not.

There is, as we have seen, a very clear set of implicative relationships amongst these constituent variables: one decision implying another. And the larger the school the greater this covariation, the extent of linking of decisions, or of organisational arrangements, increasing with organisational size. These linked decisions, of course, may be either toward increasing "openness" or "closedness" of the schooling process applied. It appears as if either certain administrative constraints or else certain consensus seeking processes within schools forces school management toward greater linking of these decisions in larger schools. In any case it clearly appears that constraining "environmental" variables, such as increasing school size, do not of themselves explain the process.

As we shall see in Chapter 4 those strategic decisions are very highly structured — they vary systematically by the sex and social class of the school's clientele, as well as by the characteristics of the school owning authority. The nature of the pupil intake, and the nature of the "schooling output", or operative objectives of the school, as well as its educational philosphy or ideology, also appear to be very important. What has been most striking about the results in this chapter is that, in most cases, such "schooling process" outcomes clearly appear to be more the result of "strategic decisions" (Child, 1972) taken by school management than of any environmental pressure or constraint — certainly not by school size *per se*.

In some schools, however, decisions to stream, for instance, had been taken at least a decade earlier. In many of these schools the whole set of schooling practices — initial entry examinations, assignment of pupils to classes, assignment of subject/levels to classes, allocation of teachers to classes, the division of labour, and the co-ordinative and hierarchical structure of the school — had become highly routinised and entrenched. Schooling arrangements had become so firmly established in their historical and well worn paths that most teachers and school management personnel had developed significant personal interests in the maintenance of the current structure of the school. It would prove very difficult to change such schooling arrangements. Such "strategic decisions", in other words, once made have very constraining influences on subsequent choices and behaviour.

Conclusion

The results of our analysis, therefore, clearly support a simple unidimensional view of the schooling process. Very rigid streaming is almost universally associated with very rigid subject distinctions and with little subject choice or teacher involvement in that choice making. But less rigid streaming or "broad banding" can occur with little subject/level distinctions — though not without any distinctions at all (Scale Type 5). Referring back to Figure 3.1 — $A_1 B_1 C_1$ is the ideal type — but only a small number of schools (see Tables 3.8 and 3.9) fit into it. But less rigid streaming or banding can be associated with only minimal subject/level distinctions — although it is never found without significant reductions in subject choice, restrictions in subject teacher involvement and moderate high boundaries between classes; i.e., Type $A_1 B_1 C_2$ (in Figure 3.1) is *not* found.

If unstreamed on the other hand — this condition never occurs with subject/level distinctions; i.e., $A_2 B_1$ does *not* occur as was predicted (Figure 3.1). Indeed, almost by definition, it cannot occur. But unstreamed schools can occur with considerable "closedness" in the "search process"; i.e., $A_2 B_2 C_1$ can and does occur. In fact it does occur far more frequently than $A_2 B_2 C_2$ (Figure 3.1), the type that was expected to occur most frequently. The main reason here is the restriction on the *size* of the curriculum. Indeed if we exclude all schools with only 1 Intermediate Certificate class, Scale Type 4 with considerable "choice" and "teacher involvement" has roughly the same number of cases as Scale Types 1 and 2 the most open and most "mixed ability" schools.

With these minor exceptions, therefore, the hypotheses originally advanced are strongly supported by the data — the 5 variables examined do fit together in a highly consistent form as hypothesised.

In the following chapter we explore the underlying reasons why different kinds of schools arrange their "schooling process" in these quite distinct ways. Before proceeding to explain such variation in the schooling process we need to initially check the meaningfulness or "face validity" of the scales used to measure it. This we do below in a preliminary way, by examining in

some detail the characteristics of the top 7 schools which are most differen
tiated by pupils' ability level and curricular allocation (Scale Type 7, Table 3.9),
as well as the bottom 11 least streamed schools.

The Most Streamed Schools

All of the 7 schools (Table 3.9) which are most streamed and differentiated
by curricular/teaching strategies are Secondary schools. They are all owned
by male religious orders, 5 by the Christian Brothers. The other 2, originally
all boys' schools, had recently taken in girls, one on a shared co-institutional
basis, the other on a completely coed basis. All but 1 of these schools are in
the free scheme. Five of these schools have more than 3 classes of pupils at
Intermediate Certificate level. In other words these are dominantly large
male Secondary schools with generally high academic aims and with curricula
which, in the top classes, are highly academic and demanding. Honours level
courses in Irish, English, Maths, are taught to the top streamed class(es); and
Pass level courses, and some technical subjects (usually Technical Drawing,
Spanish, Commerce or Home Economics) are taught in the lower streams.

These schools have either entrance tests or examinations soon after pupils
enter the school. And on the basis of these examinations — usually the
"Drumcondra" Irish, English and Maths tests, based on the Primary school
curriculum — they allocate pupils to the different streamed classes. Both this
assessment and allocation of pupils to classes is a highly centralised process —
involving both Principals and Career Guidance Teachers usually. Equally
centralised is timetabling, decisions on optional/core courses, and the allocation of subjects/teachers to classes.

On average these schools serve a middle to lower middle class clientele,
and are all located in urban areas — 3 of them in Dublin. Three of the schools
are highly selective in their intake (the Dublin schools). Of the other 4 schools,
although all are formally unselective of their intake, 2 report that they clearly
get the better pupils from the local catchment area shared with other competing schools. Since 5 of these schools are either selective or highly competitive in their intake they do not have any serious numeracy or literacy
problems amongst their pupil intake. So, in general, it is *not* greater educational ability variance in their intake that explains their rigid streaming
behaviour.

To conclude, therefore, these highly streamed schools are large, dominantly
male, Secondary schools with clearcut academic educational objectives and
with socially selective and social mobility functions. Their pupil intake is
comprised of a generally male middle to lower middle class clientele whose
dominant educational objective seems to be closely linked to achieving social
mobility. The impression one gets from these schools is that the position of

the lower ability pupil is not being equally catered for — being generally assigned a rather attenuated version of the academic curriculum.

Unstreamed Schools

Of the 11 most unstreamed or "mixed ability" schools (Table 3.9) with more than 1 class of pupils, all but 3 are Secondary schools, and these are "new" Community schools formed from amalgamating local small Secondary and Vocational schools. All these schools serve roughly the same kind of social class mix as the highly streamed schools, though 4 are somewhat higher social status — 2 being fee paying. They tend, however, to be smaller schools.

But what most distinguishes these from the former schools is the fact that they are, with 4 exceptions, all owned and operated by female religious orders and that are *all* either girls' schools or coed schools. One of the exceptions is a high status fee paying Secondary school, the others Community schools. These schools, therefore, deal with a different clientele, provide a schooling that appears to have quite different objectives to the highly streamed schools and are motivated by quite different values, particularly as these are articulated within the religious orders or managements which run these schools.

Four of the schools involved are selective in their intake, but the others are not only unselective — 4 of them being located in "one school" catchment areas — but generally appear to have a slightly higher proportion of numeracy and literacy problems in their pupil intake than the highly streamed schools. In fact 4 of them appear to serve a much more diverse social class and ability range of pupils than the highly streamed schools.

Child's (1972) view of the role of "Strategic Choice" in determining the working process of organisations receives some support in these findings. As we have already seen the rigidity of the schooling process has no significant correlation with school size. Judged in terms of extremes of schooling it also appears to have little relationship with the social class or ability characteristics of the pupil intake as such. But as we shall also see in the next chapter, such "Strategic Choices" appear to be strongly instutionally influenced.

Chapter 4

WHY SCHOOLS VARY IN THEIR SCHOOLING PRACTICE: THE INFLUENCE OF TECHNICAL AND INSTITUTIONAL FACTORS

Two contrasting sets of hypotheses can be proposed as to why schools vary so much in their schooling processes — basically "technical-rational" as against volitional and institutional forces. On technical-rational grounds it can be argued that the degree of standardisation and differentiation of schooling is a result of rational calculation by school managements about how best to deal with differences in their size, the variance in the intake characteristics of pupils, or the extent to which schools have to cope with different population subgroups with specific educational needs; e.g., a high proportion of educationally deprived pupils but also a high proportion of academically able pupils. Such "technical" solutions would, of course, assume consensus on concepts, theories, appropriate methods as well as ideologies and values in education.

Under institutional assumptions we proposed, however, that the internal working arrangements of schools are not technically determined but closely reflect the various institutional origins and charters of different school-owning authorities, as well as the important social placement or mobility, or social reproduction, roles such schools play. Within this latter perspective schooling is not seen as a straightforward rational or technical response to an unambiguously defined set of goals, problems and tasks which have straightforward scientifically validatable solutions; rather it is the result of differences in objectives and values and strategic choices made on the basis of these different priorities amongst school-owning authorities.

We hypothesised, therefore, that it is the different explicit "charters", as well as the acquired educational and social placement functions, of schools that account for the variance in the schooling process applied to a school's intake, rather than any variance in the objective "technical" characteristics of the intake. These different explicit charters — whether characterised by the tripartite, formal divisions between Secondary, Vocational or Community schools, or less formally within the privately owned Secondary school sector — usually specify, or at least imply, a particular educational orientation to a specific sex or social group as well as imply a particular type of education to

106

be applied thereto. These different educational charters are discussed in detail in Chapter 2.

Besides explicit founding charters, different school organisations have acquired distinct educational functions over time. For example, Christian Brothers' Secondary schools, although explicitly founded to serve the education of the poor, through their progressive adaptation to the State's method of funding second-level education and within the ambit of State regulation, have tended over time to move away from the provision of a basic education for the poor to an increasingly more academic grammar school education for lower middle or upper working class boys or those from small farms, the brightest of which are selected and sponsored for upward social mobility. And, as we saw in our previous study (Hannan, Breen *et al.*, 1983, pp. 188-190) tend to provide a quite specialised science-Maths or "Commerce" curriculum to achieve these ends.

On the other hand, the Mercy Order has never quite directed its energies to such specific achievement goals. This is partly because it mainly teaches girls, whose educational and occupational achievement goals are not generally seen as being as salient as those of boys. But it is also because of other differences in the basic educational goals of the religious order concerned.

We hypothesised, therefore, that rigid pupil, curricular and instructional differentiation would be most characteristic of the following types of schools:

(a) Those which teach boys rather than girls, the education of boys being far more class and'educationally differentiated (Hannan, Breen *et al.*, 1983).

(b) Schools which act as sponsoring working class, small farm or lower middle class pupils for upward social mobility.

(c) Schools which serve a wider set of educational, social placement and social mobility functions. The larger Vocational and Community/Comprehensive schools have far more comprehensive objectives than the more homogeneous functions of Secondary schools.

(d) Schools which serve a working class or lower middle class clientele, rather than an upper middle class clientele. Streaming is expected to be least characteristic of schools which aim to consolidate the position of the upper middle class.

(e) Secondary schools operated by certain male religious orders whose charters, educational goals and philosophies emphasise selection and sponsorship of lower working class or lower middle class pupils for upward social mobility: i.e., Christian Brothers, Presentation Brothers, etc.

So, institutional hypotheses indicate that three variables are of most significance; the social class origins of pupils and the social mobility function of schools, the sex of the pupil body, and a clear independent effect of the educational philosophy or ideology guiding the specific school authority. "Technical" variables, as such, are not expected to have much effect.

Analysis and Results

The analysis of the causes of variation in the schooling process focused on 7 key variables. These are dichotomised into: (a) "technical" or environmental variables — size of school, extent of literacy and numeracy problems in the pupil intake, variance in other pupil intake characteristics like social class composition or parental educational levels; and (b) "institutional" or "volitional" factors — sex of pupil body, median social class composition of pupil body, and the chartered educational objectives of the authority running the school.

Technical-Rational Factors

Basically the technical argument says that variation in educational processing results from equivalent *variation* in intake ("raw materials") — with different processes being applied to differing intakes. So the wider the variance in intake the greater the variance in processing. It is presumed under the technical argument that most school decisionmakers basically share the same set of educational values and goals and the same technically rational approach to their implementation or achievement. So larger schools and schools with greater variances should show greater differentiation in processing. The institutional argument on the other level says that differentiation depends mainly on the goals and values of the decisionmakers — it is the result of choices they make based on the underlying criteria they use in choosing one schooling solution rather than another: internal school choice and policy, rather than external or environmental factors, being the main influence.

The correlation results given below in Table 4.1 summarise the bivariate relationship between these two contrasting sets of variables. Six variables are selected to represent "technical" factors — size of school or number of pupils, extent of literacy/numeracy problems in pupil intake, and the degree of selectivity or competitiveness of pupil intake — all four variables measured in interviews with school Principals; extent of variation in the social class and educational background of pupils — which were estimated from the responses of pupils to questions about their fathers' occupational status and education at Inter Cert. level (see Hannan, Breen *et al.*, 1983, pp. 23-29 for details). We do not have any measure of pupil "ability" or "performance" at entry. Although most schools had results for entry examinations, or standardised test scores, these measures varied so widely from school to school that comparable data were not available. In addition many of the examinations or tests used were not very reliable or were of doubtful validity. It would, of course, be preferable to use such initial entry tests. However, they are highly correlated with the social class and educational background characteristics of pupils — and are, to that extent, indirectly measured here. But, in addition, we have included two measures of the extent to which a school's intake includes lower ability pupils, and two measures of the extent of the ability selectivity of the intake and of the extent to which the school is "competitive" in its intake. These school level measures do clearly "tap" the "ability selectivity" of schools. We are nevertheless only too conscious of the absence of reliable "ability" or aptitude measures for school intake. So, it is for this reason that we later use a very conservative method of estimating the influence of "schooling differentiation" on school outputs.

The results clearly indicate that the 6 individual "technical" factors are not very important predictors of the schools' propensity to differentiate their pupils or curricula. Except for size of schools there are no statistically significant correlations present. Larger schools tend to be somewhat more differentiated in the junior cycle ($r = .30$). And (Secondary) schools which are highly selective/competitive in their pupil intake and get "better" or more able pupils, are somewhat *less* inclined to differentiate. Both correlations are, however, very low and statistically insignificant. There is no consistent correlation between schooling differentiation and the extent of literacy or numeracy problems in the pupil intake. There is no consistent bivariate relationship between variation in a school's social class intake or variation in the parental educational background of pupils and propensity to differentiate. So, it is not the level of differentiation in intake that accounts for the level of differentiation of schooling process. This low correspondence between such technical-rational and environmental factors and schooling practice holds for all variables included in the overall differentiation scale (except for extent of subject choice — where larger schools have somewhat *more* choice).

Combined, these 6 "technical" factors explain less than 5 per cent of the variance in the overall scale, or 14 per cent of the variance in the Inter Cert. school process scale (see Table 4.2). The main technical variable of significance is size. Once size is controlled for, only the extent to which schools have a large lower ability intake, retains any significance. Larger schools are, as hypothesised, more likely to differentiate their schooling process. Paradoxically, however, once size is controlled for schools which have a high intake of lower ability pupils are somewhat *less* likely to rigidly stream their intake

Table 4.1: *Relationships Between "Technical" and "Institutional" Variables and the Propensity to Differentiate Pupils and Curricula. (Schools > 1 class; N = 80 Schools; Values of r = .22 or Greater, are Statistically Significant at .05 Level, Two Tailed)*

Independent Variables	Indices/Scales Used	Correlations with Schooling Process Variables (Pearson's r.)				
		Overall Scale	Inter. Cert. Scale	Individual Items in Scale		
				Streaming of Pupils	Subject Distinction	Extent of Choice of Subjects to Pupils
A. Technical Variables						
1. Size of school	(i) No. of pupils	-.13	.30*	.12	.13	-.31*
2. Extent of literacy/numeracy problems in intake	(ii) % pupil intake with literacy/numeracy problems†	.06	-.07	-.14	-.06	-.16
3. Degree of background selectivity of pupil intake	(iii) Degree to which school is selective in intake[1]	-.15	.03	.05	-.13	-.17
	(iv) Extent to which school is competitive in its intake[2]	-.10	-.11	-.12	-.08	-.02
4. Extent of variation in the pupil's social class and educational background	(v) Soc. class variance in pupil intake to school	.05	-.01	-.11	.02	-.01
	(vi) Variation in parental educ. level of pupil intake to school[3]	-.12	-.04	-.17	-.02	-.11
B. Institutional/ Volitional Factors						
5. Type/sex of school	(vii) Boys' Sec. schools	.23	.29	.20	.23	.32
	(viii) Girls' Sec. schools	-.15	-.17	-.06	-.08	-.24
6. Identity of school Authority	(ix) Community schools	-.10	-.05	-.10	-.02	-.40
	(x) Vocational schools	.22*	-.02	.13	-.02	.28
	(xi) Christian Brothers' schools	.28*	.31*	.23	.39	.31
	(xii) Mercy schools	-.11	-.12	-.07	-.13	-.06
7. Median social class and educational background	(xiii) Median soc. class of pupil body	.15	.21	-.01	.12	.11
	(xiv) Median level of parental education	-.18	-.07	.05	.01	-.09

*Statistically significant at the 5 per cent level.
†Indices of literacy and numeracy are very highly correlated (r = .95).
[1]Scale which measures extent to which school is over-subscribed in intake and selects its pupils (4 = highly selective or is completely un-selective (= 0).
[2]Scale which measures extent to which school is thought to get better and more able pupils in its intake (= 4) or to suffer from "cream off" by other local schools (= 0 or 1).
[3]Variation in fathers' educational level in Inter. Cert. classes. Results for mothers' education are even less significant.

or differentiate their curricula. Variation in the social class background of pupils is positively correlated with differentiation, as predicted, but the coefficient is not significant. So, there is no evidence that variation in the ability intake of schools – nor in the familial social or educational background of pupils – are independently and positively correlated with streaming and curricular differentiation. There is very little evidence, therefore, for the "technical" hypothesis except for the effect of school size. Indeed increasing proportions of lower ability pupils in a school appear to have a negative effect where a positive effect was predicted.

Table 4.2: *Stepwise Multiple Regression of "Technical" and Social/Institutional School Variables on the Tendency of Schools to Differentiate their Schooling Process (Inter Cert./Scale, Schools With More than 2 Classes)*

	(i)	(ii)
A. *Technical Variables*	Beta	Beta
School size (No. of pupils in entry year)	.34*	.35*
Extent of selectivity in intake[1]	−.10	−.14
Extent of literacy/numeracy problems in pupil intake	−.26*	−.15
Variation in social class intake of school	.11	.06
Variation in parental educational level of pupil intake	−.06	−.18
B. *Institutional Variables*		
Girls' school (Dummy)	—	−.33*
Boys' school (Dummy)	—	.12
Vocational/Community school (Dummy)	—	−.52*
Median social class of pupil body	—	.27*
R^2 =	.14	.32
F =	2.2*	3.4*
No. of schools**	74	74

*Statistically significant at the 5 per cent level.
**There are 80 schools with two or more classes at Inter Cert. level but only 74 with full data on *all* variables in the regression.
[1] The other scale on school competitiveness made no additional contribution and was excluded.

The reason for some of these discrepant results and for the low overall level of variance explained by such "technical" factors becomes obvious when one introduces social-institutional variables into the regression. Institutional and ideological factors clearly intervene in the ways different school authorities handle such "technical" factors. Part of the explanation, for instance, as to why schools with higher proportions of children with literacy and numeracy problems are less likely to stream rigidly, is mainly explained

by the fact that Vocational and Community schools have much higher proportions of pupils with literacy and numeracy problems (r = .45) than other
schools. They also tend to have much lower within-school variances in the
social class of intake of pupils. As a matter of policy, however, Vocational
schools (and Community schools) are much less likely to stream rigidly than
most boys' Secondary schools, although they almost universally "broad band"
when large enough.

Social-Institutional Factors

As we can clearly see from the results presented in Tables 4.1 and 4.2 —
there are much clearer relationships between institutional factors and schooling practice. Boys' Secondary schools (particularly Christian Brothers' schools)
and schools which cater mainly for lower middle or working class pupils
are far more likely to stream their pupils and differentiate their curricula
than others. Girls' schools, and schools which cater mainly for upper middle
class pupils are least likely to stream. Vocational and Community/Compre-
hensive schools are also somewhat less likely to rigidly differentiate their
schooling process — once all other factors are controlled for, although in
their case they are more likely than others to broad band. The next strongest
relationship is with the median social class level of the pupil intake to the
school — of roughly equal importance to school size. The more working
class the pupil composition, the greater the tendency to differentiate. It is
not, therefore, the *variance* in the social class intake of schools, nor variation
— in so far as we can judge — in the ability intake of pupils, that explains
variation in schooling process differentiation, but rather the *average level* of
pupil intake as well as the *policy* of the school authority.

It appears, in fact, that Secondary schools which cater mainly for potentially upwardly mobile, lower middle or working class, boys are most likely
to rigidly differentiate their schooling practice. So, boys' Secondary schools
which select or "sponsor" a proportion of their more able intake for upward
mobility appear to have the most differentiated schooling process. Many of
these schools, however, also tend to have high "dropout rates", as we shall
see later; so their schooling differentiation is also highly predictive of their
"output" differentiation. On the other hand, upper middle class Secondary
schools are least likely to stream or differentiate their curricula. Consolidating
the advantage of the upper middle class appears to require that most of their
children are "treated" relatively equally, or that the choice of the schooling
process applied is left to the pupil and his/her parents.

For example, of the 7 most highly differentiated schools, all are Secondary,
with 5 boys', and two coed schools. But 5 of the 7 are Christian Brothers'
schools, whose average parental occupation status varies between lower
middle to middle class. But what is equally important is that a substantial

number of pupils in these schools were being prepared for University entry — with 39 per cent of Leaving Cert. pupils, on average, aspiring to University entry, and 21 per cent actually going on to University after completing the Leaving Certificate.

On the other hand, however, just over 37 per cent of pupils who entered these schools drop out before the Leaving Cert., most after the Inter Cert. In other words we are dealing here with a set of schools whose schooling processes and outcomes are very highly differentiated — although the formal curriculum is, in general, highly academic. Over a third of lower ability pupils are early leavers and generally enter manual occupations, but at the opposite pole between a quarter to one-third go on to University and enter professional and upper middle class positions. Lower ability streams take a "Pass" level general curriculum; and upper streams a highly academic, Honours, and generally specialised set of courses. These schools are clearly biased towards sponsoring upward mobility for a select minority of pupils, and do not appear to pay much attention to the educational or occupational achievement of lower ability/achievement pupils.

At the other extreme are 8 Secondary schools which have completely unstreamed or mixed ability classes with undifferentiated curricula. None of these schools are boys' schools — one is coed, the others are all girls' Secondary schools. Four of the schools are upper middle class schools — 2 being fee paying. The other 4 are middle to lower middle class girls' Secondary schools — 2 run by the Mercy Order, and 1 by the Presentation Order. Most of the Principals, when interviewed, explicitly emphasised the positive values of mixed ability classes. Mixed ability teaching appeared to be a conscious strategy used to implement certain egalitarian values or to achieve certain egalitarian objectives — some Principals emphasising the advantage of such arrangements to lower ability pupils. In these 8 unstreamed schools 38 per cent of Leaving Cert. pupils aspired to go to University, and 18 per cent actually went on to University. Although third-level entry figures are somewhat lower in their case it is clear that most of the schools strongly orient their programmes in that direction; but in ways that do not marginalise the lower ability pupils. In this case only 14 per cent of pupils dropped out of school before completing their senior cycle. So, taking this into consideration, educational achievement levels are, in fact, substantially higher in this case if we take as our base the total cohort of pupils that first entered these schools.

As we can see, therefore, environmental and technical factors are much less important than institutional and ideological ones in determining a school's processing characteristics. The details of these institutional relationships are made clear in the following two tables.

Table 4.3 shows the relationship to school types and sex mix. All of the most highly differentiated schools are boys' Secondary schools, while none of the least differentiated are.

Table 4.3: *Distribution of Secondary, Vocational and Community Schools by Schooling Processing Differentiation (Inter Cert. Scale; Schools with Two or More Classes at Entry, N = 80)*

	Inter Cert. Schooling Differentiation Scale					
	Type 7	Type 6	Type 5	Type 4	Type 3, 2, 1	Total (N)
		Rigidly Differentiated			Mixed Ability Undifferentiated	
Secondary schools						
Boys'	7	5	3	6	—	21
Coed	—	3	5	—	2	10
Girls'	—	6	6	—	6	18
Vocational schools	—	7	6	5	1	19
Community and Comprehensive schools	—	4	5	—	3	12
No. of schools	7	25	25	11	12	80

χ^2 = 24.3, df. = 8, p <.005 (Table collapsed by adding Rows 2 + 3, and 4 + 5).

Almost all the larger Vocational schools are "banded" or moderately streamed -- in terms of the segregation of these pupils into different ability groups, and they maintain generally moderate curricular boundaries between these classes. Equally, most Community schools are moderately differentiated in this way. However, on average, in neither case is the degree of ability differentiation of pupils or of curricula, or restriction of subject choice, as great as in boys' Secondary schools. But in Vocational schools and in some Comprehensive schools, clear differentiation by sex of pupils occurs — a very rare occurrence in coed Secondary schools or in most Community schools. There is in general a shared view amongst Community school Principals, particularly, that rigid streaming is bad, and their ability differentiation is constructed by much less rigid methods — mostly "broad banding".

In the following table we give the distribution of Secondary schools by the religious order running the school. The sample is too small to show any statistically significant result, but the trends are in broad agreement with other results.

Almost all Christian Brothers' schools in our sample streamed their classes to some extent -- most to a very high extent. The number of schools run by other male religious orders in our sample is too small to make definite state-

Table 4.4: *Distribution of Secondary Schools by Religious Congregation Running the School and Schooling Differentiation. (Schools > 1 Class)*

Extent of Rigidity of the Schooling Process	Christian Brothers' Schools	Mercy Congregation Schools	High Status Congregations' Schools	Other Male Congregations (Presentation, De La Salle, etc.)	Other Female Congregations (Presentation, Holy Faith, etc.)	Other Schools	Total
Low (1-3)	1	3	2	—	2	0	8
Mod. (4-5)	3	7	3	2	3	3	21
High (6-7)	8	3	—	3	5	2	21
Total	12	13	5	5	10	5	50

ments. It appears, however, from our interviews with the Principals involved that the ideology underlying a school's goals or observable outputs, and the processing arrangements implemented were nowhere as clearcut as in Christian Brothers' schools. The long established role of the Christian Brothers in Irish education, which appears to have emphasised their selective sponsoring of the more able working class and lower middle class boys for upward social mobility, appears also to have been based on a strategy of selective and differentiated schooling to achieve that objective.

Like the Community school Principals, some Secondary school Principals clearly had consciously decided not to stream or differentiate their pupil body and provided a more general and more open process of schooling which would encourage each pupil to achieve their full potential through maximising choice and minimising centralised schooling decisions. This was most characteristic of convent schools and lay schools whose clientele were dominantly upper middle class. But such conscious organisation of schooling practice was not the usual pattern. The extent to which most schools differentiated their process, however, depended crucially on the social class characteristics of their intake.

The Social Class Characteristics and Social Mobility Functions of Schools

When related directly to the median social class characteristics of their pupil clientele, it is clear that the lower the mean social class of the school's pupils the more likely the school is to provide a rigid schooling process (r = .21). Working class schools are almost twice as likely as upper middle class schools to be highly streamed and differentiated.

It may well be that such middle class schools have substantially less "ability" variance in their pupil intake than working class schools have, and that it is this "ability variance" imperative which is intervening. Certainly the more middle class schools have substantially lower proportions of pupils with

Table 4.5: *Percentage Distribution of Schools Catering for Different Social Classes by Extent of Rigidity of Schooling Process (> 1 Inter Cert. Class)*

Extent of Rigidity of Schooling Process (Inter Cert. Scale)	Median Social Class of Pupil Body				
	Upper Middle Class (1+2)	Middle/Lower Middle Class (& Large Farmers) (3)	Lower Middle/ Upper Working Class (4)	Middle and Lower Working Class and Small Farmer (<30 Acres) (5+6)	Total (N)
			%		
Low (1-3):	25.0	16.7	10.0	10.0	12
Medium (4-5):	43.8	45.8	60.0	30.0	36
High (6-7):	31.3	37.5	30.0	60.0	32
Total %	100	100	100	100	100
(N)	(16)	(24)	(20)	(20)	(80)

$r = .21$, $p < .05$.

educational disabilities. However, once school size is controlled for there is a negative relationship between the estimated proportion of the pupil intake to schools with literacy and numeracy problems and schooling differentiation (see Table 4.2). And the positive association between the median social class level of a school and its score on the schooling process scale is maintained even when such factors are controlled for. Equally, although there is a moderate correlation between the median social class of a school's intake and the extent of social class variance in the school's pupil intake ($r = .23$) — the lower the social class of intake the higher the variance — there is only a very low correlation between social class variance, or parental educational variance, and such schooling differentiation practices once school size is controlled for and when all institutional factors are controlled (Table 4.2). All of this strongly indicates therefore, that such differences between schools in their schooling process cannot simply be explained by equivalent variances in their ability and social class intakes. In addition schools which select their pupil intake, or which successfully compete locally for the more able pupil clientele, are not less likely to stream or differentiate their curriculum — if any relationship exists it is in the opposite direction. In any case, such school practices are most characteristic of middle class boys' Secondary schools, which are, in fact, most likely to stream.

The typical social class level of pupils' parents within a school expresses not only the intake characteristics of pupils — indexing their familial and neighbourhood resources and influences — but also broadly indicates a school's goals or expected outputs. What it is that schools set out to achieve with their inputs or, rather, what educational outputs are typically achieved and could, in an ideal world, be avoided or changed if schools wished, is highly predicted by the class composition of a school's inputs. Upper middle class schools in our sample, for instance, almost universally "succeed" in bringing *all* their pupils up to Leaving Cert. level, and a high proportion of the graduating class go on to third-level education (30-40 per cent usually); with a much higher proportion (60-70 per cent) aspiring to go on to third level. In other words these schools have quite homogeneous educational and social placement functions — to mediate and transform high familial expectations and resources into third-level entry certifications. Besides this general uniformity in expectations, intentions, goals or expected outcomes, both the typical familial cultures of the upper middle class, and the corresponding culture of the school, emphasise those aspects of personal character and conduct which maximise individualistic achievement (see Kohn and Schooler, 1980). Self direction, personal responsibility and individualistic achievement values are maximised in such upper middle class families and in their patterns of socialisation and functioning. These values can only be maximised in mixed ability schools which allow wide levels of choice and individual expression. So, even where there may be as wide a range of ability levels in pupil intake as in lower middle class or working class schools, pressure to conform to high parental expectations and to a more demanding clientele would force such schools towards a more open schooling process arrangement.

The managers of lower middle or working class schools do not, on the other hand, face that kind of parental or familial environment. Indeed as Kohn (1983) and others have pointed out, working class culture tends to emphasise passivity, conformity and obedience, as well as substantially lower expectation levels. Where such schools, therefore, attempt to maximise educational mobility chances for the more able of their pupil intake they can do so through a much more selective procedure than in schools where parents would be better informed, and more vociferous and active. So ability variation could, in these circumstances, be translated into formal ability groupings and school determined curricular allocation and institutional procedures.

When we attempted to classify schools by using a more complex set of "input" and "output" variables combined — including the average social class level of the pupil intake, the extent of "dropout" before pupils took the Leaving Cert., and the extent to which Leaving Cert. pupils subsequently went on to University — we get a much more informative and revealing classification as given in the following table. Although this new classification is highly correlated (r = .75) with the median social class of the school intake it provides a clearer picture and is almost self-explanatory.

To some extent, however, this classification, although highly illustrative is not unambiguously interpretable. The point selected to dichotomise the schooling process scale maximises the differences. To a limited extent also, as we shall see in the next chapter, streaming *per se* appears to be a significant causal factor in dropout rates. The table, however, is so illustrative of the relationship between social class of origin, the social class of "destination" of pupils and the schooling process applied that it is worth producing it here.

At one extreme are 6 Secondary schools (3 fee paying) with a predominantly upper middle class clientele. There is almost no dropout problem in any of these schools. Almost all pupils stay on to do the Leaving Cert. and, of those who complete the Leaving Cert., between 30-50 per cent go on subsequently to University. Three of these schools have basically mixed ability classes with wide choice of subjects and levels and the least centralised direction of schooling choices, as well as maximum subject-teacher involvement in this choice-making behaviour, etc. Of the 3 schools which show most schooling differentiation none belong to the most highly streamed or differentiated category.

At the other social class extreme are 13 working class schools, 12 of which are highly streamed. These have high subject/level differentiation, with high central direction of the schooling process. Nine of these schools are Vocational schools, the rest girls' or coed Secondary schools. There are very high "dropout rates" from these schools (between 40-90 per cent of intake) and, except in the Secondary schools where a small number did go on, almost none of the Leaving Cert. pupils went on to University. Obviously, a quite differentiated set of outputs is being provided for in these schools. At the top are a tiny proportion of University entrants (<5 per cent). Next are Leaving Cert. pupils — mostly female — being positioned for entry to clerical or related lower non-manual occupations. The high performing boys are being prepared mostly for skilled manual apprenticeships. But at the bottom of the achievement scale most boys are dropping out of these schools into unskilled or semi-skilled manual employment or, in nearly half these cases, into unemployment. Although, therefore, the average level of achievement in these schools is much lower than in the former case the salient range of educational and occupational destinations for which pupils are being prepared is much greater. Whatever about the objective situation it is obvious that such "output objectives" are being perceived as much wider in scope and, therefore, are thought to require substantial differentiation in the schooling treatment applied. The extent to which there is school management centralisation of decisionmaking in this case, of course, is substantially aided by the lower level of expectations and more quiescent or less demanding behaviour of working class parents.

Between these two extremes are most schools which, although showing a clear trend towards greater differentiation in lower middle or working class schools exhibit remarkable variation in schooling practice even within the

Table 4.6: *The Relationship Between the Social Class Origins and Destinations of Pupils in School and Schooling Practice (N = 70 Schools, with > 1 Class and with Leaving Cert. Classes Where Full Information is Available)*

Social Class Origins of Pupil and Social Mobility Functions of School	Level of Schooling Differentiation (I.C. Scale)		
	Low-Moderate Differentiation (1-4)	High Levels of Pupil and Curricular Differentiation (5-7)	Total
1. Upper middle (1-2)* class pupils with very low dropout** rates (< 5%) and high educational achievement levels (Univ. entry levels > 30%)	3 (.50)	3 (.50)	6 (1.00)
2. Middle class schools (2-3) with low dropout rates (< 20%) and high educ. achievement levels (20-35% to Univ.)	6 (.60)	4 (.40)	10 (1.00)
3. Lower middle class schools, with moderate to high dropout rates (30-40%) but moderate educational achievement levels (15-25% → Univ.)	6 (.29)	15 (.71)	21 (1.00)
4. Lower middle class schools (3-4) with moderate to high dropout rates (40-60%) and low educational achievement levels (10-20% → Univ.)	2 (.25)	6 (.75)	8 (1.00)
5. Working class schools (4-5) with moderate dropout rates (c.40%) and low achievement levels (5-10%)	3 (.25)	9 (.75)	12 (1.00)
6. Working class schools (4-6) with moderate to high dropout rates (40-90%) and very low (< 5%) or no University entry	1 (.08)	12 (.92)	13 (1.00)
Total	21	49	70

R = .25; p < .05.

*The figures in parenthesis after social class code indicate the median social class or, more accurately, the socio-economic status, category involved.

**"Dropout rates" refer to proportion of original entrants who leave school before the Inter. or Group Cert. or before the Leaving Cert. level.

same social class/mobility category. The sex of the school, the religious order or secular organisation running the school, and the size of the pupil body appear to be the most differentiating variables involved. Girls' schools, schools run by female religious orders and smaller schools are least differentiated. Boys' Secondary schools, particularly Christian Brothers' schools, are most differentiated. And while both Vocational and Community schools rarely use mixed ability classes with wide pupil choice of subjects and levels they rarely also stream as rigidly as boys' Secondary schools.

The consistency with which certain school authorities stream or band or centrally control the schooling process does not appear, however, in most cases to flow from consciously articulated strategies by individual school managers or decisionmaking elites within schools. They appear to be based on shared or taken-for-granted conceptions amongst corporate school authorities of both the role or function of the school within the wider educational system or the accepted societal placement function of the school. In many, if not most cases, therefore, the "decisions" to stream and to treat or process each stream in a distinct way are now of historical interest only: the practice has become crystallised and completely taken for granted.

Conclusions

Clearly, social and institutional factors, not technical-rational ones, are the most important in explaining differences in the schooling process. Part of this effect is "environmental" — the particular social/institutional niche that a school may come to occupy in its local community. But this, of course, is mainly a chosen niche — it is not determined by factors external to the school. The sex, social class and pupil intake of schools and the social class of destination of school leavers appear to be the main structuring variables in this respect; if one conceives of this influence operating through the demands/ expectations of parents and pupils and the demands/expectations of "output customers" — employers, third-level colleges, etc. However, it is quite clear that the schooling process decisions are not simply matters of such external "environmental" influence or even of individual Principals' decisions, but are of wider corporate or institutional construction. The quite distinct "choices" made by Vocational and Community schools' Principals, as well as Christian Brothers and Mercy Sisters, clearly indicate the corporate nature of such decisionmaking which reflects the distinct charters of those schools.

Greater pupil and curricular differentiation is most characteristic of boys' Secondary schools, particularly Christian Brothers' schools, or schools which teach working class and lower middle class pupils. It is particularly characteristic of boys' working class (or small farmer) schools which select or sponsor a small proportion of the pupil intake for upward educational and social mobility. It is also characteristic of the more "comprehensive" schools which both attempt to maximise educational achievement for an academic elite, but also attempt to provide a vocational education for the able pupils: i.e., schools, particularly Community/Comprehensive and the larger Vocational schools with quite diverse operative goals. Whether such dispersion in the goals of schools — whether unintended as in some boys' Secondary schools or planned as in most "comprehensive" schools — and consequent differentiation in the schooling process applied to pupils, has equivalent polarisation effects on the output of schools is examined in the following chapter.

Chapter 5

SOME EFFECTS OF RIGIDITY IN THE SCHOOLING PROCESS

Introduction

If early selection into elite classes or tracks in a post-primary school[3] — "allow time for schools to prepare the recruits for their elite positions", as Turner (1960) says, it also allows them sufficient time to socialise those not so lucky . . . "to accept their inferiority". Both this elevation of the "most talented" and the placement of the less well endowed in vocational streams is based on theories and methods of "meritocratic selection" — generally based on various intelligence and achievement tests. These methods allow schools to differentiate pupils at a very early age and allocate them to stratified "tracks" or "streams" on the basis of "objective" allocation criteria and, by and large, to hold them to those ranked classes for most of their schooling. To a large extent, these allocations, as Rosenbaum (1976) puts it, are a "school arbitrary". Even the best measures of academic merit or talent are not 90 per cent reliable or valid as measured at any single point of time. Individuals also mature at different rates and such underlying capabilities, in any case, change over time. Most schools, however, which stream use a much less reliable and highly variable set of "ability" measurements.[4] Finally, even where the most stable and most predictable measures, such as "IQ" or "verbal reasoning ability", are used, they explain less than one-third of the variance in later examinations (Greaney and Kellaghan, 1984, pp. 159-162). In practice, however, the assignment of pupils to streams or tracks is rarely based on such rigorous criteria as standardised ability/aptitude tests alone: pupils' social class characteristics, their personal motivation and application, the organisational needs and constraints operating within a school — for example, the distribution of teachers' qualifications and of school curricular and

---

3. In our sample of most streamed schools at least 2 of the 7 Secondary schools involved had attached Primary schools in which classes were streamed from age 8 or 9.

4. Of the 7 schools which are most highly streamed, 5 have Career Guidance Teachers who gave formal pre- or post-entry assessment tests — mostly the Drumcondra range of performance and assessment tests. But a range of other formal aptitude, verbal reasoning, mathematical and reading tests are also used. Most other schools use formal entrance exams based on the courses in Irish, English and Maths in the Primary school curriculum, or post-entry examinations based on the first year curriculum.

physical resources, and student management and discipline constraints — are almost equally important (Shavitt, 1984; Barr and Dreeben, 1983; Nachmias, 1980; Hout and Garnier, 1980; Rosenbaum, 1976). In other words streaming is used to serve many other schooling objectives than merely efficiently and fairly segregating pupils by their capabilities and talents so as to maximise their differentiated achievement potentials.

Once such decisions are taken, however, such stream or "track" placements tend to be permanent, with most of the few changes that do occur moving down a stream, not up (Rosenbaum, 1976). As is clear from the review of research in Chapter 1 there is no consistent evidence that "streaming", or the use of homogeneous ability groupings, is more effective in raising the *average* achievement levels of pupils than the use of mixed ability or heterogeneous ability groupings. Such differential allocations to streams, however, have been shown to have important influences on the subsequent educational achievement of individuals, even controlling for individual pupil ability and aptitude differences, or differences in socio-economic backgrounds, etc. (Rosenbaum, 1976; Alexander and McDill, 1976; Alexander, Cook and McDill, 1978; Nachmias, 1980; Shavitt, 1984). In other words, streaming or tracking not only does not fully mediate valid "ability" or "performance" potential — in that it accurately categorises, orders and processes pupils by their potential — it severely constrains the mobility of the wrongly placed and strongly reinforces the interpersonal ranking of pupils both between and within such streamed classes (see Peterson, Wilkinson and Hallinan, 1984, for review). Streaming tends to "artificially" increase the differences or variances in achievement amongst pupils.

This process of increased differentiation within streamed schools can occur in a number of ways. A number of research studies have shown that early dropout rates are higher in lower "vocational" streams or "tracks" in schools, even controlling for all relevant ability and social variables (Shavitt, 1984; Halsey *et al.*, 1980). So rigid streaming does appear to discriminate against the lower achieving/ability classes. At first sight this would suggest that the average level of achievement of entry cohorts is depressed by rigid differentiation of schooling. However, this need not be so if the higher "ability" classes in such schools have compensating higher levels of achievement.

Such processes as tracking or streaming have been shown to enhance the correlation between social origins and educational achievement (Heynes, 1974; Bowles and Gintis, 1976; Alexander *et al.*, 1978). The correlation between socio-economic factors and scholastic aptitudes is normally so high that tracking placement tends, on average, to reinforce and enhance, rather than attenuate that correlation (Shavitt, 1984). The structural differentiation imposed by curricular tracking and streaming, therefore, mediates and, in many studies, accentuates the effects of background factors on academic achievement — with "tracking" and sorting processes within schools substantially and independently affecting educational achievement levels (Alexander *et al.*, 1978; Yuchtmann and Samuel, 1975). One of the most comprehensive British studies (Newbold, 1977) found that lower ability pupils gained more in mixed ability classes without any evidence that high ability pupils were held back. There was evidence of greater variance in achievement in streamed schools — with lower achievement, higher dropout rates and more disciplinary problems in streamed classes (pp. 42-72).

As a structural arrangement which differentiates total year groups, therefore, such potential polarisation effects of curricular differentiation are best measured by both the average attainment levels of the total entry cohort and its total within-group variance in attainment. It is quite possible for streaming, as is obvious from the above example, to have no discernible effect on the *average* attainment or achievement levels of all pupils first entering schools — such as the average number of years completed by all first year entrants before leaving post-primary schools, or the proportion successfully passing the Intermediate Certificate examination — but yet to have a substantial effect on the total (entry) year group variance in achievement. Indeed the "polarisation thesis" suggests that the greatest effect of streaming and curricular differentiation is to increase the variances — perhaps to push the top achievers up in some cases, but also to push the achievement of the bottom classes downwards (see Halsey *et al.*, 1980; Shavitt, 1984).

In conclusion, therefore, the main hypotheses being explored in this chapter are that (i) streaming has no discernible or consistent effect on the average educational attainment or achievement levels of pupils, controlling for all relevant social background and ability variables; and (ii) that streaming significantly and substantially affects the variances in levels of educational achievement, with highly streamed schools having significantly greater variances in these respects than unstreamed schools, all relevant variables having been controlled for.

Before we proceed to the analysis, however, we need to examine some particular characteristics of Irish post-primary schools which clearly differentiate them from American, British, Northern Irish or Israeli ones — where most of the relevant research work adverted to has been carried out. Comprehensive non-selective post-primary education has proceeded much further in Britain than here although the residues of selective schooling are still substantial. But in the British case such schooling takes place under the aegis of a local education authority which in earlier times in Britain tested, evaluated and assigned 11 year old pupils to selective or unselective post-primary schools; although there was always a small proportion of "public" schools free from such corporate allocation. To a large extent Northern Irish post-primary education still retains much of the earlier British pattern. American high schools are usually "stand alone" comprehensive schools, again under the aegis of a local education authority. In Ireland, however, there is neither universal local provision in a single post-primary school, nor a superordinate local education authority to "objectively" sort and assign pupils to different schools on some universally applicable criteria. No published data are available on the extent of selectivity or "free-market" competitive allocation to local schools. Obviously such "between-school" differences have clear implications for what happens within schools — both those who win and those who lose in the local education market. We have some limited information on this in our study and, since this is important for the subsequent analysis, it is provided in the following section.

The Selectivity of Irish Schools and their Variances in Output

As the results in the following table make clear only a small minority of *second*-level schools face no effective local competition — at most around 20 per cent, usually in remoter rural communities. The rest face varying degrees of competition — with parents and schools "free" to allocate children to one or other local school.

Table 5.1: *The Number of Second Level School "Centres" by the Characteristics of their Catchment Areas 1978/79*

Large Urban Areas (Dublin, Cork, Limerick, Waterford, etc.)	Characteristics of Non-Urban Catchment Areas No. of "Centres"					
	At least 2 Secondary and 1 Vocational School in Area	One Secondary and 1 Vocational	Two Secondary Schools (Boys' and Girls')	One Community/ Comprehensive School	One Secondary School	One Vocational School
	No. of Schools					
230	128	5	55	29	14	70

Sources: White Paper on Educational Development, 1980, p. 6; and *List of Recognised Secondary Schools*, 1978/79, Stationery Office, Dublin.

The usual result of that local competition is quite pronounced in terms of class, sex, ability, aptitude and social and cultural differences in pupil composition in the different local schools. This local, and usually hierarchical, division of labour has generally emerged over time into an uneasy and jealously guarded local equilibrium. The effects of differential streaming practices in this kind of schooling system — where some schools will not take lower ability pupils and other schools (mostly the smaller Vocational schools) have a concentration of all the lower ability and problem children in the local community — may be quite different to those found in the school environments of most American or British studies.

In the following table we provide the results of interviews with school Principals of their assessment of the extent to which their school suffers or benefits from such local competition as well as linked data on the extent to which the school has actually been in a position to select its intake — the extent to which the school had more first year applicants than places available and actually did reject applicants. In total 26 schools had more applicants than places and had to turn away some applicants — 9 schools being substantially over-subscribed. The third column contains information supplied by the Department of Education and estimated from published statistics[5] on the actual extent to which schools within officially defined "catchment" areas have shown relative growth or decline when compared to other schools within their area.

Only 1 in 4 schools in the sample are in official single school catchment areas, but less than 1 in 6 Principals reported that there was no other local competitive school as such (Col. 1). In examining the official figures on relative changes in a school's pupil numbers over the decade from the early 1970s to the early 1980s, around one-third of schools had fared badly in this competition — either losing numbers, or increasing their numbers at a substantially lower rate than all other local schools. Interestingly, 36 per cent of Principals reported that in such local competition their own schools had suffered "a lot" or "somewhat" from such local competition. So somewhat over one-third of schools suffer in their intake — both in relative numbers and in the ability-range of their intake. Most Vocational schools are in this position.

At the other extreme are 23 schools (almost all Secondary) which are highly competitive. These have done much better than other local schools in gaining pupil numbers over the 1970s. In addition there are 5 fee-paying Secondary schools, of their nature being highly class selective schools: i.e., a total of 31 per cent of moderately to highly selective schools. The Principals' assessment of the situation gives somewhat similar results: 18 schools (i.e., 20 per cent) gain considerably by "creaming off" the "better" pupils locally — having more applicants than places and generally using entrance examinations or tests to select pupils. Using another measure there are 25 schools which are moderately to highly selective from an over-subscribed potential

5. *List of Post-Primary Schools*: 1978, 1981. Published by the Stationery Office, Dublin.

Table 5.2: *Distribution of Sample Schools (for Which Complete Data are Available) by Extent to Which the School Faces Competition from Other Local Schools Within the Catchment Area*

(1) Extent of "Competition" Amongst Local Schools: Principals' Assessment of Extent to Which Which Own School Suffers from "Cream Off"		(2) Extent of "Selectivity" in Pupil Intake: Principals' Assessment of Selectivity of Intake; and Actual Extent to Which School Can Select from an Applicant Population Which is Greater than Number of Places Available		(3) Actual Local Competition. Extent to Which There are Other Local Schools, and Extent to Which These Have Been Doing Better or Worse than Sampled School in Pupil Numbers Growth Over the 1970s (calculated from Departmental records within official school catchment areas)	
Variable	*No. of Schools*	*Variable*	*No. of Schools*	*Variable*	*No. of Schools*
1. School suffers "a lot" from local "cream off" (school gets more lower ability pupils)	21	1. Completely unselective schools (all taken who apply)	40	1. School faces a lot of local competition and has lost numbers (1971 to 1981)	29
2. School suffers "somewhat" from "cream off"	15	2. Very little selection — some discouragement of over supply of applicants	25	2. Faces some local competition but has maintained numbers	10
3. No other school in area	14	3. Moderately selective schools — of an over-supplied applicant population	16	3. Faces local competition but has done better than others (i.e., has increased numbers at a greater rate than other local schools)	23
4. Other schools in area but do not suffer from "cream off"	22	4. Highly selective schools from a substantially over-supplied applicant population	9	4. Highly selective fee-paying schools	5
5. Own school gets better pupils	18			5. School is on its own in local area	23
Total	90	Total	90	Total	90

intake. Of the 26 schools who do not accept all applicants only a minority use assessment tests alone to select their entry, 10 do use an assessment test but most of those schools also apply other selective criteria, like locality, presence of siblings in the school, etc. The majority, therefore, use rather particularistic criteria — like relatives having been at the school or locality or ability to pay the fees in a small number of cases.

So, overall, only around one-fifth of schools are "stand alone" schools. Over a third suffer to some extent from a rather destructive local competition — in that they get the poorer and less able pupils. This is true particularly of Vocational schools. At the other extreme are between 20 to 25 per cent of schools — almost all larger Secondary schools — who gain from this selectivity, some considerably. The remaining schools hold a relatively neutral position. So, even before pupils get into second-level schools a considerable degree of segregation and differentiation has already occurred — for which individual school Principals or management take no responsibility, and over which, in fact, they individually have little control.

As we have seen already the extent to which an individual school actually differentiates its own pupil body in applying its schooling process bears almost no relationship to the extent to which it is selective in intake, and has a very limited relationship to the extent to which its intake includes a large proportion of lower ability pupils or even a wide variance in its social class composition. Such within-school differentiation is only to a limited extent, therefore, the outcome of an application of a widely shared rational-technical model of school level decisionmaking. Certainly social class or ability differences *per se* do not appear to be important variables in predicting such curricular differentiation. But the sex and class of origin of intake and the presumed class of destination of output are very important discriminators, as are certain institutional characteristics of school authorities.

Even though such selectivity factors may have little power in predicting whether and how severely schools stream they may have substantial effects on the outcomes of streaming. So in the following analysis we control for these effects.

As we have already seen, streaming and "tracking" practices within schools clearly segregate and order pupil groups by not only their "ability" but by the nature of the assigned curriculum. This "ranking" of pupils, on the basis of their general ability or achievement and schooling "treatment", tends to result in a clear stratification of pupils and of pupil-teacher interaction. This is particularly so where there is a very rigid segregation of such ranked classes of pupils, as in Scale Types 7 and 6 for example. Such differences in evaluations and expectations of pupils and teachers are likely to have very significant effects on both teachers' and pupils' achievements and general behaviour (see Rosenbaum, 1976; Oakes, 1985).

As we shall see rigid streaming and curricular differentiation has a small negative effect on dropout rates in the junior cycle. Such effects on dropout rates could normally be expected also to have direct consequences for the average level of education achieved by all pupils who first enter schools. Higher dropout rates should normally result in lower average years of schooling completed by an entry cohort. However, high dropout rates might be compensated for by disproportionately high educational achievements by the residual high ability classes. In some of the boys' Secondary schools we studied this implicit polarised school strategy was clearly in evidence: all efforts were directed to maximising the achievement of the high achievers while the low achievers were effectively ignored. However, in other schools, rigid streaming did increase the overall variance in achievement without affecting the early dropout rates: the achievement of the higher ability classes was increased without any negative effect on the lower streams. In this case, of course, the mean achievement level increased. So the means and variances can be affected in a number of different ways by streaming.

The following 6 examples of the "outputs" of highly streamed schools illustrate clearly how both the average attainment as well as dispersion in pupil attainments can differ widely from school to school, as well as indicating some of the main factors that influence these outcomes. The total entry cohort (1976/7) to each school is classified according to the level at which pupils subsequently left full-time education. Ordinal scores are assigned to each of 4 terminal attainment levels (see Figure 5.1) which roughly correspond to the number of years that the relevant pupils have spent in school before leaving, or the minimum they are expected to spend for those achieving a CAO (University) place.

The two lower-middle class boys' Secondary schools (A and B) have low early dropout rates and relatively high Leaving Cert. completions and University "place" achievements. They have roughly the same average attainment levels — but the dispersion or variance in "output" of School A is somewhat wider than in School B. Both Vocational schools (C and D) have dominantly lower working class recruitments and very high early dropout rates. They have consequently very low Leaving Cert. and University "place" achievements. Both have dispersions or variances in output that are substantially lower than School A — with achievements concentrated between the 2 lower attainment categories. The 2 working class girls' Secondary schools (E and F) have both substantially higher average attainment levels and somewhat greater variances in output, being roughly equivalent to School B. But their distributions of attainments are quite different to those of School B, with both having substantially lower average attainment levels and substantially lower schooling completion rates.

Figure 5.1: *Percentage Distribution of the Total Entry Cohort to Six Highly Streamed Schools in 1976/77, According to the Subsequent Level of Education Achieved Before Leaving School*

Achievement Level of Entry Cohort	A. Boys' Secondary Schools (Lower middle class on average)		B. Vocational Schools (Lower working class or small farmers on average)		C. Girls' Secondary Schools (Lower working class schools)	
	School A (N=210)	School B (N=136)	School C (N=212)	School D (N=221)	School E (N=178)	School F (N=184)
1. Percentage dropped out before Inter Cert. (Score = 2)*	5%	12%	38%	39%	15%	26%
2. Percentage left after Inter Cert. and before Leaving Cert. (Score = 4)*	30%	18%	55%	50%	38%	32%
3. Percentage left after Leaving Cert. (Score = 6)*	48%	58%	6%	10%	46%	40%
4. Percentage achieved University (CAO) place (Score = 7)*	17%	12%	1%	1%	2%	3%

*These are the values (scores) used to derive the mean or average achievement levels and variances of each school. There is an element of arbitrariness in assigning these particular scores, but the use of alternative scores (e.g., 2.5, 3.5, 5.0, 6.0) give almost exactly equivalent results.

Schools, therefore, vary widely in both their average attainment levels and in their overall variances in pupil output or achievement. The extent of streaming or curricular differentiation practised is only one of a number of factors which influence these outcomes: the average and range of the social class of intake of pupils, the extent of ability selectivity of that intake, the sex of pupils and the type of school attended are of equal or more importance, so that these effects need to be controlled for if we wish to examine the independent effects of streaming.

Some of the main effects of such schooling differentiation are examined in the following sections. The main hypotheses being explored are that rigid pupil/curricular differentiation by schools has no consistent effect on average attainment levels but has a significant polarisation (or variance) effect on attainments or "outputs", irrespective of, or "holding constant", all (or most) other independent variables that would be likely to have the same influences. We first examine its effects on the overall average or mean achievement levels of the total entry cohort to schools. We use 4 measures of average attainment levels – (i) the average standard (number of years) of schooling achieved by the total entry cohort; (ii) the proportion of the entry cohort achieving at least 5 Ds in "Pass" subjects at the Leaving Cert. examination; (iii) the percentage achieving at least 4 Honours at Leaving Cert. level; and (iv) the percentage achieving a (CAO) University place. In addition we examine its effect on early dropout rates.

Finally, we examine its effects on school "output variances" – specifically the standard deviation and coefficient of variation (the standardised variance) in the distribution of the total number of pupils originally entering individual schools over the subsequent total number of years (and standards) completed before leaving school. In addition we examine other more specific "output variances", particularly those for Intermediate and Leaving Certificate exam results. In almost all cases these outcomes are estimated or measured at the total school level – or rather at the individual (entry) year group level. These achievement measures are, therefore, based on *all* pupils who first entered schools.[6]

---

6. Of course, if all the relevant information had been available for individual pupils the analysis could have been done at both pupil and school level. In our case, however, relevant pupil level data are not available for those pupils not surviving to Intermediate Cert. level – particularly so in Vocational schools and working class Secondary schools. Using such residual data for the main junior and senior cycle examinations, for analysing the effects of pupil and school level, would therefore give quite biased results. Schools, for instance, with high dropout rates show higher average achievement levels and lower within-school variances for both Intermediate and Leaving Cert. examination results, controlling for all other relevant variables. Although, therefore, we would ideally prefer to model both pupil and school level effects as indicated by Aitken and Langford (1986) we are quite confident of both the validity and generalisability of the analyses carried out here.

The purpose and consequence of streaming is to differentiate amongst students — to "create" differences amongst them. If one wants to examine, therefore, the overall effects of such pupil and curricular differentiation, and particularly our hypothesis as to the polarisation effects, one first needs to measure these at the total school or year group level. Examination performance data are usually only available or comparable for particular examinations — Intermediate or Leaving Certificate for instance. Such examination results, however, are available only for that part of the entry cohort surviving to that level and, therefore, may give a quite biased picture of what has happened to the total entry cohort.

Our measures of pupil attainment are, however, limited in a number of ways. We cannot measure the potential differential effects of the schooling process on higher and lower ability pupils, for instance, since we have not measured the ability of pupils on entry to schools. We cannot then separate the effects of streaming from initial differences in ability or aptitude for individual pupils. So, in general, we cannot assess whether pupils allocated to homogeneous higher ability classes in streamed schools gain an advantage over equally able pupils allocated to mixed ability classes in other schools; nor indeed test for the opposite effects on lower ability pupils (see Alexander and McDill, 1976; Newbold, 1977). Nor can we measure the effects of streaming and curricular differentiation at a class level rather than at a total year group or school level for much the same reason (see Kellaghan, Madaus and Rakow, 1979). We cannot separate the effects of initial ability/aptitude differentiation from the effects of pupil allocation practices by schools which are based on assessing ability/performance. Since streaming is a school organised allocation of pupils to classes on the basis of their assessed "ability", highly streamed schools will have much greater between-class variance in achievement than will mixed ability schools. Indeed if done effectively mixed ability schools should show little or no difference in average performance amongst classes.

Because, however, we have data on the attainments of all pupils entering schools — for the first year entry cohort in 1976/77 — we can measure the average attainment levels and the variation in attainment levels for these pupils. Since pupils leave post-primary schools at different stages there are no comparable examinations or tests that are or can be available for all pupils. The only comparable measure applicable to all entry pupils is the total number of years or standards that pupils have completed before they leave school, and this is the main measure we will use in this research. Performance at the Intermediate and Leaving Certificate examinations will also be used, but it should be remembered that, if high pupil/curricular differentiation practices by schools have a significant "cooling out" effect

for lower ability pupils, the bottom tail of the ability/performance distribution will be cut off at an early stage in such schools. It is clear from our
own results, for instance, that high dropout rates are associated with reduced
variances and increased grades in the Intermediate and Leaving Certificate
examinations. So if streaming is associated with high dropout rates as some
research indicates, then measuring its effects from junior, or worse, senior
cycle examination results, would give quite biased estimates of its effects.

Results

The Effects of Schooling Differentiation on the Average Achievement Levels of all Pupils who Enter Schools

We use 4 main measures of the average outcome effects of a rigid and closed,
versus liberal and open, schooling process: the average number of years completed by an entry cohort to schools, the proportion of the entry cohort
who achieved at least 5 Ds as well as the proportion getting at least 4 Honours
in the Leaving Certificate examination, and the proportion of the entry
cohort who achieve a University (CAO) "place". In all cases, as we shall see,
variation in the severity of the schooling differentiation applied has no significant positive effect on those educational outcomes — tending to have a
slight overall negative effect.

In assessing the effects of streaming we decided to use the most conservative
statistical method of testing for the effect — that of hierarchical regression.
Using this method we test for the effect of streaming (its additional contribution to the explained variance) on various measures of average "cohort"
achievement (or of variances in achievement) *after* the effects of all available,
relevant and causally prior explanatory variables have already been controlled
for. The null hypothesis is that the "streaming" variable does not add significantly to the variation already explained by the preceding "causally prior"
variables. This is a conservative statistical test in that any "shared variance"
effects streaming may have with any of the preceding control variables are
arbitrarily assigned to these preceding variables. We use this method for a
number of reasons. First, many of these variables are actually causally prior
— like family background of pupils, etc. But the main reason is that we do
not have any measures of the actual "ability", etc., distributions of pupils to
the different schools, although we do have a number of measures of the
extent of ability selectivity of schools, as well as estimates of the proportion
of low ability pupils in school intake. In addition social class variables —
like the occupational status and education of parents — are moderately to
highly correlated with "ability" measures and these we can control for.

We also control for "school type" — Vocational or Comprehensive/Com-
munity schools versus Secondary schools — so that the undoubted additional

ability selectivity that has been observed to occur for Vocational schools can also be controlled for (Kellaghan and Greaney, 1970; Greaney, 1973, Rudd, 1972; Swan, 1978). We are not, therefore, testing for the effectiveness of Secondary versus Vocational schools — Breen (1986) has already done that for senior cycle performance and shown that there is no significant difference in effectiveness between Secondary and Vocational schools for boys, and only a slight difference for girls (pp. 57-90). Used as additional control variables, therefore, "school type" partials out any additional variance beyond that attributable to pupil intake and school selectivity factors, and that cannot be clearly attributable to the extent of differentiation of the schooling process itself. We are confident, therefore, that we have been able to control for the effects of most of the confounding variables in the analysis. By so weighting the cards against ourselves in testing the main hypothesis we are confident that the results achieved can be taken as valid estimates of, at least, the minimal effects of streaming.

Before we investigate the effects of streaming on the overall average achievements of the entry cohort to schools the first measure examined is that of early school leaving or "dropout" rates which can affect both the average achievement levels of a cohort as well as the overall variance in achievement.

Early School Leaving Rates

Early school leaving or "dropout" rates are calculated for a single year entry cohort (1976/77) for each school. Reliable figures are available for the number of pupils who entered in 1976/77, and the number who survived to take the Intermediate Certificate examination in 1979, or the number entering in 1975/76 for those who took a 4-year Intermediate Cert. course or a 3-year Group Cert. course. The junior cycle "dropout" rate then is the proportion of the entry cohort who left between entry and Inter Cert. examination stage. The senior cycle "dropout" rate is equivalently calculated.

Although early school leaving can generally be evaluated negatively in that leaving without qualifications leads to disproportionately high levels of unemployment (Hannan, 1986) a much higher proportion of those who leave after the Intermediate Certificate get jobs and apprenticeships; indeed many leave so that they can take up apprenticeships. The latter would be particularly true of those leaving Vocational schools. Nevertheless in all cases job opportunities improve with level of educational qualifications so it seems reasonable to treat senior cycle "dropout" rates as unwelcome.

School leaving rates are substantially greater during the senior than at the junior cycle level. For the 90 schools for which we have reliable rates, the average dropout rate per school before Inter Cert. was 10.9 per cent, with a wide variance (standard deviation of 14.3). Between Inter and Leaving Cert. levels the average dropout rate (N = 85) was 32 per cent, with an almost equally pronounced variance (standard deviation = 26). The following table provides a breakdown by school type.

Table 5.3: *The Average Dropout Rates and the Range in Dropout Rates for the 3 School Types at Both Junior and Senior Cycle Level*

	Total No. of Schools	Secondary Schools	Vocational Schools	Community/ Comprehensive Schools
Dropout rate in Junior Cycle				
Average dropout rate* (per school)	−10.9	−7.7	−16.5	−18.7
Standard deviation of school dropout rates	14.3	11.9	15.4	13.5
Number of applicable schools	90	55	25	10
Senior Cycle Dropout Rates				
Average (per school) dropout rate	−31.9	−19.8	−57.8	−41.1
Standard deviation of school dropout rates	26.0	20.5	18.2	19.0
Number of applicable schools	85	52	23	10

*Unweighted by school size.

Vocational schools and Community schools have substantially greater dropout rates than Secondary schools at both junior and senior cycle levels — being more than twice as great at junior cycle, and Vocational schools having about 3 times the rate of Secondary schools at senior cycle level. As pointed out, however, Vocational schools particularly suffer from ability selectivities and the traditional educational-occupational paths of Vocational school pupils — from the Group or Intermediate Certificate into apprenticeships, etc. — still holds in a substantial proportion of Vocational schools; although over time this particular Vocational stream has also come to suffer increasing competition from Leaving Certificate pupils (Breen, 1984). For the purposes of this study, however, we use "school type" only as a "control variable" — using the Vocational school category, for instance, as an additional control on ability selectivities — with no implication that Vocational schools *per se cause* increased "dropout" rates.

As we might expect high dropout rates are most characteristic of schools with predominantly working class compositions and of schools, like Vocational schools, in which low ability/performance pupils are concentrated. And it is these intake differences amongst schools that mainly account for differences in dropout rates. Correlations with social class and ability selectivities are much stronger at the senior cycle level than at the junior (see Appendix Table 5.1). Obviously early dropout (before the Inter Cert.) is a more problematic and less predictable phenomenon than at senior cycle — though the same set of independent variables predict in the same fashion in both cases. Only 5 independent variables have statistically significant relationships with the junior cycle dropout rate. It is substantially higher in schools where the median social class composition of the pupil body is predominantly working class, in Vocational or Community schools, in schools which have high literacy/numeracy problems in their pupil intake, and in schools which stream and rigidly differentiate their curricula. On the other hand, schools which are highly selective in their intake are less likely to suffer from dropout problems. All of these correlations become greater at the senior cycle level.

Of course many of these independent variables are intercorrelated (see Appendix Table 5.1) so that their combined effect is not as great as their individual effects suggest. The median social class level of a school is moderately to highly correlated with school type. Vocational schools are predominantly working class schools, for instance, with high ability and social selectivities in its intake. And the extent of literacy and numeracy problems in a school's intake is highly correlated with the social class composition of its intake as well as with school type. Besides these shared variances amongst the independent variables, one other pair of variables is highly correlated — size of school and size of community. The larger the school the larger the size of town or city in which it is located. Combined in a multiple regression equation, therefore, these relationships change (see Table 5.4).

The relevant significant test used to evaluate the effects of (9) the "schooling process" (streaming) scale, is one based on the incremental variance that resulted when variable 9 was added to the regression equation: whether it adds significantly to the variation in dropout rates not already explained by the independent variables 1 to 8.[7] In neither case is the coefficient statistically significant ($p < .05$), though in *both* cases it is negative. It is, however, significant at the 10 per cent level for both the junior cycle rates and senior cycle level results.

Clearly the major influence on dropout rates is accounted for by the social

7.
$$F = \frac{(R^2_{y.1-9} - R^2_{y.1-8})/1}{(1 - R^2_{y.1-9})/N-K-1}$$

where N = No. of cases and K = No. of variables.

Table 5.4: *Stepwise Regression Results (Standardised) of School Dropout Rates with (i) the Social Class and Related Characteristics of Schools; and (ii) Controlling for These, the Effects of Schooling Process on Dropout Rates. The Dependent Variables are Scored from –.70 (70 Per Cent Dropout) to +10 (Where Numbers Grew up to Intermediate Cert.[†]) (Schools with 2 or more classes at Inter Cert. level. N = 75 for Inter and N = 73 for Leaving Cert.)*

	Dropout Rates to Inter Cert.		Dropout Rates to Leaving Cert.	
	(i) Beta	(ii) Beta	(i) Beta	(ii) Beta
1. Size of school	.20	.24*	.01	.06
2. Median social class level of school	-.33**	-.24*	-.58**	-.19**
3. Extent of literacy/numeracy levels in pupil intake	-.09	-.12	-.03	-.06
4. Extent of competitiveness of school	-.04	-.04	.01	.01
5. Vocational or Community schools (=1) (else = 0)	-.33**	-.39**	-.27**	-.33**
6. Boys' Secondary school (=1) (else = 0)	-.19	-.16	-.12	-.10
7. Girls' Secondary school (=1)	-.01	-.07	.08	.02
8. Size of place (1 = Dublin; 8 = open country)	.33**	.32**	.01	.01
9. Schooling process scale (IC Scale)	—	-.18[1]	—	-.17[1]
F =	4.8*	4.7*	11.9*	11.4*
R^2 =	.36	.39	.60	.62
N =	75	75	73	73

*Using ordinary F test significant at 10 per cent level.
**Using ordinary F test significant at 5 per cent level.
  [†]In a small number of private fee-paying schools, additional pupils were taken on after first year and very few pupils left school.
  [1] The F test employed to test the effects of (9) the "schooling process (streaming) scale" is that based on the incremental variance explained when variable 9 was added to the regression equation: whether it adds significantly to the variation in dropout rates not already explained by the independent variables 1 to 8 (see footnote 7).

class composition of the pupil intake — working class schools have substantially higher rates of school leaving. This effect *increases* in significance at senior cycle level. Even controlling for such class factors, however, Vocational and Community schools have substantially higher rates of dropout than other schools: primarily reflecting the substantially greater ability and social selectivities of their intakes. Larger schools tend to do better, as do schools located in smaller towns and rural areas, though in both cases this holds only for junior cycle dropout. Clearly, therefore, the larger middle class girls'

Secondary schools have little or no dropout levels; while the smaller working class urban boys' schools, and particularly Vocational schools, have the highest dropout rates. Although these independent variables are moderately intercorrelated, they have significant independent effects. Combined they explain 36 per cent of the overall variance in dropout rates in the junior cycle, and just over 60 per cent of the dropout rates at the senior cycle. It is, therefore, surprising to find that the extent of schooling differentiation practised has an additional small negative effect at both junior and senior cycle levels, even when all these predisposing variables are controlled for. This additional effect is, however, significant only at the 10 per cent level. Although neither coefficient reaches statistical significance at the conventional 5 per cent level the fact that both coefficients are negative and almost reach significance does give some, though not unambiguous, support to the hypothesis that streaming increases the dropout rate. This effect appears to impact almost exclusively on the lower ability streams or bands. Whatever the underlying reasons — whether the negative "labelling" effect, or the differential effectiveness of the schooling process on high and low streams, pupils in streamed schools — controlling for all relevant factors — are then somewhat less likely to remain in school than in mixed ability or less rigidly hierarchically arranged systems. This result holds even when we have excluded all the "shared variance" that this measure of schooling differentiation has with the preceding control variables. This finding, though not statistically significant, does conform closely to many research findings in other countries (see Schafer and Olexa, 1971; Newbold, 1977; Halsey et al., 1980; Shavitt, 1984).

At senior cycle level over half of the variance in schools' dropout rates is accounted for by two variables: social class composition and whether the school is a Vocational/Community school or not — much of the latter variance being accounted for by their greater ability and social selectivities. The main variable, however, is the social class composition of the school, which shows a much greater impact at senior cycle level. At this level when all of the above predisposing variables have been controlled for, the schooling differentiation scale still retains a slight negative effect; though again this effect does not reach statistical significance.

As an additional test we ran separate regressions for the larger Secondary (N = 47) and Vocational (N = 17) schools. In both cases we get almost the same pattern of results — with a more substantial impact of schooling differentiation within Secondary schools. Because of the substantially reduced degrees of freedom, however, only one of the schooling differentiation coefficient is significant at the 10 per cent level — that for senior cycle dropout rates for Secondary schools.

To conclude, therefore, rigid streaming and curricular differentiation practices appear to have a slight consistent, though statistically insignificant, effect in increasing junior and senior cycle dropout rates. This effect is present, however, even where the effects of all other relevant factors have been controlled for. As already discussed this would normally have the consequence of reducing the average achievement levels of the total entry cohort. However, rigid streaming may have a compensating positive impact on the upper streams in such schools, such that the overall averages are not affected — though the variances would necessarily be increased. What these effects are on average achievement levels is examined next.

Average Number of Years of School Completed by Entry Cohort

First, the effects of a set of family background and school selectivity variables on the average level of educational attainment (average number of years completed in school) of the 1976/77 entry cohort is assessed. These measure differences amongst schools that are due to their social class and ability selectivities. As can be seen from Table 5.5 variations in these school input variables are the best predictors of the average output — combined they explain over 54 per cent of the variance in the average number of years of schooling achieved. The social class composition of pupils and the average level of education of parents, combined with the extent of ability and social selectivity of schools, explains most of the variance in average school output achievements. The addition of the three school type variables adds substantially to the explained variance with Vocational schools having a consistent negative effect. Boys' Secondary schools also have a slight negative impact — that is compared to coed schools or, particularly, girls' schools. Two "background" factors — rather than the specific "effects" of the school itself — are taken to account for both these results: the greater propensity of boys in general to leave school early — even in coed schools — and the substantially greater ability selectivity of Vocational schools (Rudd, 1972; Greaney, 1973; Swan, 1978). Vocational schools themselves are also expected to have an additional "negative" impact on average attainment levels due to their customary role in preparing boys for apprenticeships, etc. The negative effects of both school types, therefore, cannot be taken as evidence of their educational ineffectiveness. They are merely used here as additional control variables — not as tests of their educational effectiveness.

The combined effect of school input characteristics and school type variables explains 65 per cent of the total variance in the overall average attainment level of the school entry cohort. Schools of low socio-economic and parental educational composition (and with low variance in these respects), and particularly Vocational schools, have low average levels of achievement. Upper middle class Secondary schools, and particularly girls' Secondary

Table 5.5: *Regression of Average Schooling Completion Level — Average Number of Years Completed by Entry Cohort to School — With Pupil Intake Characteristics, School Characteristics and the Severity of the Pupil/Curricular Differentiation Process Applied by Schools*
(N = 71 schools; standardised regression coefficients)

Independent	(i) With Input Variables Beta	(ii) Input + School Type Characteristics Beta	(iii) Input + School Type + Schooling Process Variables Beta
School Input Characteristics			
1. Median social class of pupil intake per school	−.51**	−.54**	−.52**
2. Average parental level of education	.13	.11	.09
3. Extent of competitiveness and selectivity of school intake	.12	−.07	−.05
4. Extent of literacy/numeracy problems in pupil intake	−.11	−.12	−.14*
School Type Characteristics			
5. Boys' Secondary schools		−.20**	−.16*
6. Girls' Secondary schools		.12	.11
7. Vocational schools		−.28**	−.23*
Severity of Schooling Process Differentiation			
8. Schooling process scale			−.14*
N =	70	70	70
F =	19.2**	16.7**	15.4**
R^2 =	.54	.65	.67

*Statistically significant at the 10 per cent level.
**Statistically significant at the 5 per cent level.

schools, have high average levels of achievement. Controlling for socio-economic input composition effects, as well as school selectivity effects still leaves a substantial negative impact on Vocational schools and boys' Secondary schools, however, with no consistent effect for other school types. In both cases there may well be specific negative "school effectiveness" impacts, over and above those due to the obvious selectivity and apprenticeship roles, of Vocational schools particularly — but for this study's purposes we are not concerned with explaining why both school types have such negative effects, merely using them as control variables to exclude effects that cannot be directly attributable to streaming and curricular differentiation.

Once these school input and school type variables have been controlled for, differences between schools in the rigidity of their schooling process still retain a slight negative effect on average levels of achievement, although this effect is not significant at the 5 per cent level. It is, however, significant at the 10 per cent level. Again we ran separate regressions for Secondary and Vocational schools and got equivalent results to those of Table 5.5 — neither of which are statistically significant, however, because of the reduced degrees of freedom. We repeated this same procedure with subsequent regressions, but only where we get different results will we subsequently discuss these additional analyses.

This slight negative, though statistically insignificant, impact of streaming and curricular differentiation is consistent with the earlier effects on dropout rates — suggesting a consistent negative impact. However, it may well be that there is a compensating growth in the numbers graduating at the other end of the educational ladder — the proportion achieving Pass or Honours grades at Leaving Certificate level, or going on to University. This possibility is examined in the following two sections.

Proportion of the School Entry Cohort Reaching Leaving Certificate Level and Achieving at Least 5 Ds in the Examination

The proportion of all entry pupils who attain the minimum "passing" mark at the Leaving Certificate examination is a good measure of a school's overall academic achievement level — its success in both retaining pupils in school and ensuring they achieve a minimum level of senior certification.

As we can see from the following regression results, however, most of the between school variance in this respect is accounted for by the input characteristics of schools themselves — although some of this, of course, is partly a reflection of the direct and indirect selectivity of schools. The average socio-economic level of the pupil intake cohort, and the extent of its educational and social selectivity are the main variables predicting the school's level of "academic achievement": upper middle class, selective Secondary schools, with no literacy/numeracy problems in the intake have very high levels of achievement; while lower working class or small farm schools who suffer from the "cream off" effects of such local selective schools, and who have consequently a disproportionate fraction of the local lower ability pupils have the lowest level of "achievement". Such "output achievements", therefore, are primarily functions of input social class and ability selectivities — their combined effect explaining almost two-thirds of the variance in senior certificate output.

The addition of the three school types (dummy) variables to the regression adds substantially to the explained variance. Controlling for previous

Table 5.6: *Hierarchical Regression of the Percentage of the 1976/77 Entry Cohort Achieving 5 or More Ds in the Leaving Cert. Examination by 1981 — by School Input Characteristics, School Type and by Schooling Differentiation Scale (N = 70 schools with greater than 1 class at Leaving Cert. There were 8 schools with incomplete information on Leaving Cert. results, or in 2 cases, where schools had no senior cycles)*

Independent Variables	(i) Beta	(ii) Beta	(iii) Beta
(i) Pupil Input Characteristics			
1. Median social class level of pupil body	−.48**	−.52**	−.51**
2. Average level of mother's education	.14	.12	.12
3. Extent of literacy/numeracy problems in pupil intake	−.17*	−.16*	−.16*
4. Extent of competitiveness and selectivity of intake	.16*	−.02	−.01
(ii) School Type			
5. Boys' Secondary school	—	−.09	−.08
6. Girls' Secondary school	—	.25**	.25**
7. Vocational school	—	−.19*	−.18*
(iii) Extent of Schooling Differentiation			
8. Schooling process scale	—	—	−.04
N =	70	70	70
F =	26.7**	25.2**	21.9**
R^2 =	.62	.74	.74

*Statistically significant at the .10 level.
**Statistically significant at the .05 level.

social background and selectivity factors, girls' Secondary schools have substantially greater success than all other schools — particularly boys' Secondary, Community and coed schools. And Vocational schools have somewhat lower achievements in these respects than all other schools. Combined, the three additional school type variables add 12 per cent to the explained variance — so that both pupil input and school type variables together explain three-quarters of the variance in the minimum Leaving Cert. achievement level of the entry cohort per school.

The addition of the schooling process variable in this case adds nothing to the variance explained — it has no discernible independent effect on such average achievement levels. Certainly, judged in terms of the proportion of the entry cohort it succeeds in getting as far as the Leaving Cert. and obtaining a minimum level of achievement in the examination, it has no discernible average effect. Whereas, therefore, such schooling process effects do appear to influence early dropout rates and the overall average attainment level — though none of those effects is individually statistically significant — it has no independent effect at all on the proportion achieving minimal Leaving Certificate grades.[8] However, it may very well increase the small proportion achieving very high standards at the Leaving Cert. level — one of the main rationales used by schools for using rigid streaming methods. The proportion of the entry cohort achieving 4 or more Honours level grades in the Leaving Cert. examination is a good measure of such elite achievement. The results of a regression using this as the dependent variable are given in Appendix Table 5.2. Here the social class of intake of schools, parental educational level, the extent of selectivity of intake, and school type are highly predictive of school achievement levels. However, once the effects of such school input and school type variables have been controlled for the extent of pupil/ curricular differentiation used by schools has no effect on output. So schooling process differentiation is not predictive of such elite achievement levels.

However, it may well be that elite segregation of the highly academic streams in rigidly differentiated schools may have positive social and social psychological effects for them, independent of any purely academic effect. Such effects might still influence such elite aspirations and achievements as third-level entry. This possibility is examined in the following section.

Proportion Achieving University Entrance Levels

As a measure of the academic "success" of a school the proportion of its entry cohort of pupils who achieve University entry is not, of course, an unambiguous measure of a school's effectiveness — since so much depends on the particular social class characteristics of a school's prospective University students. Unfortunately, we do not have any estimate of technical college (or RTC) entry, a much less socially selective flow. Nevertheless, like our preceding measure of academic "success", this measure does give some additional information on the relative effects of streaming or curriculum differentiation on the overall academic effectiveness of schools. Table 5.7 provides the relevant multiple regression results.

As can be seen the family background socio-economic characteristics explain two-thirds of the variance in academic achievement levels — with

8. Separate regressions run for Secondary and Vocational schools gave similar results for Secondary schools but showed a slight, though statistically insignificant, positive effect for Vocational Schools (N = 17).

Table 5.7: *Hierarchical Regression of Proportion of the 1976/77 Entry Cohort Who Achieved Acceptance to University (CAO) Place, with School Input Characteristics, School Type, and Schooling Differentiation Scale (Standardised regression coefficients)*

Independent Variables	(i) Beta	(ii) Beta	(iii) Beta
(i) Pupil Input Characteristics			
1. Median social class level of pupil intake	−.48*	−.46*	−.43*
2. Average level of mother's education	.40*	.33*	.32*
3. Extent of literacy/numeracy problems in pupil intake	−.03	.00	−.01
4. Extent of selectivity of school intake	−.01	−.01	.01
(ii) School Type			
5. Boys' Secondary school	—	.23*	.27*
6. Girls' Secondary school	—	.04	.04
7. Vocational school	—	−.00	.05
(iii) Extent of Schooling Differentiation			
8. Schooling process scale	—	—	−.15*
N =	72	72	72
F =	32.5*	21.0*	19.9*
R^2 =	.66	.70	.72

*Statistically significant at the 5 per cent level. (In the case of variable 8 this is the "incremental F" test.)

parental educational variables (particularly mothers') being almost equally as important as socio-occupational variables. Once these are controlled for, other school selectivity variables retain no effect. However, the addition of the three school type variables adds another 4 per cent to the explained variance — primarily due to the substantial positive effect of boys' Secondary schools. Even controlling for such social class background variables boys' Secondary schools are substantially more likely to have higher rates of University entry than other schools — even though girls' schools are more likely than boys' to bring pupils up to at least Pass Leaving Cert. level. Their pupil composition is, of course, much more selective than girls' schools. Given that roughly the same proportion of each sex goes on to University, this finding suggests a much stronger self-selective academic bias within boys' Secondary schools, as well as greater school "effectiveness" in this respect. However, as we saw earlier, this elite achievement may well be purchased at the expense of lower achievers within these schools, as boys' schools also show evidence of higher dropout rates and lower average attainment levels for the total entry cohort.

Controlling for all these schools' input and school type variables leaves 30 per cent of residual variance. The school process scale does add another 2 per cent to the explained variance. Although small this is highly statistically significant. As in the preceding cases, the sign of the coefficient is also negative: the greater the rigidity of pupil curricular differentiation the *lower* the achievement level. Clearly this, and the previous results, indicate that, considered at a total school level or from the point of view of *all* pupils who initially enter, there is *no* overall positive attainment effect of rigid streaming. The hypothesis of a positive effect can be clearly rejected, while that of a negative effect receives some consistent support. Such differentiated schooling, therefore, has no apparent effect on increasing the *average* levels of education received by a school's entry cohort, nor the proportions meeting minimum standards at the Leaving Certificate examination; and it has a slight, though statistically significant, negative effect on the proportions going on to University.[9]

In conclusion, therefore, the argument put forward for streaming or "tracking" by schools — that it allows them to maximise the educational achievements of their student intake, can be clearly rejected — particularly for that proportion achieving elite standards as well as for lower achievers. Certainly in terms of the average attainment levels of a cohort, or in the percentage of an entry cohort who attain moderate to high levels of Leaving Cert. results — and clearly in the percentage going on to University, "streaming" has no consistent and independent positive effect. So one cannot support it on that basis. Nor does streaming, on average, minimise early dropout rates. Assigning low ability pupils to special homogeneous ability classes and using particular curricula to suit their needs — again one of the main arguments put forward for streaming — also, on average, does not work either. The hypothesis of a positive effect on dropout rates can be clearly rejected. In fact, there is some consistent though statistically insignificant evidence that it is inclined to increase their alienation and early dropout.

On most grounds, therefore, one has to reject as invalid the posited claims for "streaming" that it maximises the achievement potential of both the high and low ability pupil. Indeed, by and large — though not strongly so — we would have to come to the tentative conclusion that it tends, on average, to depress achievement levels within schools. We examine the extent to which it influences polarisation or wider differentiation in achievement in the following section.

9. In the separate regressions for school types the effect of schooling process differentiation in Vocational schools was even more clearly negative, though not significant.

The Effects of Streaming and Curricular Differentiation on School Output Variances

The main hypothesis being tested in this section is that the use of streaming and curricular differentiation by schools increases the variation in attainment amongst pupils over that occurring in its absence, controlling for all other relevant factors that affect variation in achievement. The null hypothesis is that of no independent effects. We first use two overall measures of school output variances. Initially the standard deviation in output is used as the main dependent variable. This measures the dispersion of individual school leavers over the years or standards of education reached by the time they left school. The standard deviation in attainments of the total entry cohort was calculated from school records and Principals' interviews for the total number of pupils first entering schools in September 1976 up to the time of completing the Leaving Cert. examination in June 1981[10] (see Figure 1.1 for illustrative examples). Since the average number of years completed by entry cohorts varied widely from school to school the standard deviation is not the best measure of relative within-school inequalities in attainments, so the co-efficient of variation — as a measure of relative variation — is also used: i.e., the standard deviation divided by its mean (see Blalock, 1960, pp. 67-74). Both measures are distributed normally with the coefficient of variation being more satisfactory (see Appendix Table 5.4). For variables like age or educational level, etc., the coefficient of variation is a very satisfactory, scale invariant, measure of inequality (see Allison, 1978). It allows us to compare the within-school inequalities of attainment/achievement on a scale which uses the same units of measurement but which is standardised by the average level of attainment/achievement, allowing us to compare inequalities in attainment between schools which vary, for instance, from ones with very high Leaving Certificate completion rates to ones with very low; or those with higher or lower average grades in the Leaving Certificate. However, standard deviations do provide measures of absolute differences between schools — along the same scale — so it is worth examining first.

These two measures of within school variance or inequality in achievements refer to the total population of students who first entered each school. Whether, however, streaming also brings about wider variances in achievement at both the Intermediate and Leaving Certificate examinations is also checked. Of course, both examinations are taken by increasingly more selective components of the original entry cohort of pupils. Nevertheless, the process of streaming and curricular differentiation is also applied to them — although less rigidly so as one moves up to the Leaving Certificate level.

10. Schools with 5-year cycles. Schools with 6-year cycles were measured from September 1975 to June 1981.

Standard Deviation in the Number of Years of Schooling Completed

There were 71 larger schools — with more than 1 class at Inter Cert. level — for which we had complete information on all variables relevant to this analysis. Fifteen schools were excluded because they were too small. Two additional Vocational schools were excluded because they did not operate a senior cycle programme — their junior cycle leavers going on to other schools. And there were 7 schools for which we did not have sufficient reliable information on all the variables concerned to include in the regression. These 71 schools are used in the rest of the analysis. Independent checks — using less stringent criteria for inclusion — carried out indicate that the results can safely be generalised to the total relevant sample.

The family and social background characteristics of pupils first entering schools combined explain a quarter of the variation of within-school variances in output. The social class characteristics of the school are the main discriminating variables — particularly the median level of social class of intake and the extent of class differentiation of pupil intake, as well as the degree of ability and social selectivity applied by the school. Lower middle class or working class schools and particularly those with wide social class variability in intake — the newer "open" and more comprehensive schools — have substantially larger variances in output, as one would expect. However, greater direct selectivity in intake is *not* reflected in lesser variance in "output" — in fact quite the reverse. The more "selective" schools — generally among the boys' Secondary schools — have, in fact, wider variances in output once social class and related variables are controlled for. At the other extreme, to the more open or more "comprehensive", schools are the upper middle class, generally fee paying, schools with very little variance in output — usually only between those who leave after completing the Leaving Cert. and those who go on to University.

The addition of the three dummy variables for school type adds 7 per cent to the total variance explained, which is highly statistically significant. However, none of the individual school types shows any statistically significant relationship to output variance once the preceding social class and ability selectivities have been controlled. Combined, these two sets of variables explain around a third of the variance in output, with boys' Secondary schools and Vocational schools showing somewhat greater output variance than the girls' or Community or coed Secondary schools (the controls), and girls' Secondary schools in particular having somewhat less variance.

The addition of the school process variable substantially and significantly increases the variance of output by almost 8 percentage points even with all the preceding variables controlled for. The null hypothesis can be clearly rejected: rigid streaming and curricular differentiation substantially increases

Table 5.8: *Regression of "Variance in Output" of Schools — the Standard Deviation in the Number of Years of Schooling Completed Before Leaving School by 1975/76 Entry Cohort — on Pupil Intake Characteristics, School Characteristics and Extent of Streaming and Curricular Differentiation Within Schools. Schools > 2 Classes*

Independent Variables *	(i) With Input Variables	(ii) Input + School Type Variables	(iii) Input, School Type Plus School Process Variables
	Beta (Standardised)	Beta (Standardised)	Beta (Standardised)
(i) School Input Characteristics			
1. Variance in fathers' level of education	.18	.29**	.30**
2. Variance in fathers' occupational status	.27**	.26**	.24**
3. Median social class level of pupil intake	.24*	.26**	.24*
4. Average level of maternal education of pupil intake	−.18	−.19	−.17
5. Extent of selectivity of intake	.30**	.36**	.39**
6. Extent of literacy/numeracy problems in intake	.07	.08	.12
(ii) School Characteristics			
7. Boys' Secondary schools	−	.13	.04
8. Girls' Secondary schools	−	−.11	−.11
9. Vocational schools	--	.25	.16
(iii) Severity of Schooling Process Differentiation			
10. Schooling process scale	−	--	.29**
N =	71	71	71
F =	3.29**	3.02**	3.7**
R^2 =	.24	.31	.38

*F statistically significant at 10 per cent level.
**Statistically significant at the 5 per cent level.

Variables:
1 = Variance in fathers' level of education (1 = Primary school only; 8 = University degree), based on responses by pupils in Inter Cert. classes in schools.

2,3 = Fathers' occupational status as reported by pupils in Inter Cert. classes in school (1 = professional → 8 = unskilled manual). Variance and median estimated from responses of pupils in Inter Cert. classes.

4 = Average measured from same variables as in 1.

5 = Selectivity of school (1 = school is "creamed off" substantially → 5 = school gets better pupils and is selective).

6 = Literacy/numeracy levels from Principals'/Career Guidance Teachers' estimates (1 = <5%, 4 = >25%).

7-9 = Dummy variables.

10 = School process scale for both junior and senior cycle — Guttman scale (see Chapter 4).

output differentiation. This strong conclusion supports a lot of more recent research work on the effects of streaming and tracking which show that although these practices have no "main effect" on student achievement, they have significant polarisation effects — tending to create greater inequalities between students at the ends of the ability and social class continuum (see Hallinan, 1987, pp. 41-69 for review; and Peterson, Wilkinson and Hallinan, 1984, pp. 229-240).

Coefficient of Variation in School Output — A Standardised "Within School" Measure of Inequality

The following table gives the equivalent regression analysis for the coefficient of variation measure. As can be seen much more of the variance is explainable using this more discriminating inequality measure.

Table 5.9: *Hierarchical Regression of "Inequality in Output" of Schools — Coefficient of Variation in the Numbers of Years Pupils Spend in Individual Schools — on Pupil Input Characteristics, School Characteristics and Extent of Streaming and Curricular Variation in Schools*
(N = 71 schools with > 1 Inter Cert. class)

Independent Variables	(i) Beta	(ii) Beta	(iii) Beta
(i) School Input Characteristics			
(All measured for pupils in Inter Cert. classes)			
1. Variance in fathers' level of education	.19	.28*	.29*
2. Variance in fathers' occupational status	.14	.17	.15
3. Median social class level of school intake	.36*	.38*	.36*
4. Average level of mothers' education of school intake	-.18	-.18	-.16
5. Extent by selectivity in school intake	.13	.31*	.27*
6. Extent to which literacy/numeracy problems occur in school intake	.10	.11	.14
(ii) School Characteristics			
7. Boys' Secondary schools	—	.18	.11
8. Girls' Secondary schools	—	-.11	-.11
9. Vocational schools	—	.36*	.28*
(iii) Severity of Schooling Process			
10. Schooling process scale	—	—	.26*
N =	71	71	71
F =	4.4*	4.9*	5.4*
R^2 =	.30	.42	.48

*Statistically significant at the 5 per cent level.

Again there were 71 schools with 2 or more classes in the Inter Cert. for which we had full information on all variables included in the regression. School input characteristics explained almost one-third of the variance in output — mostly due to the social class composition of the school: the lower the median social class of the pupil body and the general level of education of parents, and the generally greater the variance in both of these respects, the greater the relative variance in output. Upper middle class schools with pupils whose parents have high levels of education — and with little variance in both these respects — have very little variance in output. Almost all pupils who first enter these schools complete the Leaving Cert. and the only variance remaining is due to the dichotomy between those who leave education at that stage and those who go on to University. At the other extreme, schools with a lower working class intake, with poor parental educational characteristics, but with wide variance in the social class and educational mix amongst parents, experience very wide variance in output.

The addition of the three "school type" variables to the regression equation adds significantly to the amount of variance explained — by 12 percentage points. But only Vocational schools show a significant effect — by about 10 per cent on their own. So, to a large extent, independent of intake factors, Vocational schools have a significantly greater variance in educational output. Given their historical vocational charters and their recently acquired more academic functions — attempting to maximise Leaving Cert. achievement with a highly unselective pupil intake, but at the same time to maximise the vocational opportunities (apprenticeships, etc.) of those leaving after junior cycle exams — this is hardly a surprising finding. Nevertheless, this dispersion in the objectives and outputs of such schools — Group and Inter Cert., technical and apprenticeship objectives of boys, girls' commercial/ secretarial objectives, and a small academic Leaving Cert. stream, etc. — may have serious consequences for the organisational effectiveness of such small and unselective schools.

It is interesting that, when one controls for the effects of school type, "school selectivity" becomes highly significant; controlling for most relevant pupil intake and school type variables; schools that select also significantly differentiate their output.

Even with all these statistical "controls" the effects of rigid streaming and curricular differentiation are quite pronounced. The introduction of the "schooling process" variable into the regression equation adds a substantial 6 per cent to the amount of variance explained in the overall inequality measure.

Of course, we have not controlled for all the relevant pupil composition variables — particularly ability variables. However, given the various social class and educational input characteristics controlled for, as well as variables measuring school selectivity and type, the quite substantial addition to variance explained by the introduction of the streaming/differentiation variable provides very strong support for the polarisation hypothesis.

So, both measures of the level of inequality in attainment within schools show that to the extent that schools stream, and make clear distinctions amongst categories of pupils in the type of curriculum and teaching process applied, they substantially increase the variances in educational attainment over and above that which occurs where schools do not use such methods. That these organisationally created distinctions in achievement are not to the overall or average benefit of all pupils is clear from the results given in the previous section; they tend to increase the early dropout rate, do not increase the proportions achieving Pass or Honours grades at the Leaving Cert. level, and tend to have a slight negative effect on the proportions of the original cohort going on to University. Before coming to final conclusions on this issue, however, it seemed worthwhile to check whether such rigid school processing has an equal polarising effect at the Intermediate and Leaving Certificate levels for those selective proportions of the initial entry cohort who survive to these levels.

Intermediate Certificate Examination Performance

For those who survive to the Intermediate Certificate examination level differential allocation to academic or Pass level "general education" or vocational "tracks" within highly streamed schools has an obvious and direct effect. But whether this formal school allocation process actually creates greater variances in, for example, the number of higher or Honours papers taken at the Intermediate Certificate level than actually occurs "spontaneously" in unstreamed schools — where the interaction of pupils, parents and teachers at individual classroom level mainly determines which level of Irish, English or Maths is taken from the "set" of Honours and Pass level courses taught — is an open question. Most recent research work carried out abroad (Shavitt, 1984; Nachmias, 1980; Hout and Garnier, 1980) shows both that the allocation process tends to have clear social class and ethnic biases independent of ability/performance, and that greater output variances occur where such formally determined curricular allocation processes occur (see also Alexander, Cook and McDill, 1978).

At the Intermediate Certificate level we have three relevant measures of variance in performance: variation in the number of Honours levels taken, and variation in the number of "academic" subjects[11] as well as variation in

11. Academic subjects are defined as Honours Irish, English and Maths and the recognised academic subjects of French, German and other languages, History, Geography, Science, Art, Music.

the takeup of vocational subjects.[12] Pupils were interviewed in the Christmas to Easter term before they took the 1981 Intermediate Certificate examination — so we do not have the results of that examination.

There are 71 schools with 2 or more classes for which we have complete data for the regressions. The average standard deviation in the number of Honours subjects taken is 1.1 per school, but there are very wide differences amongst schools in this respect (standard deviation = .28). The variable is again normally distributed, although the distribution is tightly clustered around the mean. There is, of course, a high correlation ($r = .71$) between this variable and within-school variation in the total number of academic subjects taken by pupils in the Intermediate Cert. course. The average school standard deviation in this case is very wide at 5.1, but showing wide differences amongst schools in this respect (standard deviation = 1.4). Both variables are normally distributed. We first examine the absolute differences amongst schools in the discriminations they make between Pass and Honours students at Intermediate Certificate level.

School input or pupil composition effects account for over a third of the differences between schools in their extent of Honours/Pass level distinctions (see Appendix Table 5.5). This is mainly due to the extent of social selectivity of schools: schools with wider social class and parental educational intake have substantially greater distinctions amongst Pass and Honours pupils. But schools that select their pupils on ability grounds and that, in fact, get proportionately *fewer* pupils with literacy and numeracy problems have also much wider variances in output. The absolute differences in the level of Honours/Pass distinction are not, therefore, due to a large intake of lower ability pupils. The addition of "school type" variables adds substantially to the explained variance: boys' schools, but particularly Vocational schools, have significantly *less* within-school variance in these respects than girls' or coed Secondary schools or Community schools. The Honours/Pass distinctions within Vocational schools is usually between those who take 1 or no Honours course, whilst within the more selective boys' Secondary schools the distribution of those taking Honours courses is very much biased toward the other end of the distribution.

Adding in the schooling process scale to the regression contributes somewhat to the explained variance, but very moderately and not significantly so, highly differentiated schools showing only minor additions to the within-school variance. The process of streaming and curricular differentiation by schools, therefore, does not tend to create significantly greater achievement differences amongst Inter Cert. pupils than would otherwise occur.

12. "Vocational Subjects" = the three technical subjects, plus Domestic Science and Commerce.

With two important exceptions we get much the same results when we use the variance in the number of academic subjects taken at the Intermediate Certificate level as the dependent variable (see Appendix Table 5.6). In this case the average familial social class and educational backgrounds of the pupil body clearly have a much greater impact — the more working class the composition of the school the greater the variance amongst pupils in their uptake of academic subjects. Schools with wider socio-economic intakes do have much wider output variance, but the differences are not statistically significant once school type is controlled for. As in previous cases schools which have a high intake of low ability pupils, or pupils with serious literacy/ numeracy problems, also have lower variances in output; primarily because they are located in Vocational schools and these teach relatively fewer academic subjects and have much lower variances in these respects.

The addition of two school type variables has much the same effect as in the previous case, substantially increasing the variance explained. Controlling for all the preceding variables, boys' Secondary schools and Vocational schools show substantially less variance in the uptake of academic subjects than girls' or coed Secondary schools or Community schools. Everything else being equal, boys' Secondary schools maximise the number of academic subjects taught to most pupils — not surprising since they teach few vocational or aesthetic subjects — and Vocational schools minimise such takeup or indeed, provision.

With all of the preceding pupil input and school type variables controlled for school differentiation, however, does add substantially and significantly to the explained variance. Streaming and its associated curricular differentiation clearly polarises academic subject takeup, as is the primary intention.

Peculiarly, within-school variation in the number of vocational subjects taken by Intermediate Cert. pupils has no independent relationship to the rigidity of streaming and its associated curricular differentiation. Almost all the explained variation is accounted for by the type of school involved — Vocational and Comprehensive schools show substantially more variation than all others while Secondary schools, and particularly girls' schools, show substantially less. But, controlling for all relevant variables, the rigidity of the streaming process retains no statistically significant effect; any effect present being negative.

As already discussed the standard deviation is not a good measure of relative within-school inequality. Although it does provide a measure of the absolute inequality differences amongst schools. Since, however, the mean attainment levels differ radically from school to school a much more effective measure of relative inequality is the "coefficient of variation" (see Allison, 1978). In the following table, therefore, we regress within-school inequality in the number of academic subjects taken on school input, school type and schooling process variables.

Here the effects of social class are much more pronounced than with the (absolute) standard deviation — so that it dominates all other effects. Working class schools show substantially greater inequality in the uptake of academic subjects even when all other relevant variables have been controlled or allowed for. Combined, the pupil input variables account for a third of the variance in this school inequality measure — with working class schools showing much greater inequality in these respects than others. Of course working class schools are also far more likely than others to be Vocational or Community schools, and slightly more likely to be coeducational Secondary schools. All of these provide much more "comprehensive" curricula — a wider mixture of technical/vocational and academic subjects — than Secondary schools. The latter, of course, usually have more Honours and academic subjects. So given the "elite" academic sponsorship role that such schools possess they also obviously create much greater inter-pupil differentiation in the uptake of academic versus vocational subjects.

Once social class and other pupil intake variables are controlled for only boys' Secondary schools exhibit any significant difference in the provision/ uptake of academic subjects — exhibiting significantly *less* inequality in academic subject uptake than others. Of course boys' Secondary schools also *display* significantly less variation in academic/vocational subject pro- vision than other schools. Combined pupil intake and school type variables account for 38 per cent of the variance in this school inequality measure.

Once, however, pupil intake and school type variables have been controlled for, the schooling process scale does add substantially to the explained variance — an additional 8 per cent in fact — which is highly statistically significant. Even with all of the preceding statistical controls, schools that rigidly differentiate their pupils and curriculum exhibit significantly greater inequality in academic subject provision/uptake. Such schools, therefore, impose greater inequality *than* would otherwise occur. The same tendency is evident when inequality in the number of Honours subjects is used as the dependent variable, though in this case the effect is only statistically significant at the 10 per cent level.

Even at the more selective Intermediate Certificate level, therefore, school imposed pupil/curricular differentiation processes clearly have an impact on academic inequality within schools. Such school policy effects are most obvious in increasing inequality in academic subject takeup, and to a less significant extent in Honours level subject takeup. Other variables, however, are more important — particularly the social class of intake and type of school. Working class schools and Community/Comprehensive schools as

Table 5.10: *Hierarchical Regression of Inequality in Junior Cycle Academic Uptake — the Coefficient of Variation in the Number of Academic Subjects Taken up by Pupils — or Pupil Intake, School Type and Schooling Process Variables (N = 71 schools with > 1 Inter Cert. class)*

Independent Variables	*(i)* With School Input Variables	*(ii)* School Input and School Type Variables	*(iii)* School Input, School Type and Schooling Process Variables
	Beta	Beta	Beta
(i) School Input Characteristics			
1. Median social class by pupil intake	.50*	.47*	.41*
2. Average level of mothers' education of pupil intake	.06	.19	.25
3. Variance in social class of intake of pupils	.17	.16	.12
4. Variance in parental educational level of pupil intake	−.01	.01	.08
5. Selectivity of schools	−.13	−.15	−.13
6. Extent of literacy/numeracy problems in pupil intake	−.10	−.15	−.09
(ii) School Types			
7. Boys' Secondary schools	—	−.27*	−.36*
8. Vocational schools	—	.05	−.13
(iii)			
9. Schooling process scale	—	—	.31*
N =	71	71	71
F =	5.4	4.9	6.0
R^2 =	.33	.38	.46

*Statistically significant at .05 level.

well as coed Secondary schools have greater variation and inequality in academic, Honours and vocational subject takeup. This is partly a function of subject provision (which, of course, is policy determined) but also a function of what appears to be, in some schools, a clear "sponsorship role" being adopted for an elite of upwardly mobile lower-middle or working class pupils. That this is likely to be a "school determined" rather than an "environmentally imposed" outcome is suggested by the finding that the non-selective schools and schools with *lower* proportions of educationally disadvantaged pupils exhibit *higher* absolute levels of within-school variation in the takeup of Honours and academic subjects. That such school imposed policy has a substantial impact on subject takeup is very evident when the independent effects of streaming/curricular differentiation were examined — where such practices clearly increased inequality in academic subject takeup.

Inequality Effects at Leaving Certificate Level

Measured at the Intermediate Certificate level, when very little dropout has occurred in most schools, the effects of rigid pupil/curricular differentiation are, in general, polarising — even when we control for most relevant pupil composition and school type variables. By Leaving Certificate level, however, we are left with a quite selective sub-population of pupils in most schools: the average school dropout rate to Leaving Certificate level is 39 per cent but it varies extremely widely across the different school types — with an overall standard deviation of 25. So, although such rigid streaming and curricular differentiation may have quite discriminatory effects at junior cycle level the experience of the quite selective cohort reaching Leaving Certificate level may be quite different. In addition, as we saw in Chapter 3, streaming and curricular differentiation is much less pronounced at senior cycle level.

As can be seen from the results presented in Table 5.11 these expectations are, to a large extent, met. Variations in the schooling process variable have no independent effect, once the main school composition and school type variables have been controlled for. With this restricted Leaving Certificate sample, however, the combined set of independent variables has somewhat different effects than at Intermediate Certificate level or earlier. Although schools with wider socio-economic variance in intake have somewhat wider variance in output, working class schools and schools where the parental educational level of the pupil intake is low have significantly *less* variance than middle class ones. Presumably by Leaving Cert. level, with the very high level of dropout suffered by working class schools (see Tables 5.3 and 5.4), only a limited range of the more able of the initial student group is left; whereas, with almost no dropout amongst the upper middle class schools the total initial range of student ability is still present. As a result, working class schools show little variation around a generally low average level of achievement, whereas middle class schools exhibit much wider variance around a generally higher average level of achievement. The more selective schools again, as previously, experience somewhat more variance in examination results. So the more "middle class" schools, who retain their more comprehensive ability ranges and particularly those with wider socio-economic intakes, experience much greater variation in examination achievements at the Leaving Certificate level.

Table 5.11: *Regression of Within-School Differentiation (Standard Deviation) in Leaving Cert. Grades Received on the (i) School Input, (ii) School Type, and (iii) Schooling Process Variables*
(N = 71 schools)

Independent Variables	(i) Effects of School Input Variables	(ii) Effects of School Input and School Variables	(iii) Effects of School Input and School Type and Schooling Process Variables
	Beta	Beta	Beta
(i) School Input (Pupil) Variables			
1. Median social class of pupil intake	−.34*	−.30*	−.32*
2. Average maternal educational level amongst pupil intake	.30*	.12	.14
3. Variance in social class of pupil body	.09	.10	.09
4. Variance in fathers' level of education of pupils	.12	.03	.05
5. Extent of selectivity of school	.26*	.20	.20
6. Extent of literacy/numeracy problems in pupil intake	.09	.13	.16
(ii) School Type Variables			
7. Boys' Secondary schools	---	.19	.16
8. Vocational schools	—	−.29*	−.27*
(iii)			
9. Schooling process scale	—	—	.10
N =	71	71	71
F =	11.1*	10.1*	9.1*
R² =	.51	.56	.57

*Statistically significant at the .05 level.

Boys' Secondary schools, however, show somewhat greater variation in output than all other schools, even controlling for all preceding variables. Vocational schools show substantially less. While the latter conforms to our findings for the Intermediate Certificate results, the former does not. Why the much more selective boys' Secondary schools should show more variance in this respect than the much more "comprehensive" girls', coed Secondary

and Community schools is not at all clear. The bivariate correlations, however, with school type are very pronounced at Leaving Certificate level, substantially more pronounced, in fact, than for any of the Intermediate Certificate variance measures. Although much more selective at that stage than
girls' schools, in boys' Secondary schools the top achievers tend to do better,
but the bottom worse than in other schools. As for Vocational schools they
show consistently less variance than any other schools — for reasons already
discussed. Middle class boys' Secondary schools, of course, suffer minimally
from dropout and are most likely of all schools to stream rigidly when large
enough. But streaming is not the full explanation: even controlling for the
rigidities of streaming, boys' Secondary schools still show substantially
greater variance in examination performance than others.

However, when we control for school type, and for pupil composition
effects, the rigidity of streaming retains no additional, statistically significant,
effect. By this stage the worst of such streaming effects have worked themselves out of the system and streaming in any case is much less rigidly
enforced.

We get much the same result when we use the more accurate, coefficient
of variation, inequality measure (see Appendix Table 5.7); except in this
case the only variable that retains any significant effect on within-school
inequality is the ability/selectivity of schools — where schools with a high
intake of lower ability pupils exhibit substantially greater inequality in
examination achievement. Although boys' Secondary schools tend to exhibit
higher inequality than girls' or coed schools and Vocational schools less, and
while highly differentiated schools also exhibit somewhat greater inequality
than mixed-ability schools, these effects are minor and not statistically
significant. So that by the end of the senior cycle, when substantial selective
dropout has already occurred, such school-imposed discriminations appear
to have little additional effect.

Conclusions

1.   Both main hypotheses proposed are supported by the analysis of
        results: streaming and curricular differentiation does not increase the
        average level of educational attainment of an entry cohort to schools.
        There is, indeed, some tentative evidence that it decreases average
        attainment levels. The process of pupil and curricular differentiation,
        however, does increase the variance and level of inequality in the
        achievement levels of the total entry cohort over and beyond that
        which would occur in its absence. In dropout rates, in the average
        number of years or standards of schooling completed before leaving,

and in the percentage of the entry cohort to schools attaining University entrance levels — a rigid schooling process tends to have a slight but consistent negative impact. And in terms of all measures of differentiation or polarisation of overall pupil attainment or achievement, a differentiated schooling process also has a consistent polarisation effect.

2.   At the Intermediate Certificate level — when some dropout has already occurred, particularly in working class schools — such rigid schooling differentiation has clearcut polarising effects on the takeup of academic subjects and some, though statistically insignificant, effects on the number of Honours subjects taken. Again there is no evidence here that it increases average achievement levels.

3.   For that select proportion of the cohort, however, who survive to do the Leaving Certificate examination there is no statistical support for the hypothesis that streaming increases polarisation in levels of examination achievement; although it does tend to decrease the proportion of the entry cohort going on to University. Clearly, therefore, by this stage the maintenance of rigid distinctions amongst ranked classes of pupils, constructed of "homogeneous ability" groups, neither maximises examination achievements nor minimises academic and social distinctions amongst pupils. It does, however, tend to decrease University entry proportions.

4.   Appendix Table 5.8 contains the relevant regression of each *individual* pupil's overall level of Leaving Cert. examination performance (scored using the UCD, CAO, method) on individual level family background variables, preceding educational performance level (Intermediate Cert. results), and school type variables, as well as the schooling process scale. The latter has no independent effect for either boys' or girls' level of examination performance. This holds even with preceding examination performance excluded from the equation. So, being in a streamed versus unstreamed school has no *average* academic advantage for pupils at Leaving Cert. level. For any measures of average academic achievement we have used, therefore, streaming has no discernible positive academic effect for the total number of pupils attending school; or even for the selective sub-populations that remain in school until Leaving Certificate level; indeed in many respects it tends to have an overall negative effect. It has, however, a clear and consistent polarising effect — particularly at junior cycle level.

5.   In a later paper we will examine the effects of streaming or "tracking" on individual pupils who are placed in upper or lower streams or bands

at senior cycle level, where schooling is highly differentiated. Most preceding research has shown a clear negative impact of being placed in a lower stream controlling for all relevant family background and ability/performance variables; as well as a positive effect for placement in a higher stream. Unfortunately we do not have all the necessary information to test these hypotheses at junior cycle level, where streaming appears to have its greatest impact. Some preliminary work at senior cycle level — using the Intermediate Certificate results as a proxy measurement for the preceding ability/performance characteristic of pupils — shows some support for these hypotheses. This is a very "strong" finding given that "streaming" is likely to have its greatest effects at junior cycle level and these effects are controlled for by holding Intermediate Certificate results constant. If upheld in later work this finding would help to explain how differentiated schooling brings about greater differentiation and inequality in educational attainment.

Chapter 6

SUMMARY, CONCLUSIONS AND IMPLICATIONS OF STUDY

Introduction

This study had three objectives: (i) It investigated the nature and extent of distinctions made by school authorities amongst their pupils, as well as distinctions in the type of curriculum and teaching process applied to different pupil categories. (ii) It sought to identify the reasons why different kinds of schools differ so widely in the nature and severity of the schooling distinctions made. (iii) And thirdly, it examined some of the main consequences of these school-imposed distinctions on pupils' educational attainments.

The majority of Irish second-level schools "create" distinctions amongst categories of their pupils by "measuring" their presumed educable capabilities, by assigning them to different "streams" or "bands", and by making clear distinctions amongst these categories of pupils in the type of curriculum and instructional process applied to them. The nature and extent of pupil and curricular differentiation varies widely amongst schools, but there are clear underlying structural and cultural, or ideological, reasons why this is so. In making these distinctions school decisionmakers do have objectives — although many of these are more clearly implied in school practice rather than being expressions of conscious policy. In many schools such schooling distinctions have been in place for a long time, the objectives and outcomes of which are so taken for granted that they are accepted as "natural" and inevitable. Many studies have shown that such school practices as "streaming" or "tracking" have substantial differential effects on the educational performance and subsequent occupational achievement of individuals who are placed in different streams, taking into account all initial ability differences amongst pupils. So these practices operate in many cases to transmit and even amplify social class and related inequalities from generation to generation; yet in many cases again school decisionmakers appear not to see or be concerned about these consequences even though they may be quite obvious to well informed outsiders.

These and related policy issues surrounding such school imposed differentiation have been the subject of considerable public controversy in the United States, Britain and many European countries since, at least, the mid-1960s.

161

In Ireland, however, there has been barely a murmur above the level of the individual school. Conferences of teachers' unions, religious orders involved in teaching, school-owning and managerial authorities, policy discussion documents emanating from the Department of Education, or the recently established Curriculum and Examination Board, have not dealt at all with these issues. Why? The way in which a school applies its curriculum is almost as important as the content and structure of the curriculum itself. Yet the process by which schools apply or organise their curriculum and instructional processes – not to mention the actual pedagogical practice within the secrecy of the classroom – have not been the subject of any discernible open discourse or dispute. Why? It is clearly not because school decisionmakers and the teaching profession all agree with each other on this question – such decisionmakers, in fact, vary widely in their practices and relevant philosophy. It is not because there is no platform for debate – the relevant annual conferences are well attended and have attentive conference and mass media audiences. Clearly these matters are not issues that have high agenda priority. Why?

There is a closely related school practice that has equal importance for pupils' life chances and that has equally low priority – the socially prejudicial allocation of pupils amongst schools. This issue of selectivity versus "comprehensivisation" has equally been the subject of much research and of heated debate and political controversy in the United Kingdom (see *Oxford Review of Education*, 10, 1, 1984), as has the issue of selective academic schools in the United States (Coleman, 1982; see *Harvard Educational Review*, 1981 for review of earlier edition).

There are, we believe, five main reasons why this public inattention exists.

1.   There is almost no Irish research on the subject which could be used as a stimulus to the debate. (An exception is Kellaghan, 1967.) This in itself, of course, is even more puzzling, since academic researchers should be very open to the international literature and be less ideologically influenced. There is, however, very poor funding of educational research at second level and no apparent central policy on the matter.

2.   The schooling processes involved and their educational consequences are not, however, publicly visible – so pupils and parents who suffer from the current system have no way of publicly comprehending and registering their dissatisfaction. Those who suffer most in any case are likely to be least influential.

3.   The State, either at central or local level, does not accept responsibility for the way schools are operated: either for the allocation of different categories of pupils to different types of schools, or for differential

streaming or tracking within schools. State policy indeed had, at an earlier stage, implicitly colluded in the development of "selective" schooling: i.e., in the expansion of the Vocational school sector — by "filling in the gaps" so to speak, left by the selective provision of Secondary schools. Only in recent times by the development of Comprehensive/Community schools in newly developing urban areas, or in the few comprehensive amalgamations occurring in the smaller towns, has the State operated an effective local comprehensive provision policy. The more vigorous policy of comprehensifisation pursued in the early 1970s was so successfully fought off by local vested interests that the State effectively withdrew its earlier policy. This is — or used to be — in marked contrast, for instance, to the behaviour of the British state; except, peculiarly, in Northern Ireland where comprehensive schooling appears to be almost equally unpopular.

Schools, the great majority of which are privately owned, do have to conform to State regulations in regard to the nature and content of the curriculum applied — though this still allows schools considerable degrees of freedom (Hannan, Breen *et al.*, 1983). Schools also are centrally regulated by timetables and by attendance and public examination requirements as well as certain certification procedures. And they have to conform to particular organisational rules in order to be publicly funded. There is also a minimal monitoring inspectorial arrangement. But, by and large, second-level schools, although funded almost completely by the State, are, within these broad parameters, free to run their own affairs untouched by external State authority. They are also, by and large, free to compete with each other for local academic talent.

4. By and large, the ideological "climate" and class forces within Ireland are such that the pursuit of egalitarian citizenship rights has no active political priority or urgency. Partly as a result, the educational process over the past 20 years has clearly worked to the benefit of the majority of middle class, and moderate to large farmer class, as well as upper working class families — the majority of families and voters.[13] Consequently any deleterious effects it might have had on the minority of working class or poorer families (only 8 per cent of children come from the families of unskilled manual workers) are not publicly

---

13. In 1981, 20 per cent of children under 15 years (N = 1,043,729) were present in families of non-manual workers, 13 per cent in families of farmers, 24 per cent in the families of skilled manual workers, and 17 per cent in families where the chief breadwinner was a semi-skilled manual worker or a service worker (other non-manual). Only 8 per cent were in families of unskilled manual workers, *Census of Population of Ireland, 1981*, Vol. 7.

"seen" or projected and have been ignored. So any dissatisfaction present is publicly voiceless and unorganised.

Equality of opportunity was certainly a stated goal of reform of the 1960s but it has never been actively pursued by the State in the same way that it has in Britain, the Scandinavian countries or even the United States, for instance. In the former countries equal educational opportunity had a high priority in successive post-war social democratic politics. In the United States equality of citizenship rights and equality of opportunity also has had a long history of interventionist political and State action, although not based on successful class movements as in the UK or Scandinavia. Given inconsequential class politics and a low priority in the agenda of successful populist movements, political forces have never been committed enough nor strong enough to even attempt the institutional reforms necessary to initiate serious equality of opportunity reforms.

5.   The philosophy underlying and legitimating the State's considerable expansion of educational provision since the mid-1960s, has been rooted in theories of "human capital" formation, within the context of a pragmatic economic and technical rationale about the means to obtain these ends (*Investment in Education Report*, 1966). The main educational objectives paid attention to, have been those of technical knowledge and skill acquisition or socialisation; i.e., the traditional view that the main objectives of schooling are the socialisation of individuals, with priority attached to cognitive development (see Dreeben, 1968). Here the main social effects of schooling are thought to result from the aggregation of individual effects — having no, or unimportant, institutional or organisational intervening effects. As Meyer (1977) or Ramirez *et al.*, (1980) indicates, this view ignores completely the social allocation functions of schools, which may operate to consolidate or even amplify processes of transmission of social inequalities from generation to generation. Schools have substantial institutional powers to allocate pupils and certify pupil achievements. Both different types of school, and streams or bands within schools, publicly differentiate and validate the educational/ occupational achievement paths of different pupils. This institutional power of schools to control or channel the future life chances of their pupils (Meyer, 1977) has thus far remained unexamined and uncontrolled. Educational achievement has been found to be the most predictive variable of occupational and economic attainment in industrialised countries (Cummings, 1979; Treiman and Terrel, 1975; Blau and Duncan, 1967). And in newly industrialised countries this

correlation is even more pronounced (Meyer, Turner and Zagorski, 1979) as well as in Ireland (Whelan and Whelan, 1984). Variations in the institutional power and effectiveness of highly structured schooling in these respects need to be paid much more attention.

Examining Schooling Differences

Our conceptual approach to the study is based on models used in the study of organisations. The main approach is that of Perrow (1967, 1970) which emphasises that the determining characteristics of organisations like schools is the way they process their materials — i.e., their "technology": the way they select and categorise their pupil intake — the number and complexity of the types of categories into which pupils are sorted, and the extent of standardisation and centralisation of decisions as to what kind of educational process is appropriate to each category. At one extreme are schools which sort their pupils into a small number of categories whose distinct natures are perceived to be rather similar and well understood, thus enabling each category to be separately processed with few individual exceptions occurring. This is an organisational "solution" characteristic of highly streamed schools with highly programmed, routinised and centralised schooling processes. At the other extreme, are a small number of mostly upper class, mixed-ability schools where each pupil is an "exceptional case"; and "schooling process" decisions are left for negotiation between individual pupils, teachers and parents. As Perrow (1970) points out, the inherent nature of the materials does not determine the organisational process. This is, as Child (1972) points out, mainly a matter of the "strategic choices" made by decisionmakers within organisations, within the set of environmental constraints present. Child's (1972) work emphasises the role of choice amongst alternative organisational solutions — i.e., in "choosing" and in categorising pupils, in the choice of curricula and teaching resources, and in their deployment to the different categories of pupils; as well as in structuring relationships amongst teachers, pupils and parents and so on.

This voluntaristic conceptual approach is used not only to guide the way in which we categorised our own research materials but also to determine the main hypotheses proposed to explain why different schools adopted different "schooling process" solutions. Two contrasting sets of hypotheses were proposed: (i) Such strategic schooling decisions are determined largely by technical-rational or environmental considerations. (ii) They are influenced largely by "institutional" and voluntaristic factors — i.e., highly structured differences in the founding charters or "missions" of different school-owning authorities, as well as in their historically acquired roles in the schooling and social placement of each succeeding generation (Meyer, 1970; Kamens,

1977). The former set of hypotheses stresses these commonsense theories which are usually employed by school decisionmakers to explain why they stream or rigidly differentiate their pupils and curricula. The latter stresses the institutional and voluntaristic factors which are proposed here as the main explanatory factors.

Under "technical-rational" and commonsense assumptions the degree of differentiation of the total schooling process is seen as a function of:

(i)   Size of school: the larger the school the greater the differentiation.
(ii) Extent of variance in the ability level of the pupil intake — the larger the variance the greater the differentiation.
(iii) Comprehensiveness: the more comprehensive the local catchment of the school the greater the differentiation.

Under "Institutional/Volitional" assumptions we hypothesised that the extent of schooling differentiation was directly related to:

(a)   The explicit founding "charter" or "mission" of the school or group of schools; and the inspirational philosophy guiding the authority (community) which governs or owns the school(s);
(b)   Social class of the clientele and the social placement (mobility) function of the school — both often acquired rather than planned;
(c)   The sex of the pupil body — with boys' education hypothesised to be much more instrumentally differentiated than girls' education.

The Structure and Charters of Irish Second-Level Schools

Irish post-primary schools vary widely in their "objectives" — both those stated and consciously pursued, and those which are clearly implicit in the kind of educational "inputs" chosen and "outputs" produced. Schools vary widely in their "choice" of the social characteristics of persons/pupils they educate — mainly by sex, social class, religion and ability selectivities. To a large extent these "choices" are institutionally determined — given in the founding charters or State legitimated functions assigned to the different school types. But these different educational "missions" have also emerged as strategic adjustments by individual school-owning authorities to changing national and local environmental opportunities and constraints. Given a range from the upper middle class Protestant or Catholic fee-paying Secondary schools to Christian Brothers' selective boys' Secondary schools or Mercy or Presentation "comprehensive" and coed schools, to "selective" lower working class Vocational schools, it is obvious that the charters or "missions" of different school-owning authorities vary widely and systematicaly. As a result, within most communities a highly stratified system of selective schooling emerges from the free competition between the different school types in each local catchment area. The analysis of such local selectivities by different school authorities within our own survey of schools showed wide social class and ability selectivities amongst schools which were highly structured and institutionally determined (Chapters 2 and 4). As became quite clear in Chapter 4 these marked differences in the role and functions of different schools were the most predictive of their "school processing" decisions.

The Extent and Structure of Pupil/Curricular Differentiation

We used five separate measures of pupil and curricular differentiation in the analysis: (i) the extent of "ability" differentiation of pupils amongst classes ("streaming"); (ii) the extent of curricular differentiation by class of pupil — between Honours and Pass level and by type of subject; (iii) the extent of choice of subject and level options available to pupils; (iv) the extent to which subject teachers were involved in subject/career choices; and finally (v) the extent to which clear boundaries existed between different classes of pupils within schools.

A majority of schools practise some form of "streaming" — with around 40 per cent of schools having relatively rigid streaming at Intermediate Cert. level, and only 1 in 4 schools having mixed ability classes as such. And almost 40 per cent of schools allocate Honours and Pass levels, and differentiate subject types, by the pupils' class rank within streams or "bands". Although almost all schools have substantially more subjects than are taken by the average pupil in the school, most schools place considerable constraints on subject and level choices. In fact, around 40 per cent of schools allow almost no choice at all at junior cycle level. In most cases this is not due to the scarcity of subjects/levels available. Even where subject/level choices are present, however, the process is often organised by school "management" rather than by subject teachers. It is no surprise to find, therefore, that in only 1 in 4 schools are subject teachers highly involved in such choice making, or parents facilitated in discussing subject/level "choices" with subject teachers. As a result of these processes of school-imposed pupil/curricular differentiation, over a third of all schools (with more than 1 class) maintain very rigid boundaries and distinctions between ranked classes of pupils on the basis of their presumed "abilities" or educational potential.

The relationships amongst these 5 crucial "schooling process" variables are highly structured. On average there is a moderate to high level of intercorrelation amongst the 5 variables. But what is equally significant is that the larger the school the greater these intercorrelations become. This does *not* mean that the larger the school the greater the tendency to differentiate pupils and curricula, to reduce pupil-parent choice and to increase the boundaries between classes. What it does mean is that if a choice is made to "stream" pupils, then certain curricular, "choice", pupil-teacher-parent relationship characteristics and distinctions between ranked classes of pupils necessarily follow: i.e., that once a "streaming" choice is made it has organisational effects which appear to follow almost inevitably. On the other hand, where schools decide to relax their rigid streaming practices this decision also has an opposing set of "knock-on" organisational consequences.

Of the 80 schools in our sample with 2 or more classes at Intermediate Cert. level, 7 were extremely rigidly streamed with all the above organisationally differentiated characteristics: rigid streaming of pupils, rigid curricular distinctions, little choice, no subject-teacher involvement in any choice making that occurs, with very little parental involvement, and very high resistant boundaries between ranked classes of pupils. An additional 25 schools had less rigid streaming or had 2/3 "bands", with some "mixed ability" classes within each "band". There were less rigid, but still substantial, subject/level distinctions between the streamed/banded classes, somewhat less restricted pupil-teacher-parent choice making as well as less rigid boundaries between classes. At the other extreme were 12 schools which were "mixed ability", 5 of which allowed such wide choices that almost no pupil-class distinctions existed.

There is a small direct and positive correlation between school size, tendency to stream, differentiate the curriculum, and organisationally standise and regulate the schooling process. So, at least to that extent, such schooling differentiation is directly environmentally determined. The correlation, however, is very low — explaining less than 6 per cent of the variance in the schooling process scale; and the relationship of school size to "choice" and to the strength of between-class boundaries is actually of the opposite sign.

Why Differentiate?

Other than school size other "technical" variables — such as the ability and social selectivity of schools, and the extent of variation in the social and cultural backgrounds of pupils — do not predict the extent of schooling differentiation practised. With other variables controlled school size does have a moderate effect — about double that of its direct effect. But almost all the other "technical" variables have actual *negative* effects. Schools which select their intake, that have a larger proportion of literacy/numeracy problems amongst their intake and have wider overall variation in the social/ educational background of pupils, are *less* likely to stream rigidly. So, other than size, the "technical" hypothesis has to be clearly rejected. The proposition put forward by most school decisionmakers for streaming — that the wide variance in the ability and aptitude levels of their pupil intake forces them to rigidly differentiate the schooling applied — receives no support in this study.

On the other hand, the hypothesised effects of institutional and social class factors receive major support. The median social class level of the pupil intake, the sex of the pupil body and the type and identity of the school authority are the main variables predicting variation in the extent of differentiation of the schooling process applied. Boys' Secondary schools (particularly Christian Brothers' schools), and working class or lower middle class schools are far more likely to stream and differentiate their curricula. Vocational and Community schools, largely by explicit policy, do not stream as such but almost universally "broad band" their wider ability intake when large enough and do not make as rigid distinctions in applying their curricula. It is boys' Secondary schools — which cater for a lower middle class, small farmer or upper working class clientele and which select or "sponsor" a proportion of their more able pupil intake for upward social mobility — which have the most differentiated schooling process. These schools, however, also tend to have moderate to high "dropout" rates so that clearly the lower ability/aptitude pupil is not being equally catered for. These schools maximise the achievement of the top while appearing to "cool out" the lower achievers, socialising them for failure (Willis, 1977).

At the other extreme upper middle class Secondary schools, particularly those catering for girls, are least likely to differentiate their schooling process. The cultural consolidation of the advantages of an upper middle class background is being achieved by a highly individualised schooling in which a lot of autonomy is allowed, or developed, at the individual pupil level.

The difference in the schooling "treatment" of boys and girls can perhaps best be understood within Bernstein's view that the increasingly instrumental and rational-technical orientation of education (for boys) has led to an increasing pressure to differentially sort, instruct, certify and legitimate the different types and qualities of educational output, or "market slots" being aimed at by schools (see Cherkaoui, 1977). At its most extreme, in some Secondary schools educational achievements and examination success are defined narrowly, instrumentally and externally. Here the "better pupils" are being selected and sponsored for upward mobility into the higher "places" available. Those who do not succeed in this narrow and unidimensional achievement game are being "cooled out" in the bottom classes, where the education provided is not being specifically geared to any particular "market slot".

Within many working class schools, or schools catering mainly for the children of poorer farmers, etc., whether Vocational or Secondary, a very severe process of schooling differentiation is applied which succeeds only in sponsoring a small minority of the pupil intake for upward mobility – in terms of good Leaving Cert. results and third-level entry – but who have a large group of low achievers who either drop out early or fail their junior cycle examinations. Here again clear evidence of disproportionate attention to the top and relative inattention to the lower achievers was obvious.

At another pole are the girls' convent Secondary schools where the "expressive-moral" functions of education are assigned equal value with the instrumental-achievement ones. Here socialisation into the wider moral order is a much more important goal than in boys' schools. As an organised "moral milieu" such schools are very important in Ireland, whose integrative goals place high priority on socialisation with the moral order as well as on the personal development of their pupils. Here schooling differentiation is mini-mised. This gender-based division of labour along the instrumental/expressive-moral axis broadly reproduces distinctions present in the larger society.

This social class, gender, and wider institutional basis to schooling differen-tiation indicates both the "pressure" of external, highly institutionalised expectations on school authorities as well as the importance of the "strategic response" of school decisionmakers to their external environment. As an example, it is clear that upper middle class parents are far more demanding, more informed about their children's schooling, and less intimidated by school authorities than working class parents. Yet it is clear that many middle class schools do formally differentiate or differentially "sponsor", the brighter children of the middle class while the less able – and such "less able" pupils may well be at or near the average ability level for the total cohort in many selective Secondary schools – receive a very attenuated academic type education: i.e., school policy actively intervenes despite parental pressure. At the same time many working class and lower middle class schools – particularly convent schools – with comprehensive ability intakes do not differentiate their intake as a matter of policy. Indeed many of these schools had specifically rejected it as a policy. So, both these wider institutional forces and schools' strategic choices are clearly involved in schooling process decisions.

The Effects of Streaming and Curricular Differentiation

The research literature reviewed suggested two main hypotheses: (i) no consistent effect of streaming and curricular differentiation by schools on the average attainment or achievement level of all pupils first entering schools; (ii) that increased schooling differentiation would have a significant polarisation, or increased inequality, effect on the attainments of such an entry cohort controlling for, or holding constant, all other relevant variables.

"Holding constant all other relevant variables" is a statistically necessary requirement since schools vary so much in their pupil intake characteristics. It is not easily achieved, however, and is not fully satisfactorily achieved in this study. In their social class intake schools vary from the 1 in 12 which are upper middle class, mainly fee-paying schools, with little social class variance and minimal numbers of pupils with serious numeracy and literacy problems, to the very comprehensive class and ability intakes of a substantial proportion of convent Secondary schools and Community schools. At the other extreme are the majority of Vocational schools with intakes predominantly from working class or even lower working class families and, suffering from the "cream off" effects of other local schools, having high proportions of lower ability pupils. These school intake differences do not appear to have changed much from the early 1970s (Kellaghan and Greaney, 1970; Rudd, 1972; Greaney, 1973).

We do not unfortunately have measures of the "ability" characteristics of pupils on entry to post-primary schools — although we do have relatively good measures of the extent of ability and social class selectivity of schools. To some extent, therefore, our results have to be treated with some caution. However, we do use a very conservative method of assessing the relative effects of streaming and curricular differentiation which, if used where evidence was available of the actual "ability" characteristics of intake pupils, would underestimate the full impact of the schooling process variable. Taking all these points into consideration, plus the robustness and consistency of the main results, we remain confident of the generalisability of our results.

The results of extensive analyses of the effects of streaming and curricular differentiation within our sample of schools and pupils strongly support both sets of hypotheses: controlling for most relevant variables such schooling differentiation has no consistent effect on the average achievement level of the entry cohort — although there is a tendency toward increased early dropout rates as well as reduced proportions going on to University in highly differentiated schools; but such school-imposed differentiation substantially increases the inequality in output of schools, both for the total entry cohort but also for that part of the entry cohort which survive to Intermediate Certificate level. For the most selective part of the cohort that survived to the Leaving Certificate, such variations in the schooling process applied had no consistent variance or inequality effects.

Implications

(i)   It is clear that the differentiation of pupils and curricula is a school-imposed "arbitrary" that mainly reflects the values, goals and "operative objectives" (or "avoidable outcomes") of school-owning and managing authorities. It is not given or determined by purely objective and technical considerations. This schooling policy or approach, however, has not generally resulted from explicit, conscious and thought-through strategies by school decisionmakers to achieve a chosen set of ordered objectives. In many cases, in fact, such "decisions" are of historical relevance only, the persistence with streaming and curricular differentiation having more to do with the functions or interests it serves for the more important or influential actors involved — e.g., school management, teachers, parents and pupils in upper streams and so on.

From a school management or from teachers' points of view there is no doubt that "streaming" and its associated practices is an easier schooling solution than mixed ability teaching, and that it can be clearly and "objectively" explained or rationalised by taken-for-granted "commonsense" rationales. The centralisation and "objectification" of schooling decisions, the routinisation of schooling procedures, the concentration of the teachers' role on "knowledge transmission" to homogeneous ability classes, and the difficult-to-avoid consequence of this process of streaming classes along one single academic performance dimension, are all organisational tendencies characteristic of rigidly streamed schools. Where present at its extreme the almost explicit denigration of the educable capacities of pupils in lower streams results in high dropout and failure rates. But the habitual practices of such schools allow most of its workers to overlook or ignore these outcomes. And when streaming of pupils is accompanied by streaming of teachers the outcomes are even more severe (see HMI, *Mixed Ability Work in Comprehensive Schools*, DES London, 1978).

Given that such rigid streaming practices bring about greater educational inequalities than would otherwise occur those presumed schooling rationales need to be vigorously questioned.

(ii)   However, it is clear that the greater inequality in educational attainment observed in streamed or rigidly banded schools can occur in a number of ways. Within the same set of streamed or banded schools — holding most other relevant social and educational variables constant — their greater variation in educational outcomes occurs despite significant differences in the average achievement levels occurring within each category. For instance, amongst the most highly streamed boys' Secondary schools, which have lower middle class (average) clienteles, the modal attainment level for some schools is the Leaving Certificate level, while in others it is the Intermediate Cert. category. The dropout rate in the former schools is substantially lower than the latter. In lower working class Vocational schools using stringent "banding" arrangements, the modal attainment level in all cases are those who completed the Group or Intermediate Certificate level. In some of those cases, however, the early dropout rate was extremely high and the Leaving Certificate achievement level was minimal; while in other cases the early dropout rates were minimal and Leaving Certificate attainments were moderate. Overall, however, average achievement levels were not increased, while high achievements for a small elite were "paid for" by the very poor attainments of the low achievers.

Nevertheless, although in almost all streamed or banded schools the variances were much greater than in mixed ability schools these greater within-school inequalities *can* occur in ways that either benefit or damage lower ability pupils. There is almost as much difference in achievement means and variances *within* each schooling differentiation category as there is between them.

It appears, therefore, that what schools actually do with, or how well they use, streaming or curricular differentiation practices is almost as important as the choice of one form of streaming or mixed ability schooling rather than another. Both the objectives actively pursued by schools and the organisational ethos and management effectiveness of schools *within* each "schooling process" category are also very important "choices". So, the importance of strategic decisionmaking as well as management effectiveness extends far beyond the choice of whether to stream or not.

It may appear somewhat paradoxical to report the case of at least 1 school which chose "streaming" to maximise the achievement of their lower ability pupils — but it is put forward to illustrate the important role of enlightened and committed human action in the achievement of important and agreed goals. This particular Secondary school — using the word school mainly to denote the community of teaching and management personnel involved — having jointly discussed and worried about their high early dropout and exam failure problems for some time, decided to start streaming their intake with the objective of directing maximum teaching effort to the lower ability pupils. To this end they (teachers and management staff combined) decided to: (a) allocate a much higher teacher-pupil ratio to the bottom two classes (15/1) than to the top (30 to 32 to 1); (b) allocate teachers who were committed to or were most suitable and effective in teaching lower ability pupils; (c) institute special remedial classes in English, Irish and Maths; (d) develop an approach toward teaching the conventional academic junior cycle curriculum which maximise pupil interest/involvement; (e) expand contact with parents, etc., to increase home support, etc. As a result, after 5 years the dropout and failure rates had been substantially improved and the whole ethos and effectiveness of the school had substantially improved. The roles of planning, staff discussion, teacher commitment and effective leadership and "management", etc., were central to this successful innovation. The example also illustrates the central role that such conscious, planned, rational and committed human action plays in an effective organisation. This example also illustrates, of course, some of the consequences of the opposite organisational syndrome: of taken-for-granted, routinised or habitualised roles, conventional practices and imbedded special interests in maintaining rigidly and conventionally streamed schooling processes. So that, when school authorities change from conventional streaming practices to mixed ability teaching procedures without substantive planning, preparation, training and teacher commitment to the new process it will not work (HMI, 1978, op. cit., pp. 27-34, 57-62).

(iii) One cannot, therefore, unambiguously recommend moving directly to "mixed ability" teaching to all highly streamed schools as a solution to their "dropout", discipline or motivational problems with pupils in the lower streams, not without considerable rethinking, reorientation, retraining and a substantive change in teacher-pupil-parent relationship. Even where a school does not change completely from streaming over to "mixed ability" teaching — e.g., by retaining "remedial classes" (by withdrawal from the normal classes) and "setting" of Honours/Pass levels — the school as a "teacher-learner community" will need to undergo substantial change in attitudes and behaviour before a successful transition can be managed. This transition may be felt quite severely by some teachers and school Principals. As we saw in Chapter 3 the organisational processes involved in proceeding in a "streaming" or "mixed ability" direction are quite different and quite complex. So if a school decides to proceed toward mixed-ability teaching the change will demand not only willingness to change but teacher commitment and management effectiveness in managing the process.

Where the ability range of intake is very wide, of course, loose "banding" with remedial classes and with considerable "setting" of levels and subjects, using malleable class boundaries, might be easier and more attainable goals than completely mixed-ability teaching. These schooling arrangements considerably increase learning opportunities, avoid rigid boundaries between classes, and minimise the rigid stratification of classes (and teachers) that is characteristic of highly streamed schools. In general it would be better to "unstream" gradually and successfully than fail gloriously at mixed-ability teaching.

(iv) Rigid streaming appears to have almost inevitable effects on the nature and organisation of teacher-teacher and teacher-pupil, and even pupil-pupil relationships. It tends to isolate the pupil-teacher relationship to that of the rather technical classroom teacher-pupil role. It tends to centralise decision-making and reduce teacher and pupil-parent interaction. It would, therefore, tend to make it more difficult to create that organisational climate and ethos that appears to be most characteristic of highly effective school organisations. Where schools have been rigidly streamed and wish to go in the opposite direction they face substantial "inertial" forces which will be very difficult to overcome. Good and effective schooling does appear, however, to require that kind of organisational climate and structure that is almost incompatible with rigid streaming. From the result of this research we would unambiguously recommend that schools move away from that pattern. How far they should go toward full mixed-ability teaching will depend on management and teacher commitment as well as skilled help and advice.

(v) The dearth of advisory services on management training courses for school managers and Principals in their pursuit of more effective teaching/ schooling processes is a major lacuna in Irish education. Given the substantial decline since the late 1970s in the number of school inspectors[14] as well as the continued diversion of their time and energies to other non-school roles, there is apparently less help available now to individual schools or teachers from this source than at the beginning of the 1970s. There have been some in-service courses on school management — but very few and infrequent. We would, therefore, recommend strongly that such services/courses be provided — even by the provision of some funding for in-service courses or training workshops provided by outside "experts". In the context of an expenditure provision of almost IR£450 million for post-primary education in 1986 a modest expenditure of even £50,000 to £60,000 pa — one eighth of 1 per cent of the annual budget — on such schooling management programmes — in concert with the school owning/managing bodies — would, we feel, have a substantial impact.

(vi) There is no single educational forum in which school decisionmakers can discuss schooling issues and problems, and develop policy responses such as are dealt with here in this report. The absence of any local or national educational authority, or even voluntary Schools Council, means that there

14. In 1980 there were 86 inspectors concerned with all of post-primary education on the Department of Education's list, with 11 additional vacancies listed. By 1986 these had been reduced to 73 with only 1 vacancy listed. (State Directory, 1980; 1986). Even between 1979 and 1984 the number of second-level teachers had increased by over 2,000. (See Statistical Report, Department of Education, 1979/80, and 1983/84.)

is no single forum which facilitates and encourages management development or planning and policy-making functions at any level higher than the individual school, religious order or VEC, etc. Up to this point neither the CMRS nor the IVEA, as national representative school-owning bodies, have devoted much attention to these issues. In its expenditure decisions the Department of Education does not accord these issues much importance. The remit of the Curriculum and Examination Board does not cover this area of schooling practice. In fact the terms of reference implicitly accept a rather narrow and technical view of schooling practice — concerned with the content of what is taught or the formal procedures of provision and examination, etc. Indeed most direct State educational provision generally seems to be based on such a technical, "objectivist", formal instructional viewpoint — since it makes such little provision for developing the management competencies of school authorities, has retained a minimal monitoring or management role for the State itself, and makes such little provision for in-service courses.

The results of this research clearly indicate the importance of such school organisational processes. Without changed State policy, however, we cannot expect much change in individual schools' behaviour.

(vii) Finally, the scarcity of research on second-level schooling in Ireland is a serious impediment to the development of good policy-making. This research itself is a by-product of other work which had received major funding from the Department of Education, however, the State needs a much more active policy in stimulating and funding policy relevant research.

The absence of a central monitoring and policy development body and the poverty of educational research at second level both indicate an extraordinary degree of institutionalisation of traditional or conventional schooling/teaching arrangements in Ireland, such that what schools do are very widely accepted as "natural" and historically given processes which have no viable alternative — they have such a concrete "objective reality" in most people's consciousness that current practice is completely taken for granted (see Bourdieu and Passeron, 1977, pp. 1-69). The role of research is to question that "reality" and reveal its underlying nature, meanings and consequences. Without that critical examination of everyday, taken for granted, practice, policy making cannot be very effective. But in the absence of effective policy-making and decisionmaking bodies even the best and most policy relevant research is of academic interest only.

REFERENCES

ALDRICH, H.E., and J. PFEFFER, 1976. "Environments of Organisations" in A. Inkeles, J. Coleman and N. Smelser, (eds.), *Annual Review of Sociology*, Vol. 2, pp. 79-105, Palo Alto: Annual Reviews Inc.

ALEXANDER, L., and A. COOK, 1982. "Curricula and Coursework: A Surprise Ending to a Familiar Story", *American Sociological Review*, Vol. 47, pp. 626-640.

ALEXANDER, L., A. COOK, and E.L. McDILL, 1978. "Curriculum Tracking and Educational Stratification", *American Sociological Review*, Vol. 43, pp. 47-66.

ALLISON, P.D., 1978. "Measures of Inequality", *American Sociological Review*, Vol. 43, No. 6, pp. 865-880.

ALEXANDER, KARL L., and EDWARD L. McDILL, 1976. "Selection and Allocation Within Schools: Some Causes and Consequences of Curriculum Placement", *American Sociological Review*, Vol. 41, pp. 963-980.

AMATO, J., 1980. "Social Class Discrimination in the Schooling Process: Myth and Reality", *The Urban Review*, Vol. 12, Part 3, pp. 121-130.

ARANYA, N., D. JACOBSON, and S. SHYE, 1976. "A Smallest Space Analysis of Potential Work Mobility", *Multivariate Behavioural Research*, Vol. 11, pp. 165-173.

ARCHER, M.S., 1979. *Social Origins of Educational Systems*, London: Sage Publications.

ATKINSON, V., 1969. *Irish Education: A History of Educational Institutions*, Dublin: Allen Figgis.

AVERCH, Harvey, *et al.*, 1972. *How Effective is Schooling?*, Santa Monica, CA: Rand Corp.

BARKER-LUNN, J.S., 1970. *Streaming in the Primary School*, Slough: National Foundation of Educational Research.

BARR, REBECCA, and ROBERT DREEBEN, 1983. *How Schools Work*, Chicago: University of Chicago Press.

BELL, L.A., 1980. "The School as an Organization: A Re-Appraisal", *British Journal of Sociology of Education*, Vol. 1, No. 2.

BERG, G., and E. WALLIN, 1982. "Research into the School as an Organization. II: The School as a Complex Organization", *Scandinavian Journal of Education Research*, Vol. 26, No. 4.

BERNSTEIN, B., 1971. "On the Classification and Framing of Educational Knowledge", in Young, M.F.D., (ed.), *Knowledge and Control*, London: Macmillan.

BERNSTEIN, B., (ed.), 1977. *Class, Codes and Control*, Vol. 1, Surrey: Unwin Brothers. (Paper).

BIDWELL, E., and J.D. KASARDA, 1975. "School District Organization and Student Achievement", *American Sociological Review*, Vol. 40, No. 1, pp. 55-70.

BIDWELL, C.E., and J.D. KASARDA, 1980. "Conceptualising and Measuring the Effects of School and Schooling", *American Journal of Education*, Vol. 88, pp. 401-430.

BLALOCK, H.J., 1960. *Social Statistics*, New York: McGraw-Hill.

BLAU, P.M., 1970. "The Formal Theory of Differentiation in Organizations", *American Sociological Review*, Vol. 35, April, pp. 201-218.

BLAU, P.M., 1977. "A Macrosociological Theory of Social Structure", *American Journal of Sociology*, Vol. 83, No. 1, July, pp. 26-54.

BLAU, P.M., and O.D. DUNCAN, 1967. *The American Occupational Structure*, New York: Wiley.

BOURDIEU, P., 1973. "Cultural Reproduction and Social Reproduction", in Richard Brown, (ed.), *Knowledge Education and Cultural Change*, London: Tavistock.

177

BOURDIEU, P., and J.C. PASSERON, 1977. *Reproduction in Education, Society and Culture*, London: Sage Publications.

BOWLES, S., and H. GINTIS, 1976. *Schooling in Capitalist America: Educational Reform and the Contradictions of Economic Life*, New York: Basic Books.

BREEN, R., 1984. *Education and the Labour Market: Work and Unemployment Amongst Recent Cohorts of Irish School Leavers*, Dublin: ESRI, General Research Series, Paper No. 119.

BREEN, R., 1986. *Subject Availability and Student Performance in the Senior Cycle of Irish Post-Primary Schools*. Dublin: ESRI, General Research Series, Paper No. 129.

BRINKERHOFF, M.B., and P.R. KUNG, 1972. *Complex Organisations and their Environment*, Duluque, Ills.: Brown & Co.

BURKE-SAVAGE, R.S.J., 1950. *Catherine McAuley: The First Sister of Mercy*, Dublin: Gill & Sons.

CAMPBELL, W.J., 1965. "School Size: Its Influence on Pupils", *Journal of Education Administration*, Vol. 3, No. 1.

CAMPBELL, J., 1981. *Sociology of Education*, Vol. 54, No. 1.

CANTER, D., 1983. "The Potential of Facet Theory for Applied Social Psychology", *Quality and Quantity*, Vol. 17, pp. 35-67.

CHANDLER, A., 1962. *Strategy and Structure: Chapters in the History of the Industrial Enterprise*, Cambridge: MIT Press.

CHERKAOUI, M., 1977. "Bernstein and Durkheim: Two Theories of Change in Education Systems", *Harvard Education Review*, Vol. 47, No. 4, pp. 556-568.

CHILD, J., 1972. "Organizational Structure, Environment and Performance: The Role of Strategic Choice", *Sociology*, Vol. 6, pp. 1-22.

CHILD, J., 1972. "Technology, Size and Organizational Structure", *Sociology*, Vol. 6, pp. 369-393.

CHILD, J., 1972. "Organization Structure and Strategies of Control — A Republication of the Ashton Study", *Administrative Science Quarterly*, Vol. 17, pp. 163-177.

CHILD, J., 1973. "Strategies of Control and Organizational Behaviour", *Administrative Science Quarterly*, Vol. 18, pp. 1-17.

CHILD, J., 1973. "Predicting and Understanding Organizational Structure", *Administrative Science Quarterly*, Vol. 18, pp. 168-185.

CHILD, J., 1974. "What Determines Organizational Performance?", *Organizational Dynamics*, (Summer), pp. 2-18.

CLARK, B.R., 1980. "Academic Differentials in National Systems of Higher Education", *Comparative Education Review*, Vol. 22, No. 2, pp. 242-258.

CLIFFORD, P., and A. HEATH, 1984. "Selection Does Make a Difference", *Oxford Review of Education*, Vol. 10, No. 1, pp. 85-91.

COLEMAN, J.S., 1961. *The Adolescent Society*, Glencoe: Free Press.

COLEMAN, J.S., 1964. *Equality of Educational Opportunity*, Washington, D.C.: Government Printing Office.

COLEMAN, J., T. HOFFER, and S. KILGORE, 1982. *High School Achievement: Public, Catholic and Other Private Schools Compared*, New York: Basic Books. See *Harvard Educational Review*, Vol. 51, No. 4, Nov. 1981, for review.

COOLAHAN, J., 1981. *Irish Education: History and Structure*, Dublin: IPA.

CORISH, A.J., (ed.), 1971. *A History of Irish Catholicism*, Vol. 5, Catholic Education, Dublin: Gill and Macmillan.

CROWTHER REPORT, 1959. London: HMSO.

DAHLLOF, U.S., 1971. *Ability Grouping, Content Validity and Curriculum Process Analysis*, N.Y.: Teachers' College Press.

DAVIES, B., 1977. "Meanings and Motives in Going Mixed Ability" in B. Davies and R.G. Cave, (eds.), *Mixed Ability Teaching in Secondary School*, London: Wardlock.

DAVIES, B., 1981. "Schools as Organizations and the Organization of Schooling", *Educational Analysis*, Vol. 3, Part 1, pp. 47-67.

DEPARTMENT OF EDUCATION, 1969. Ar nDaltai Uile — All Our Children, Dublin: Department of Education.

DEPARTMENT OF EDUCATION, 1982/83. *Statistical Report 1982/83*, Dublin: Stationery Office.

DOUGLAS, J.W.B., 1964. *The Home and the School*, London: McGibbon and Kee.

DOWLING, PATRICK J., 1971. *A History of Irish Education — A Study of Conflicting Loyalties*, Cork: Mercier Press.

DREEBEN, R., 1968. *On What is Learned in Schools*, Reading, Mass.: Addison Wesley, pp. 66-73.

ELBOIN-DROR, R., 1973. "Organizational Characteristics of the Education System", *Journal of Educational Administration*, Vol. II, No. 1, pp. 3-21.

ELIZUR, D., and S. SHYE, 1976. "The Inclination to Reimmigrate: A Structural Analysis of the Case of Israelis Residing in France and in the USA", *Human Relations*, Vol. 29, pp. 73-84.

ELVIN, E., 1981. *The Educational Systems in the European Community: A Guide*, Windsor, Berks.: NFER-Nelson Publ. Co.

FITZPATRICK, J.D., 1945. *Edmund Rice*, Dublin: M.H. Gill & Son.

GAMORAN, A., 1987. "The Stratification of High School Learning Opportunities", *Sociology of Education*, Vol. 60, No. 3, pp. 135-155.

GARNIER, M.A., and M. HOUT, 1976. "Inequality and Educational Opportunity in France and the United States", *Social Science Research*, Vol. 5, pp. 225-246.

GERTRUDE, Sr. MARY, 1967. *Heroine of the Faith: Margaret Aylward*, Dublin: Holy Faith Sisters.

GOOD, T.L., and S. MARSHALL, 1984. "Do Students Learn More in Heterogeneous or Homogeneous Ability Groups?" in Peterson *et al.*, (eds.), *The Social Context of Instruction*, Orlando, Florida: Academic Press, pp. 15-38.

GRAY, J., A.F. McPHERSON, and D. RAAFE, 1983. *Reconstruction of Secondary Education: Theory, Myth and Practice since the War*, London: Routledge and Kegan Paul.

GRAY, J., D. JESSON, and B. JONES, 1984. "Predicting Differences in Examination Results Between Local Education Authorities: Does School Organisation Matter?", *Oxford Review of Education*, Vol. 10, No. 1, pp. 45-52.

GREANEY, V., 1973. "A Comparison of Secondary School Entrants, Vocational School Entrants and Terminal Leavers", *Irish Journal of Education*, Vol. 7, No. 2, pp. 79-101.

GREANEY, V., and T. KELLAGHAN, 1984. *Equality of Opportunity in Irish Schools*, Dublin: The Educational Co. of Ireland.

GUTTMAN, L., and S. LEVY, 1975. "Structure and Dynamics of Worries", *Sociometry*, Vol. 38, pp. 445-473.

HADOW REPORT ON SECONDARY EDUCATION, 1926. *The Education of the Adolescent*, London: HMSO.

HADOW REPORT ON PRIMARY EDUCATION, 1931. *Report on Primary Education*, London, HMSO.

HALLINAN, M.T. 1984. "Summary and Implications", in P.L. Peterson, L.C. Wilkinson and M. Hallinan (eds.), *The Social Context of Instruction*, Orlando, Florida: Academic Press.

HALLINAN, M.T. (ed.), 1987. *The Social Organisation of Schools*, New York: Plenum Press.

HALLINAN, M.T., and A.B. SORENSON, 1981. "The Formation and Stability of Instructural Groups", Paper presented at the ASA annual meetings, Toronto, August 1981. Published in *American Sociological Review*, Vol. 48, pp. 838-851, 1983.

HALLINAN, M.T., and A.B. SORENSON, 1985. "Class Size, Ability Group Size and Student Achievement", *American Journal of Education*, Vol. 94, No. 1, November, pp. 71-89.

HALSEY, A.H., A.F. HEATH, and J.M. RIDGE, 1980. *Origins and Destinations: Family Class and Education in Modern Britain*, Oxford: Clarendon Press.

HANNAN, D.F., R. BREEN, and B. MURRAY, D. WATSON, N. HARDIMAN, K. O'HIGGINS, 1983. *Schooling and Sex Roles: Sex Differences in Subject Process and Student Choice in Irish Post-Primary Schools*, Dublin: ESRI, General Research Series, Paper No. 113.

HANNAN, D.F., 1986. *Schooling and the Labour Market*, Shannon C.D.U. for the Department of Education and the Irish Pilot Projects.

HARGREAVES, D., 1967. *Social Relations in a Secondary School*, London: Routledge and Kegan Paul.

HER MAJESTY'S INSPECTORATE, 1978. *Mixed Ability in Comprehensive Schools*, London: Department of Educational Sciences.

HEATH, A., 1984. "In Defence of Comprehensive Schools", *Oxford Review of Education*, Vol. 10, No. 1, pp. 115-132.

HEYNES, D., 1974. "Social Selection and Stratification within Schools", *American Journal of Sociology*, Vol. 79, No. 6, pp. 1434-1451.

HOUT, M., and M.A. GARNIER, 1980. "Curriculum Placement and Educational Stratification in France", *Sociology of Education*, Vol. 52, No. 1, pp. 146-156.

INVESTMENT IN EDUCATION, 1966. Report of the Survey Team Appointed by the Minister for Education, Dublin: Stationery Office.

JACKSON, B., 1964. *Streaming: An Education System in Miniature*, London: Routledge and Kegan Paul.

JENCKS, C., S. SMITH, H. ACLAND, M.J. BANE, E. COHEN, H. GINTIS, B. HEYNS, and I. MICHELSON, 1972. *Inequality: A Reasessment of the Effects of Family and Schooling in America*, New York: Basic Books.

KAMENS, D., 1977. "Legitimating Myths and Educational Organisations: The Relationship Between Organisational Ideology and Formal Structure", *American Sociological Review*, Vol. 42, No. 2, pp. 208-219.

KARABEL, J., and H. HALSEY (eds.), 1977. *Power and Ideology in Education*, New York: Oxford University Press.

KELLAGHAN, T., 1967. "The Organisation of Classes in the Primary School", *Irish Journal of Education*, Vol. 1, No. 1, pp. 15-36.

KELLAGHAN, T., and V. GREANEY, 1970. "Factors Related to Choice of Post-Primary Schools in Ireland", *The Irish Journal of Education*, Vol. 4, No. 2, 69-83.

KELLAGHAN, T., G. MADAUS, E.A. RAKOW, 1979. "Within School Variance in Achievement: School Effects or Error?", *Studies in Education Evaluation*, Vol. 5, pp. 101-107.

KELLY, A.V., 1978. *Mixed Ability Grouping, Theory and Practice*, London: Harper and Row Ltd.

KENNY, C., and D. CANTER, 1981. "A Facet Structure for Nurses' Evaluations of Ward Designs", *Journal of Occupational Psychology*, Vol. 54, pp. 93-108.

KERCKHOFF, A.C., 1974. "Stratification Processes and Outcomes in England and the USA", *American Sociological Review*, Vol. 39, pp. 789-801.

KERCKHOFF, A.C., 1975. "Patterns of Educational Attainment in Great Britain", *American Journal of Sociology*, Vol. 80, pp. 1428-1437.

KERCKHOFF, A.C., 1976. "The Status Attainment Process Socialisation or Allocation", *Social Forces*, Vol. 55, No. 2, pp. 368-381.

KERCKHOFF, A.C., 1986. "Effects of Ability Grouping in British Secondary Schools", *American Sociological Review*, Vol. 51, No. 6, pp. 842-858.

KERCKHOFF, A.C., R.T. CAMPBELL, and J.M. TROTT, 1982. "Dimensions of Educational and Occupational Attainment in Great Britain", *American Sociological Review*, Vol. 47, June, pp. 347-364.

KOHN, J., and C. SCHOOLER, 1983. *Work and Personality: An Inquiry into the Impact of Social Stratification*, Norwood, N.J.: Ablex Publishing Corp.

LACEY, C., 1970. *Hightown Grammar: School as a Social System*, Manchester University Press.

LACEY, C., 1984. "Selective and Non-Selective Schooling: Real or Mythical Comparisons", *Oxford Review of Education*, Vol. 10, No. 1, pp. 75-84.

LEVY, S., 1976. "Use of Mapping Sentence for Coordinating Theory and Research", *Quality and Quantity*, Vol. 10, pp. 117-125.

MADAUS, G.F., and T. KELLAGHAN, 1976. "School and Class Differences in Performance in the Leaving Certificate Examination", *The Irish Journal of Education*, Vol. 10, No. 1, pp. 41-50.

MADAUS, G.F., T. KELLAGHAN, *et al.*, 1979. "The Sensitivity of Measures of School Effectiveness", *Harvard Educational Review*, Vol. 49, No. 2, pp. 207-230.

MADAUS, G., P. W. AIRASIAN, and T. KELLAGHAN, 1980. *School Effectiveness*, New York: McGraw-Hill.

McELLIGOTT, T.J., 1966. *Education in Ireland*, Dublin: IPA.

MEYER, M.W., 1970. "The Charter: Conditions of Diffuse Socialization in Schools" in W. Scott (ed.), *Social Processes and Social Structure*, New York: Holt, Reinhart and Winston.

MEYER, M.W., 1977. "The Effects of Education as an Institution", *American Journal of Sociology*, Vol. 85, No. 1, 55-77.

MEYER, M.W., 1987. "Implications of an Institutional View of Education for the Study of Educational Effects", in M.T. Hallinan (ed.), *The Social Organisation of Schools*, New York: Plenum Press.

MEYER, M.W., and B. ROWAN, 1977. "Institutionalised Organisations: Formal Structure as Myth and Ceremony", *American Journal of Sociology*, Vol. 83, pp. 340-363.

MEYER, M.W., and B. ROWAN, 1978. "The Structure of Educational Organisations", in M. Meyer *et al.* (eds.), *Environments and Organisations*, San Francisco: Jossey-Bass.

MEYER, M.W., W.R. SCOTT *et al.* 1978. "Instructural Dissensious and Institutional Consensus in Schools", in Meyer *et al.* (eds.), *Environments and Organisations*, San Francisco: Jossey-Bass.

MEYER, M.W., N. TURNER, and K. ZAGORSKI, 1979. "Education and Occupational Mobility: A Comparison of Data on English and American Men", *American Journal of Sociology*, Vol. 84, pp. 978-986.

MILLER, K.A., M.L. KOHN, and C. SCHOOLER, 1986. "Educational Self-Direction and Personality", *American Sociological Review*, Vol. 51, No. 3, 372-389.

NACHMIAS, C., 1980. "Curriculum Tracking: Some of its Courses and Consequences under a Meritocracy", *Comparative Education Review*, Vol. 24, No. 1, pp. 1-20.

NEA, 1968. *Ability Grouping, Research Summary*, Washington, D.C.: National Education Association.

NEWBOLD, D., 1977. *Ability Grouping: The Banbury Enquiry*, Windsor, Berks.: National Foundation of Education Research.

NORWOOD REPORT, 1943. *Report of the Committee of the Secondary Schools Examinations Council*, London: HMSO.

OAKES, J., 1985. *Keeping Track: How Schools Structure Inequality*, London: Yale University Press.

OPPENHEIM, A.M., 1966. *Questionnaire Design and Attitude Measurement*, London: Heinemann Educational Books.

ORGANISATION FOR ECONOMIC COOPERATION AND DEVELOPMENT, 1966. *Investment in Education — Report of the Survey Team*, Dublin: Stationery Office.

PERROW, C., 1961. "The Analysis of Goals in Complex Organisations", *American Sociological Review*, Vol. 26, pp. 854-866.

PERROW, C., 1965. "Hospitals, Technology and Goals", in James March (ed.), *Handbook of Organizations*, Chicago: Rand-McNally, pp. 910-971.

PERROW, C., 1967. "A Framework for Comparative Organizational Analysis", *American Sociological Review*, Vol. 32, pp. 194-208.

PERROW, C., 1970. *Organizational Analysis, A Sociological View*, Monterey, C.A.: Brooks Cole.

PERROW, C., 1972. *Complex Organizations, A Critical Essay*, Glenview, Ill.: Scott Foresman.

PERSELL, C., 1977. *Education and Inequality: The Roots and Results of Stratification in American Schools*, New York: Free Press.

PETERSON, P.L., L.C. WILKINSON, and M. HALLINAN (eds.), 1984. *The Social Context of Instruction*, Orlando, Florida: Academic Press.

PUGH, D.S., *et al.*, 1969. "The Context of Organisation Structures", *Administrative Science Quarterly*, Vol. 13, pp. 65-105.

RAMIREZ, F.O., and M.W. MEYER, 1980. "Comparative Education: The Social Construction of the Modern World System", *Annual Review of Sociology*, Vol. 6, pp. 369-399.

RICHER, S., 1976. "Reference Group Theory and Ability Grouping: A Convergence of Sociological Theory and Educational Research", *Sociology of Education*, Vol. 49, No. 1, pp. 65-71.

ROSENBAUM, J.E., 1975. "The Statification of Socialisational Processes", *American Sociological Review*, Vol. 40, No. 1, pp. 48-54.

ROSENBAUM, J.E., 1976. *Making Inequality: The Hidden Curriculum of High School Tracking*, New York: Wiley.

RUDD, J., 1972. *Report on National School Terminal Leavers*, Dublin: Department of Education.

SADLER, P.J., and B.A. BARRY, 1970. *Organisation Development*, London: Longmans.

SANDS, M., and KERRY, T., (eds.), 1982. *Mixed Ability Teaching*, London: Croom Helm.

SCHAFER, W.E., and C. OLEXA, 1971. *Tracking and Opportunity*, Scranton, Ohio: Chandler.

SHAVITT, Y., 1984. "Tracking and Ethnicity in Israeli Secondary Education", *American Sociological Review*, Vol. 49, No. 2, pp. 210-220.

SHYE, S., 1978. *Theory Construction and Data Analysis in the Behavioural Sciences*, San Francisco: Jossey-Bass.

SIMPSON, C., 1981. "Classroom Structure and the Organisation of Ability", *Sociology of Education*, Vol. 54, No. 1, pp. 120-131.

SORENSON, A.B., 1970. "Organisational Differentiation of Students and Educational Opportunity", *Sociology of Education*, Vol. 43, pp. 355-376.

SORENSON, A.B., 1977. "The Structure of Inequality and the Process of Attainment", *American Sociological Review*, Vol. 42, pp. 965-978.

SORENSON, A.B., 1987. "The Organisational Differentiation of Students in School as an Opportunity Structure", in M.T. Hallinan (ed.), *The Social Organisation of Schools*, New York: Plenum Press.

SORENSON, A.B., and M.T. HALLINAN, 1977. "A Reconceptualisation of School Effects", *Sociology of Education*, Vol. 50, pp. 273-289.

SWAN, D., 1978. *Reading Standards in Irish Schools*, Dublin: The Educational Company of Ireland.

TORGERSON, W.S., 1958. *Theory and Methods of Scaling*, New York: John Wiley.

TREIMAN, D., and K. TERRELL, 1975. "The Process of Status Attainment in the United States and Britain", *American Journal of Sociology*, Vol. 81, pp. 563-583.

TURNER, R., 1960. "Sponsored and Contest Mobility and the School System", *American Sociological Review*, Vol. 25, pp. 855-867.

WALSH, T.J., 1969. *Nano Nagle and the Presentation Sisters*, Presentation Generalate, Co. Kilkenny.

WEBER, M., 1946. *From Max Weber, Essays in Sociology*, (Trans. and ed. by Hans Gerth and C. Wright Mills), New York: Oxford University Press, Inc., pp. 196-244.

WEBER, M., 1947. *The Theory of Social and Economic Organization*, (Trans. A.M. Henderson and T. Parsons), New York: Oxford University Press.

WHELAN, C., and B. WHELAN, 1984. *Social Mobility in the Republic of Ireland: A Comparative Perspective*, Dublin: ESRI, General Research Series, Paper No. 116.

WHITE PAPER, 1980. *White Paper on Educational Development*, Dublin: Stationery Office.

WILLIS, P., 1977. *Learning to Labour: How Working Class Kids Get Working Class Jobs*, Farnborough: Gower Press.

WILLMS, T.D., 1986. "Social Class Segregation and its Relationship to Pupils' Examination Results in Scotland", *American Sociological Review*, Vol. 51, No. 2, pp. 224-241.

WOODWARD, J., 1965. *Industrial Organization: Theory and Practice*, London: Oxford University Press.

WOODWARD, J., 1970. *Industrial Organization: Behaviour and Control*, London: Oxford University Press.

YATES, I., 1966. *Grouping in Education: A Report Sponsored by the UNESCO Institute for Education*, Hamburg, Stockholm: Almquist and Wiksell.

YOUNG, A.G., 1975. "Northcliffe Community High School", in A.V. Kelly (ed.), *Case Studies in Mixed Ability Teaching*, London: Harper and Row, pp. 26-39.

YUCHTMANN, E., and Y. SAMUEL, 1975. "Determinants of Career Plans: Institutional Versus Interpersonal Effects", *American Sociological Review*, Vol. 40, pp. 521-531.

ZUCKER, L.G., 1977. "The Role of Institutionalisation in Cultural Persistence", *American Sociological Review*, Vol. 42, No. 5, pp. 726-742.

APPENDIX I

PRINCIPAL'S QUESTIONNAIRE

Economic and Social Research Institute

Curricular Differences Project

School Number _____

Interviewer   _____

Date   _____

Principal's Schedule - 4

1. Name of School _____

2. Address   _____

   _____

3. a) Name of Interviewee: _____ Position _____

   b) Sex: M   F

   c) Status of Interviewee   Lay _____ (1)

      Religious

      Diocesan priest   (2)

      Religious order priest   (3)

      Teaching brother   (4)

      Teaching sister   (5)

      Protestant minister   (6)

      Other (specify)   (7)

      _____

4. Type of School:

   a) Secondary _____ 1
      Vocational _____ 2
      Community/Comprehensive __ 3
      Community College _____ 4

   b) Catholic Lay-run _____ 1
      Catholic Religious run _____ 2
      Protestant _____ 3
      Interdenominational _____ 4
      VEC _____ 5

   c) Fee-paying _____ 1
      Non-fee paying _____ 2

d)   Boarding only _____ 1

Boarding and day _____ 2

Day only· _____ 3

e)   Boys _____ 1

Girls _____ 2

Coed. _____ 3

Coinstitutional _____ 4

		Boys	Girls
f) No. of Pupils?:	Boarders	_____	_____
	Day pupils	_____	_____

5.   Year school was established?   _____

School Ownership and Management

6. Who owns the school?	Lay Catholic	_____ 1
	Order of nuns	_____ 2
	Order of priests	_____ 3
	Order of brothers	_____ 4
	Secular (diocesan) priests	_____ 5
	Church of Ireland/Protestant	_____ 6
	Other - Interdenominational	_____ 7
	VEC	_____ 8
	Community Comp.	_____ 9

7.   If owned by religious order:

Name of order _____

IF NOT .... Q. 10

8.   (a)   How many schools run by the order in Ireland? _____

(b)   Are they organised into a single unit (or number of units?) _____

(c)   What is the unit of which this school is a member? _____

(d)   What is the name of the higher authority? _____

(e)   Compared to other orders, would you say that the order is more tightly organised and controlled, or more loosely organised and controlled?

        1)   Much more tightly organised and controlled   (   )

        2)   About equally organised and controlled   (   )

        3)   More loosely organised with much more local autonomy   (   )

IF AN ORDER

9. Does the order as such have a particular educational philosophy (or set of general objectives) which it follows in each school?

> Yes 1   No 2   Q. 13
>
> (a) Is the policy spelled out in any particular document?   No 1
>   Yes 2   Details: _____
>
> (b) Does it see its mission as directed between any particular social group? _____

10. Individual schools vary in the kinds of changes or improvements which they aim to bring about in their pupils from first entry to the school to finally leaving it. In terms of the main working objectives of this school: what are the two most important objectives, or important changes which this school aims to bring about in the pupils? If the school is coed., please indicate if there are different aims for boys and girls.

1. _____

2. _____

11. In what concrete ways does the school go about achieving those goals?
(e. g. through curricular provision, organisational structures, resources etc.) (2 examples)

1. _____

2. _____

12. Are there any specific rules or policies laid down by the higher body (including the VEC) that must be adhered to by the school in the following areas?

(i) School organisation of pupils (classing, streaming, setting, etc.)   Yes ( )   No ( )

IF YES (Specify) _____

(ii) Curricular provision and subject packaging   **Yes ( )**   No ( )

IF YES (Specify) _____

13. Has the school?

  (i) a Board of governors   Yes ( )   No ( )

  (ii) a Board of management Yes ( )   No ( )

  (iii) a Board of trustees   Yes ( )   No ( )

  (iv) some individual arrangement Yes ( )   No ( )

  IF NO TO ALL GO ON TO QUESTION 14.

  IF YES (v) What is the composition of the Board or of individual management? _____

  _____

   (vi) How are the members appointed/elected? _____

  _____

   (vii) How long does their appointment last? _____

14. Who appoints the Principal?   VEC   ( )

             Religious superior/provincial ( )

             Board (local)   ( )

             Elected by (local) religious
             community   ( )

             Other (specify) _____

             _____ ( )

15. How long does the appointment last? _____

17. Does the school have a manager apart from the Principal? Yes ( ) No ( )

  (If a religious run school). Is this the head of the house/convent? Yes ( ) No ( )

18. (a) Does the school have a Vice-principal?   Yes ( )   No ( )

     (b) Who appoints the Vice-principal?   The principal with an
                                                         appointment board   ( )

                                                         VEC   ( )

                                                         Religious superior   ( )

                                                         Board of governors   ( )

                                                         Other (specify)   ( )

                                                         _____

                                                         _____

     (c) For how long? _____

     (d) Is the Vice-principal normally appointed from among the school staff?   Yes ( )   No ( )

19. Internal/External decision-making

     In the context of running the school, what kind of decisions are taken by you within the school,
     and what kind of decisions have to be referred to a higher authority? For example, if you were
     to add another subject to the curriculum - remaining within the teacher quota - would this decision
     be made in the school (internally) or would you have to refer it to higher authority?

		Make Internally	Refer
(i)	Add another subject to the curriculum, remaining within teach quota	( )	( )
(ii)	Add another subject to the curriculum, involving employing teacher above the quota, and above your normal budget	( )	( )
(iii)	Are parents to donate or increase donations to the school/or, if fee-paying, increase the fees	( )	( )
(iv)	Introduce new method of allocating pupils to classes - e.g. from mixed ability to streaming or visa-versa	( )	( )
(v)	Make a major alteration in school buildings, but within normal expenditure	( )	( )
(vi)	Major expenditures beyond budget (e.g. £10,000)	( )	( )

TEACHERS

20. (a) How many teachers does the school employ, within the quota?   _____

     (b) Has the number of these teachers changed within the past 5 years?

          Yes 1   No 2

          IF YES (a) by what no? (±) _____

          (b) Did this result in subjects being lost ( ) or added to the curriculum ( )?

          If Yes to either: what subjects (added) _____

                    or lost   _____

21.   (a)   How many ex-quota teachers are employed:

               Total, Full-time _____   Religious? _____

               Total, Part-time _____   Religious? _____

       (b)   How are these ex-quota teachers financed?

               School funds (fees)   Yes ( )   No ( )

               Funds from the Order   Yes ( )   No ( )

               Funds raised by parents   Yes ( )   No ( )

               Unpaid   Yes ( )   No ( )

               Other _____

Staff Organisation

23.   Does the school have formal staff meetings?

               | Yes .... 1 | No 2

       IF YES: (a)   How often are they held?

                         1 or more per month 1

                         2 or 2 per term 2

                         2 or so per year 3

                         1 per annum 4

                         Never, or at least not every year.. 5

24.   What are the number and type of "posts of responsibility" in the school?

	No. Male	No. Female		What is his/her main responsibilities?
(a) Vice Principal	_____	_____	(a)	_____
				_____
				_____
(b) No. of A Posts?	_____	_____	(b)	_____
				_____
				_____
				_____
(c) No. of B Posts?	_____	_____	(c)	_____
				_____
				_____
(d) "Special Function Allowance" Teachers	_____		(d)	_____
				_____
				_____

25.   How successful are these posts of responsibility in the administration of the school?

Very successful	(1)
Somewhat successful	(2)
Slightly successful	(3)
Unsuccessful	(4)

26.   (a) Are the teachers organised into subject departments or faculties in the school?

Yes ( )   No ( )   28

(b) IF YES, what is the main function of these depts/faculties? _____
_____
_____

27.   (a) Are there any other teacher or administration offices or structures within the school?

(e. g. year groups, junior or senior cycle groups etc; Class Teachers; Deans; Wardens etc.)

Yes (1)	No (2)

(b) If YES, please describe their functions and evaluate their effectiveness, giving some reason for your evaluation:

Office or Structure(s)	Responsibility or Purpose	How effective is it			
		Very	Somewhat	Slight	Not
		1	2	3	4

29.   Concluding on the distribution of responsibility amongst the different staff members: (a) who actually is the main decision maker?; and (b) who would usually be consulted when these decisions are being made?

	Individual teacher(s)	Class Head (master) or year Head	Dean or equivalent	Faculty H. D. or Equiv.	Career Guidance teacher	Vice Principal	Principal
(1) If school has the position check (✓) and describe ("title")	( )	( )	( )	( )	( )	( )	( )
(2) Time tabling (i) Decide (ii) Consulted	(i) (ii)	(i) (ii)	(i) (ii)	(i) (ii)	(i) (ii)	(i) (ii)	(i) (ii)
(3) Allocation of Teachers - who takes which classes? (i) Decide (ii) Consulted	(i) (ii)	(i) (ii)	(i) (ii)	(i) (ii)	(i) (ii)	(i) (ii)	(i) (ii)
(4) Adding/Dropping a subj. from the Curric.	(i) (ii)	(i) (ii)	(i) (ii)	(i) (ii)	(i) (ii)	(i) (ii)	(i) (ii)
(5) Allocating senior students to which classes	(i) (ii)	(i) (ii)	(i) (ii)	(i) (ii)	(i) (ii)	(i) (ii)	(i) (ii)

CAREER GUIDANCE/PASTORAL CARE

30. Does the school have a career guidance teacher?

Yes 1   No 2   30

(a) No? _____   Sex _____

(b) Is he/she/they quota 1   _____

    or ex quota 2   _____

(c) How long has the school had a career guidance teacher? _____

31. In their choice of subjects at (a) junior and (b) senior cycle level, who is the main person in the school that helps them decide?

(a) At junior cycle? _____

(b) At senior cycle? _____

(c) And who do they consult with most when leaving school about choosing job/careers?

_____

_____

32. Is anything else organised for the pupils to prepare them for the world of work?

Yes ( )   No ( )

IF YES; What?

Visits to firms in locality   ( )

Lectures from representatives of firms,
Industries   ( )

Careers Exhibition   ( )

Mock Interviews   ( )

Other: _____

33.   Does the school run pre-employment courses?

No 1   Yes 2

(a) For which years/classes? _____

_____

(b) Details of Courses: _____

_____

IF A COED. SCHOOL: Are there separate courses for boys and girls?

Yes ( )   No ( )

IF YES: Details? _____

_____

34.   (a) Does the school have a pastoral care programme or some other system of dealing with pupil personal development or welfare (other than career guidance)?

Yes ( )   No ( )   35

(b) IF YES, could you describe how it operates? _____

_____

_____

(c) What are the aims of the program? _____

_____

_____

(d) Who is involved in running the program? _____

_____

. 1, What subjects are taught in the school this year in the Junior Cycle - i.e. Inter. and Group Cert.

SUBJECTS	Not Taught	Taught but not for exams	Taught for Group Cert.	Taught for Inter Cert.
Inter. and Group				
Irish - Higher				
Irish - Lower				
English - Higher				
English - Lower				
Maths - Higher				
Maths - Lower				
History and Geography				
Science				
French				
German				
Spanish				
Home Economics				
Commerce				
Woodwork				
Metalwork				
Mechanical Drawing				
Art				
Music				
Italian				
Latin				
Greek				
Hebrew				
Civics				
Physical Education				
Religious Education				
Group Cert. only				
Book-keeping				
Commercial Arithmetic				
Rural Science				
Shorthand - General				
Typewriting - General				
Shorthand - Secretarial				
Typewriting - Secretarial				
Cookery				
Needlework				
Laundry and Household Management				
Domestic Science				

'2. What subjects are taught in the school this year at Senior Cycle level – i.e. for the Leaving Cert.

'Please indicate whether subjects are taught at Ordinary or Higher Level.

SUBJECTS	Not Taught	Taught but not for exam.	Taught for Leaving Cert. Ordinary Level	Higher Level
Irish				
English				
Maths				
History				
Geography				
Physics				
Chemistry				
Physics & Chemistry				
Biology				
French				
German				
Spanish				
Home Economics – General				
Home Economics – Social and Scientific				
Accounting				
Business Organisation				
Technical Drawing				
Arts & Crafts				
Music				
Applied Maths				
Mechanics				
Economics				
Economic History				
Agricultural Science				
Agricultural Economics				
Italian				
Latin				
Greek				
Hebrew				
Building Construction				
Engineering Workshop – Theory and practice				
Civics				
Physical Education				
Religious Education				

37.　(a)　Have any subjects been dropped from the curriculum in the past 5 years?

Yes ( )　　　No ( )

(b)　IF YES, what were these subjects? _____

(c)　To whom (in terms of sex and ability) were these subjects taught? _____

(d)　Why were they dropped? _____

_____

(e)　What happened to the teacher(s) who used to teach them? _____

_____

38.　Have any new subjects been added to the curriculum in the past 5 years?

Yes ( )　　　No ( )

(a)　IF YES, what were they? _____

(b)　To whom (in terms of sex and ability) were these subjects taught? _____

(d)　Was a new teacher employed to teach them?　　Yes ( )　　No ( )

IF YES, how was the teacher financed? _____

_____

(e)　Did the addition of these subjects involve expenditure on new facilities?

Yes ( )　　No ( )

IF YES, how was this financed? _____

_____

39.　(a)　If you could add a new subject to your curriculum, what would you add?

1. _____

2. _____

(b)　What would you have to do/get to be able to do this? _____

_____

(c)　What is the main constraint you see in adding subjects like this to your curriculum? _____

_____

Admission Procedures

40.   (a) Is there a primary school attached to this school   Yes ( )   No ( )

   IF YES, what proportion of each year's pupil intake comes from there?

Under 25%	( )
25% – 50%	( )
50% – 75%	( )
Over 75%	( )

41.   Do you have a stable number of "feeder" primary schools whose pupils come to this school?

Yes 1   No 2

(a) No. ? _____

(b) Are they all local schools?   Yes 1   No 2

	Male Female
42. How many applicants were there in 1979	1980 _____
How many finally came?	1980 _____

43.   Are all the pupils who apply to this school usually accepted?

Yes 1   No 2

If NO, what criteria are used in deciding who to accept and who not to accept?

44.   (a) Are pupils assessed for aptitude or ability before, or after, entry to the school?

YES, before entry ( )   YES, after entry ( )   Neither ( )

(b) IF YES before, is this assessment used to select those who are accepted by the school?

Yes ( )   No ( )

(c) IF YES (both), is this assessment used in allocating students to classes in first year?

Yes ( )   No ( )

46.   (a)   On what basis are pupils allocated to classes on entry to the school?

                              Alphabetically/randomly   1

                              Perfromance in "assessment test"   2

                              Subjects chosen   3

                              Other (specify)   4

                              _____

                              _____

        (b)   On what basis are pupils allocated to classes, on entry into 2nd year? (1 - 4) _____

                       _____

47.   Are entry classes then: (a) All mixed ability (   ); (b) All streamed (   ); (c) Banded (   )

        (Describe) _____

                       _____

                       _____

                       _____

48.

(1) The Structure of Classes

	Entry (First) Year 1980/81*				Entry (First) Year or viz. 1978/79 1978/80				Entry (First) Year 19				Group Cert. Classes 1980/81*				Inter Cert. Classes 1978/79				Inter Cert. Classes 1980/81*				Leaving Cert. Classes 1980/81*			
	M		F		M		F		M		F		M		F		M		F		M		F		M		F	
	Class Level	Ability Level	Class Level	Ability Level	Class Level	Ability Level	Class Level	Ability Level	Class Level	Ability Level	Class Level	Ability Level	Class Level	Ability Level	Class Level	Ability Level	Class Level	Ability Level	Class Level	Ability Level	Class Level	Ability Level	Class Level	Ability Level	Class Level	Ability Level	Class Level	Ability Level
No. of Pupils																												
No. of Classes																												
Division and Level of Classes (Streaming Banding)																												
• Do these first																												
▪ Get no. of students in each year																												
▬ Then ask f; (a) had changed from 1978/79																												

* What was year of entry of current term al G. C. class? 1979/80.

If different from 1978/79 (3 year G. C.) Get entry details also

SUBJECT CHOICE

48. IF A COED, SCHOOL, In their first and second years, are some subjects taken only by boys, some only by girls?

Yes 1   No 2

IF YES; a) which subjects:

	Boys	Girls
1st year 1.		1.
2.		2.
3.		3.
2nd year 1.		1.
2.		2.
3.		3.

b) Taking the first 2 subjects mentioned as taken only by boys: can girls take these subjects if they wanted to?   Yes 1   No 2

c) IF NO; Why not? _____

d) Have any girls asked to take any of these subjects in the past 2 years? Yes ( ) No ( )

e) IF NO; What would be needed to allow the school to let girls take these subjects? _____

_____

f) Taking the first 2 subjects mentioned as taken by girls only: can boys take these subjects if they wanted to?   Yes 1   No 2

g) Have any boys asked to take any of these subjects in the past 2 years? Yes ( ) No ( )

h) What would be needed to allow boys to take these subjects? _____

49. (a) Do pupils have a choice of subjects in the junior cycle?

Yes 1   No 2

(b) If YES, when do they have to choose?

on entry to 1st year ( )

on entry to 2nd year ( )

Other _____

(b) If NO, do all pupils take the same subjects?

Yes ( ) 50   No ( )   (b)

(c) Do all classes take the same subjects Yes ( ) No ( )

IF YES ———→ d(ii)

G. C.

(d) From what set of options did the present I. C., G. C. classes choose their subjects (ii) Describe the different subject packages for different classes.

I. C. Class: 1980/81	CORE	Level of 1. 2. 3. Irish English Maths	OPTIONAL PACKAGES
1.			
2.			
3.			
4.			
5.			

G. C. Class 1980/81

1.			
2.			
3.			
4.			
5.			

49. **(d)** Were the optional packages (if any) constructed before ( ) or after ( ) pupils were first given a choice?

(e) How long have these packages remained unchanged? _____

(f) Does the school involve the parents in the pupil's choice of junior cycle subjects?

Yes ( )	No ( )

If YES: In what way? _____

_____

When does this occur? _____

_____

50. When do pupils decide on the level at which they will take Irish, English, Maths for the Inter Cert?

_____

51 a) On what basis are pupils allowed to take higher level English/Maths or Irish? _____

_____

b) IF APPLICABLE: What I. C. classes are allowed to take the higher level courses? _____

_____

52. Are separate classes held for higher and lower level pupils, in these subjects? (Irish, English, Maths)

Yes ( )	No ( )

If NO, what arrangements are made? _____

_____

·53. In their choice of subjects, and of subject levels in the junior cycle, are pupils given any guidance?

Yes ( )	No ( )

If YES, what form does this take? _____

_____

<u>Allocation to Classes and Subject Choice; Senior Cycle</u>

54.   In the transition to senior cycle, are students reallocated to different classes?

Yes ( )   No ( )

If YES, (a) on what basis are the new classes formed?

Ability test   ( )

Performance in I.C.   ( )

Subject group choice   ( )

Other _____

(b) What % would change in this way? _____

54. (2)   (c) Are Senior cycle classes then all mixed ability ( ) streamed ( ) banded ( )

55.   Do pupils have a choice of subjects in the senior cycle?

Yes 1   No 2

IF NO, Do all pupils take the same subjects?

Yes ... 1   No ... 2   (b)

Do all classes take the same subjects Yes ( ) No ( ) ⟶(b)

(b) From what set of options do senior cycle pupils choose their subjects. (Taking the present L.C. class)

Class	CORE SUBJECTS	Level of Irish English Maths	OPTIONAL PACKAGES
1.			
2.			
3.			
4.			
5.			
6.			
7.			

<u>NB</u>: This question has to be answered in <u>all</u> cases; i.e. <u>Core /options for each class.</u>

56. (a) At what point do students decide on their senior cycle subjects? _____

57. (a) Are they given any guidance in their choice?   Yes ( )   No ( )

If YES, what form does this guidance take? _____

_____

b) Who is involved in giving the guidance? _____

58. Does the school involve parents in the pupil's choice of L. C. subjects?

Yes ( )   No ( )

What form does this take? _____

_____

When does this occur? _____

_____

59. At what stage do pupils finally decide on the level at which they will take subjects for the Leaving Cert?

_____

_____

60. Are separate classes held for higher and ordinary level pupils in each subject?

Yes ( )   No ( )

If NO, what arrangements are made? _____

_____

61. What L. C. classes are allowed to take the honours courses in Maths, Science, English/Irish/French?

_____

_____

62. Does the school lay down any conditions about particular subject choices in the senior cycle?

(Probe for Physics, Chemistry, Accountancy, H. Maths)

Yes ( )   No ( )

If YES, what subjects are involved? What are the conditions?	If Coed Do girls take this subject	
H. Maths	Yes	No
Physics	Yes	No
Chemistry	Yes	No
Acct.	Yes	No
T. Drawing	Yes	No
Building Construction	Yes	No

63. Taking the current packaging of core and optional subjects in the junior and senior cycle levels: (If no optional subjects, take "core" to mean subjects given).

	Junior Cycle		Senior-Cycle	
	Core	Optional Packages	Core	Optional Packages
(a) When was the last change made?	19	19	19	19
(b) Given a continuation of the present circumstances of the school - student numbers, teachers, classrooms etc. how difficult would it be to change the way the core and optional packages are arranged if you wanted to?	Impossible 1 Very diffic. 2 Difficult 3 Easy 4	1 2 3 4	1 2 3 4	1 2 3 4
(c) What is the main constraint on changing the core?				
(d) What is the main constraint in changing the optional packages?				
(e) How satisfied are you with the present set of core/optional packages.	Very satisfied 1 Satisfied 2 Not satisfied 3	1 2 3	1 2 3	1 2 3

Classroom Behaviour : Standards/Expectations

64. Does the school have a general standard of classroom discipline?

Yes ( )   No ( )

If YES, is there a written set of "School Rules" given to pupils ( ) and parents ( )?

(b) Are parents asked to sign these "Rules"? Yes ( )   No ( )

65. Does the school have a set of standards or expectations for classes in the following:

		Does school have a set of standards of what should be done?	
(i)	Setting of Homework:	Yes ( )	No ( )
(ii)	Checking Homework:	Yes ( )	No ( )
(iii)	Teaching Methods:	Yes ( )	No ( )
(iv)	Content of Lessons:	Yes ( )	No ( )

66. Is there any direct or indirect checking carried out to see that this occurs?

_____

Pupil Organisation

67. Is there a 'prefect' or similar type of system in the school?

Yes ( )   No ( )

If YES, describe _____

68. Is there a student council or representative body?

Yes ( )   No ( )

If YES, what kind of things does it deal with? _____

69. Are pupils organised in any other way (e.g. 'house' system)?

Yes ( ) No ( )

If YES, give details _____

70. Within the school, (a) how frequently do the following discipline problems arise, and (b) who is the main person to deal with the problem?

Pupils who:	(a) Frequency			(b) Who sanctions?
	Very Frequent	Occas- ionally	Rare	
(i) Are guilty of what one could call normal classroom misbehaviour? (e.g. talking in class, occasionally failing to do homework, late occasionally etc.)	1	2	3	
(ii) Somewhat more serious infractions e.g. being persistent in the above behaviour but not involving violence verbally or physically etc.)	1	2	3	
(iii) Serious misbehaviour: abusive to teacher or pupils; violence to teacher or pupils, serious damage to property, drugs or alcohol etc.)	1	2	3	

Pupil Characteristics

71. In your assessment, about what proportion of 1st year students in the school come from homes disrupted by poverty, alcoholism, unemployment, desertion, etc. ?

Very few or none	( )
5% - 10%	( )
10% - 25%	( )
Over 25%	( )

72. In your assessment, what proportion of 1st year pupils have serious literacy or numeracy problems?

	Literacy	Numeracy
0 - 5%	1	1
5 - 10%	2	2
10 - 15%	3	3
15 - 25%	4	4
Over 25%	5	5

73. (Fee-paying schools only)   Fees: Boarding £_____   Day £_____

    a) Are any scholarships or fee-exemptions granted?   Yes ( )   No ( )

    b) If YES, % of students getting exemptions?   _____%

74. (Non-fee paying schools)   Are parents asked to donate annually to the school?

                                      Yes ( )   No ( )

    a) If YES, how much are they asked to donate? _____

    b) For what purpose are the donations used? _____

                     _____

                     _____

75. a) Are there any other local schools to which pupils here might go?

                                    Yes ( )   No ( )

    b) Is there any competition for pupils between the local schools? _____

    c) To what extent do the other schools tend to "cream off" the better pupils? A great deal ( );
          Somewhat ( ); Not to any extent ( ); We get the better pupils ( ).

Parent Organisation

76.. Are parent or parent-teacher meetings held in the school?

Yes ( )   No ( )

If YES, (b) how often are they held?

Once a term   ( )

Twice a year   ( )

Once a year   ( )

Other _____

If NO, (c) do parents as a group have formal meetings with the principal or other staff?

With principal: Yes ( ) No ( ): With Staff: Yes ( )   No ( )

(d) How often?   once a year ( ),   2/3 times a year ( ),   more often ( ).

77. Are parents organised into a council or association?

Yes ( )   No ( )

Council   ( )

Association ( )

If YES, what is its function? _____

_____

Principal

78. How long have you been principal in this school? _____

79. . Were you principal in another school before you came here?

Yes ( )   No ( )

For how long? _____

63. Taking the current packaging of core and optional subjects in the junior and senior cycle levels: (If no optional subjects, take "core" to mean subjects given).

		Junior Cycle		Senior-Cycle	
		Core	Optional Packages	Core	Optional Packages
(a)	When was the last change made?	19	19	19	19
(b)	Given a continuation of the present circumstances of the school - student numbers, teachers, classrooms etc. how difficult would it be to change the way the core and optional packages are arranged if you wanted to?	Impossible 1 Very diffic. 2 Difficult 3 Easy 4	1 2 3 4	1 2 3 4	1 2 3 4
(c)	What is the main constraint on changing the core?				
(d)	What is the main constraint in changing the optional packages?				
(e)	How satisfied are you with the present set of core/optional packages.	Very satisfied 1 Satisfied 2 Not satisfied 3	1 2 3	1 2 3	1 2 3

Classroom Behaviour ; Standards/Expectations

64. Does the school have a general standard of classroom discipline?

Yes ( )   No ( )

If YES, Is there a written set of "School Rules" given to pupils ( ) and parents ( )?

(b) Are parents asked to sign these "Rules"?   Yes ( )   No ( )

83. Are you a member of any of the following teachers' or principals' organisations? Please circle the

number of each organisation of which you are a member.

Catholic Headmasters' Association	1
Conference of Convent Secondary Schools	2
Catholic Lay Schools' Assocation	3
Association of Irish Headmasters	4
Association of Principals and Vice-principals of Community and Comprehensive Schools	5
Conference of Major Religious Superiors	6
J. M. B.	7
TBA	8

84. Do you attend meetings of the associations of which you are a member?

Every meeting 1   Most meetings 2   Seldom 3   Never 4

85. Apart from these meetings, have you had contact with any of the above organisations over the past year?

Yes ( )   No ( )

If YES, which ones and what did you contact them about? _____

_____

86. Have you had any contact with the Secretariat of Secondary schools, over the past year?

(a) Secretariat of Secondary Schools   Yes ( )
(b) Dublin Dioc. Secretariat   Yes ( )
(c) C. of I. /Protestant Secretariat   Yes ( )

IF YES, to any of the above what was it that you contacted them about? _____

_____

87. Over the past year, has the school had any non-routine contact with the Department of Education?

Yes ( )   No ( )

a) Which sections? _____
b) What business? _____

Thank you very much for your help. The information you gave will be treated as strictly confidential. The
school will not be identified in any way in any publication. We merely wish to get an aggregate picture of the
total school system in Ireland of the major curricular characteristics of P. P. schools in general and of the main
constraint on curricular change. We will leave a short self completion questionnaire with you which we would
like you to return as soon as you conveniently can.

APPENDIX II

TABLES

Appendix Table 4.1: *Intercorrelations Amongst Independent Variables in Multiple Regression (Table 4.2)*

	1 Size of School	2 Select School	3 Compet. School	4 Lit. Probs.	5 Var. Soc. Class	6 Var. Ed. Parents	7 Boys' Schools	8 Girls' Schools	9 Voc/C. Schools	10 Soc. Class
1. Size of school	1.00									
2. Selectivity in school intake		1.00								
3. Competitiveness of schools		.12	1.00							
4. Extent of literacy problems of pupil intake	.12	-.10	-.32	1.00						
5. Variation in social class intake of pupil intake	-.27	-.26	-.30	.24	1.00					
6. Variation in educ. level of parents of pupil intake	-.10	-.09	+.25	-.07	.16	1.00				
7. Boys' school	.13	.19	+.13	-.32	-.20	.04	1.00			
8. Girls' school		.05	.27	.03	-.16	.13	-.35	1.00		
9. Voc./Community school	.14	-.20	-.59	.45	.22	-.31	-.28	-.37	1.00	
10. Median social class of pupil body	.13	-.30	-.46	.52	.36	-.12	-.35	.01	.51	1.00

Appendix Table 5.1: *Intercorrelations Amongst Independent Variables as in Table 5.4*
(N = 76 schools, junior cycle)

| Independent Variables | Correlations With Dropout Rates[†] | | Independent Variables | | | | | | | | |
	(a) Junior Cycle	(b) Senior Cycle	1	2	3	4	5	6	7	8	9
1. Median social class of I.C. class in school	-.45*	-.68*	1.00								
2. Vocational/Community school**	-.45*	-.58*	.59	1.00							
3. Extent of literacy/numeracy problems in pupil intake	-.33*	-.38*	.53	.44	1.00						
4. Extent of selectivity of school	.34*	.46*	-.51	-.21	-.33	1.00					
5. Boys' Secondary schools**	-.02	.13	-.33	-.28	-.32	.13	1.00				
6. Girls' Secondary schools**	.14	.23*	.04	-.37	.04	.27	-.37	1.00			
7. Size of schools (no. of pupils)	-.01	.11	-.04	-.07	.01	.02	.10	.27	1.00		
8. Size of community	.14	-.17	.14	.12	-.04	.03	-.23	-.21	-.67	1.00	
9. School process scale (ICSCALE)	-.21*	-.21*	.13	-.05	-.10	-.06	.27	-.18	.20	-.14	1.00

*Coefficients significant at the .05 level.

**Dummy variables: 1 = Vocational or Community school; 0 = other.

[†]Dropout Rates: At junior cycle the denominator is the total number of pupils who entered first year in schools in 1976/77, the numerator being the number who left before reaching the Inter Cert. level/year. It is scored from −60 per cent (where 60 per cent of the entry cohort had left by Inter Cert.) to 0, where none had. Therefore, the *higher* the numerical value the lesser the dropout rate. The same procedure is used for calculating the senior cycle dropout rate with the denominator here being the number of pupils in school at the Inter Cert. year. Here there are some positive numbers when there was a flow into senior cycle classes in some private fee-paying schools.

Appendix Table 5.2: *Hierarchical Regression of Percentage of School Entry Cohort Achieving at Least Four Honours Grades in the Leaving Certificate Examination by a Set of School Entry (Pupil) Characteristics, School Type Characteristics and School Differentiation Scale*

Independent Variables	(i) School Input Effects	(ii) School Input and School Type Effects	(iii) School Input and School Type and Schooling Process Effects
	Beta	Beta	Beta
Pupil Input Effects:			
1. Median social class of pupil intake	−.38*	−.40*	−.41*
2. Extent of literacy/numeracy problems in intake	−.06	−.07	−.07
3. Extent of selectivity in intake	.20**	.07	.06
4. Average level of mothers' education	.24**	.17	.17
Type of School:			
5. Boys' Secondary schools	—	−.09	−.10
6. Girls' Secondary schools	—	.11	.11
7. Vocational schools	—	−.20**	−.21**
8. Schooling process scale	—	—	.05
N =	70	70	70
F =	15.4*	10.3*	8.9
R^2 =	.49	.54	.54

Appendix Table 5.3: *Correlation Matrix of Independent Variables Used in Regression Equation in Tables 5.3 to 5.10 (Schools > 1 class: N = 75)*

Column headings:

1. Av. No. years
2. % to Univ.
3. Total Dropout Rate to LC
4. St. Dev. in No. Years
5. Coeff. of Var. in No. Years
6. Median Soc. Class (163)
7. Av. of Mos' Ed. (218)
8. Av. of Fas' Ed. (214)
9. S^2 In Fas' Ed. (216)
10. S^2 In Fas' Ed. (256)
11. S^2 In Fas' Occ. Status (265)
12. Lit. Problems in Intake (171)
13. Num. Problems in Intake (174)
14. Ext. of Sch. Select. I (114)
15. Ext. of Sch. Select. II (116)
16. Ext. of Sch. Select. III (118)
17. Boys Sec. D1
18. Girls Sec. D2
19. Voc. Sch. D3
20. Sch. Size (120)
21. Sch. Process Scale (112)

Independent Variables	1	2	3	4	5	6	7	8	9	10	11	12	13	14	15	16	17	18	19	20	21
1. Av. yrs. of education completed in school by entry cohort	1.00																				
2. Percentage to Univ. of entry cohort	.70	1.00																			
3. Total dropout rate to Leaving Cert. from entry cohort	.70	-.65	1.00																		
4. Std. Deviation in no. yrs. of education achieved by entry cohort	-.97	-.24	.37	1.00																	
5. Coeff. of variation in no. of yrs. of educ. achieved	-.47	-.45	.67	.91	1.00																
6. Median social class of pupil intake	-.77	-.75	.71	.31	.50	1.00															
7. Av. of mother's ed. of pupil intake	-.71	.73	-.56	-.28	-.44	-.69	1.00														
8. Av. of father's ed. of pupil intake	.56	.75	-.53	-.32	-.44	-.71	.89	1.00													
9. Variation in mother's level of educ. of intake	.60	.04	-.25	.19	.01	-.07	-.01	.01	1.00												
10. Variation in father's level of educ. of intake	.22	.37	-.38	.09	-.07	-.41	.49	.44	.50	1.00											
11. Variation in father's occ. status of intake	.34	-.37	.29	.28	.32	.35	-.27	-.34	.17	-.05	1.00										
12. Estimate of literacy problems in intake	-.32	-.43	.45	.16	.30	.53	-.42	-.41	-.02	-.26	.22	1.00									
13. Estimate of numeracy problems in intake	-.41	-.45	.40	.14	.26	.50	-.39	-.37	-.02	-.23	.19	.98	1.00								
14. Extent of school selectivity I	-.45	.38	-.52	.07	-.15	-.51	.35	.28	.26	.41	-.27	-.32	-.29	1.00							
15. Extent of school selectivity II	.48	.12	-.19	-.06	-.08	-.29	.43	.51	-.17	.07	-.24	-.09	-.09	.13	1.00						
16. Extent of school selectivity III	.20	.17	-.28	-.21	-.26	-.30	.13	.18	.07	.06	-.10	-.26	-.26	.09	.00	1.00					
17. Boys' Sec. school	.27	.61	-.25	.07	-.06	-.45	.53	.50	.10	.40	-.13	-.45	-.45	.26	.15	.11	1.00				
18. Girls' Sec. school	.29	-.09	-.28	-.09	-.16	.02	-.08	-.03	-.03	.19	-.15	.01	.02	.30	.03	-.04	.32	1.00			
19. Voc. school	-.66	-.51	.66	.11	.36	.51	-.66	-.54	-.45	-.67	.19	.34	.31	-.58	-.23	-.17	-.33	-.31	1.00		
20. School size	.18	.20	-.13	-.07	-.13	-.04	.23	.33	-.04	-.22	-.27	.01	.06	.02	.43	-.10	-.01	.26	-.37	1.00	
21. School process scale	-.29	-.19	.24	.42	.42	.19	-.15	-.19	-.06	-.13	.06	.01	.01	-.12	-.15	-.16	.17	-.20	.22	-.15	1.00

Appendix Table 5.4: *Distribution of Schools With More Than Two Classes According to Their Standard Deviations and Coefficients of Variation in the Number of Years of Schooling Completed by Pupils Before Leaving School*

Standard Deviation in the Number of Years of Schooling Completed by Pupils Within Schools		Coefficient of Variation in Number of Years of Schooling Completed by Pupils Within Schools	
Values	*Number of Schools*	*Values*	*Number of Schools*
.25-.49 =	3	.055-.09 =	3
.50-.74 =	1	.100-.149 =	5
.75-.99 =	11	.150-.199 =	10
1.00-1.24 =	22	.200-.249 =	17
1.25-1.49 =	19	.250-.299 =	14
1.50-1.74 =	15	.300-.349 =	12
1.75-1.99 =	3	.350-.399 =	10
2.00-2.41 =	1	.400-.449 =	5
Total number of schools	76	Total number of schools	76
Kurtosis = 1.12; Skewness = −.120		Kurtosis = −.55; Skewness = −.088	

Appendix Table 5.5: *Hierarchical Regression of Within-School Differences (Standard Deviation) in the Number of Honours Papers Taken on the Intermediate Certificate Course by (i) Family Background, (ii) School Type and (iii) Schooling Process Variables (Standardised Betas: N = 71; Schools > 1 class)*

Independent Variables	(i) (With School Input Characteristics)	(ii) (With School Input and School Type Characteristics)	(iii) (With School Input, School Type and Schooling Process Variables)
	Beta	Beta	Beta
A. *Pupil Composition Variables*			
1. Median social class of pupil intake	−.05	−.03	−.06
2. Average level of mothers'education in pupil intake	−.10	−.19	−.15
3. Variance in social class of pupil intake	.13	.15	.13
4. Variance in parental level of education of pupil intake	.34*	.21	.25*
5. Extent of selectivity of schools	.25*	.14	.15
6. Extent of literacy/numeracy problems in pupil intake	−.27*	−.27*	−.24*
B. *School Types*			
7. Boys' Secondary schools	—	−.14	−.19
8. Vocational schools	—	−.35*	−.31*
9. Schooling process scale	—	—	.16
N =	71	71	71
F =	4.6	4.6*	4.4*
R^2 =	.30	.37	.39

*Statistically significant at the 5 per cent level.
**Statistically significant at the 10 per cent level.

Appendix Table 5.6: *Regression of the Within-School Standard Deviation in the Number of Academic Subjects Taken in the Inter Certificate on the School Input, School Type and Schooling Process Variables*
(N = 71 schools > 1 class)

Independent Variables	(i) Effects of School Input Variables	(ii) School Input and School Type Variables	(iii) School Input and School Type Plus Schooling Process Variables
	Beta (Std.)	Beta	Beta
School Input Variables			
1. Median social class of pupil body	.33*	.33*	.27*
2. Average maternal educational level of pupil body	−.15	−.10	−.17
3. Social class variance in pupil intake	.16	.17	.13
4. Variance in parental education level amongst pupil intake	.24*	−.08	.15
5. Selectivity of pupil intake to school	.13	−.05	−.03
6. Extent of literacy/numeracy problem in intake	−.40*	−.43*	−.37*
School Type Variables			
7. Boys' Secondary schools	—	−.35*	−.44*
8. Vocational schools	—	−.47*	−.40*
9. Schooling process effects	—	—	.30*
N =	71	71	71
F =	3.4*	6.0*	6.0*
R^2 =	.24	−.43	.50

Appendix Table 5.7: *Regression of Within-School Inequality (Coefficient of Variation) in Leaving Certificate Examination Results on Pupil Intake, School Type and Schooling Process Variables (N = 71; larger schools)*

Independent Variables	(i) With Pupil Intake Variables	(ii) With Pupil Intake and School Type Variables	(iii) With Pupil Intake, School Type and Schooling Variables
	Beta	Beta	Beta
A. *School Intake Characteristics*			
1. Median social class of pupil intake	−.19	−.15	−.17
2. Average parental education level	.22	.09	.12
3. Variance in social class intake	.03	.04	.02
4. Variance in parental education level	.12	.04	.07
5. Selectivity of schools	.19	.14	.14
6. Extent of literacy/numeracy problem in pupil intake	.25*	.28*	.30*
B. *School Type Variables*			
7. Boys' Secondary schools	—	.12	.08
8. Vocational schools	—	−.24	−.21
C. *Schooling Process Variable*			
9. Schooling process scale	—	—	.13
N =	71	71	71
F =	2.9*	2.5*	.24*
R^2 =	.21	.24	.26

Appendix Table 5.8: *Regressions of Individuals' Leaving Cert. Grades on Certain Family Background, School Type, Preceding (Inter Cert.) Performance, and Streaming Characteristics of School Attended (Separate Regressions for Boys' and Girls' Schools With Greater Than 1 Class at Leaving Cert. Level)*

Independent Variables	Boys		Girls	
	(i) Beta	(ii) Beta	(i) Beta	(ii) Beta
A. *Family Background Variables*				
1. Fathers' education level	.07*	.07*	.02	.02
2. Mothers' education level	.01	.01	.04	.04
3. Fathers' occupational status	−.02	−.02	−.04*	−.04*
4. Number of children in family	−.02	−.02	.01	.01
B. *School Type*				
5. Boys' Sec./Girls' Sec. school	.03	.03	−.05*	−.05*
6. Vocational school	.00	.00	−.05*	−.05*
7. Extent of selectivity of school intake	.02	.02	−.01	−.01
C. *Preceding Performance Level*				
8. Grade at Inter Cert.	.75*	.75*	.75*	.75*
D. *Extent of School Processing*				
9. Extent of streaming/differentiation at Leaving Cert. level		−.00		−.01
R^2 =	.61	.61	.60	.60
D.F. =	8/1091	9/1090	8/1556	9/1555
F =	215.4*	191.3*	259.0*	233.0*

*Statistically significant at .05 level or less.

Books:

Economic Growth in Ireland: The Experience Since 1947
                                    Kieran A. Kennedy and Brendan Dowling
Irish Economic Policy: A Review of Major Issues
                            Staff Members of ESRI (eds. B. R. Dowling and J. Durkan)
The Irish Economy and Society in the 1980s (Papers presented at ESRI Twenty-first Anniversary Conference)   Staff Members of ESRI
The Economic and Social State of The Nation
                            J. F. Meenan, M. P. Fogarty, J. Kavanagh and L. Ryan
The Irish Economy: Policy and Performance 1972-1981
                                        P. Bacon, J. Durkan and J. O'Leary
Employment and Unemployment Policy for Ireland
                    Staff Members of ESRI (eds., Denis Conniffe and Kieran A. Kennedy)
Public Social Expenditure – Value for Money? (Papers presented at a Conference, 20. November 1984)
Medium-Term Outlook: 1986-1990. No. 1   Peter Bacon
Ireland in Transition   Kieran A. Kennedy (ed.)

Policy Research Series:

1. *Regional Policy and the Full-Employment Target*   M. Ross and B. Walsh
2. *Energy Demand in Ireland, Projections and Policy Issues*   S. Scott
3. *Some Issues in the Methodology of Attitude Research*   E. E. Davis *et al.*
4. *Land Drainage Policy in Ireland*   Richard Bruton and Frank J. Convery
5. *Recent Trends in Youth Unemployment*   J. J. Sexton
6. *The Economic Consequences of European Union. A Symposium on Some Policy Aspects*
                            D. Scott, J. Bradley, J. D. FitzGerald and M. Ross
7. *The National Debt and Economic Policy in the Medium Term*   John D. FitzGerald

Broadsheet Series:

1. *Dental Services in Ireland*   P. R. Kaim-Caudle
2. *We Can Stop Rising Prices*   M. P. Fogarty
3. *Pharmaceutical Services in Ireland*   P. R. Kaim-Caudle
                assisted by Annette O'Toole and Kathleen O'Donoghue
4. *Ophthalmic Services in Ireland*   P. R. Kaim-Caudle
                assisted by Kathleen O'Donoghue and Annette O'Toole
5. *Irish Pensions Schemes, 1969*   P. R. Kaim-Caudle and J. G. Byrne
                                    assisted by Annette O'Toole
6. *The Social Science Percentage Nuisance*   R. C. Geary
7. *Poverty in Ireland: Research Priorities*   Brendan M. Walsh
8. *Irish Entrepreneurs Speak for Themselves*   M. P. Fogarty
9. *Marital Desertion in Dublin: An Exploratory Study*   Kathleen O'Higgins
10. *Equalization of Opportunity in Ireland: Statistical Aspects*
                            R. C. Geary and F. S. Ó Muircheartaigh
11. *Public Social Expenditure in Ireland*   Finola Kennedy
12. *Problems in Economic Planning and Policy Formation in Ireland, 1958–1974*
                                            Desmond Norton
13. *Crisis in the Cattle Industry*   R. O'Connor and P. Keogh
14. *A Study of Schemes for the Relief of Unemployment in Ireland*
                                    R. C. Geary and M. Dempsey
    with Appendix   E. Costa
15. *Dublin Simon Community, 1971-1976: An Exploration*   Ian Hart

16. *Aspects of the Swedish Economy and their Relevance to Ireland*
                          Robert O'Connor, Eoin O'Malley and Anthony Foley
17. *The Irish Housing System: A Critical Overview*
                          T. J. Baker and L. M. O'Brien
18. *The Irish Itinerants: Some Demographic, Economic and Educational Aspects*
                          M. Dempsey and R. C. Geary
19. *A Study of Industrial Workers' Co-operatives*
                          Robert O'Connor and Philip Kelly
20. *Drinking in Ireland: A Review of Trends in Alcohol Consumption, Alcohol Related Problems and Policies towards Alcohol*   Brendan M. Walsh
21. *A Review of the Common Agricultural Policy and the Implications of Modified Systems for Ireland*   R. O'Connor, C. Guiomard and J. Devereux
22. *Policy Aspects of Land-Use Planning in Ireland*
                          Frank J. Convery and A. Allan Schmid
23. *Issues in Adoption in Ireland*   Harold J. Abramson

Geary Lecture Series:
1. *A Simple Approach to Macro-economic Dynamics* (1967)   R. G. D. Allen
2. *Computers, Statistics and Planning-Systems or Chaos?* (1968)   F. G. Foster
3. *The Dual Career Family* (1970)   Rhona and Robert Rapoport
4. *The Psychosonomics of Rising Prices* (1971)   H. A. Turner
5. *An Interdisciplinary Approach to the Measurement of Utility or Welfare* (1972)
                          J. Tinbergen
6. *Econometric Forecasting from Lagged Relationships* (1973)   M. G. Kendall
7. *Towards a New Objectivity* (1974)   Alvin W. Gouldner
8. *Structural Analysis in Sociology* (1975)   Robert K. Merton
9. *British Economic Growth 1951-1973: Success or Failure?* (1976)
                          R. C. O. Matthews
10. *Official Statisticians and Econometricians in the Present Day World* (1977)
                          E. Malinvaud
11. *Political and Institutional Economics* (1978)   Gunnar Myrdal
12. *The Dilemmas of a Socialist Economy: The Hungarian Experience* (1979)
                          János Kornai
13. *The Story of a Social Experiment and Some Reflections* (1980)
                          Robert M. Solow
14. *Modernisation and Religion* (1981)   P. L. Berger
15. *Poor, Relatively Speaking* (1983)   Amartya K. Sen
16. *Towards More Rational Decisions on Criminals* (1984)   Daniel Glaser
17. *An Economic Analysis of the Family* (1985)   Gary S. Becker

General Research Series:
1. *The Ownership of Personal Property in Ireland*   Edward Nevin
2. *Short-Term Economic Forecasting and its Application in Ireland*   Alfred Kuehn
3. *The Irish Tariff and The E.E.C.: A Factual Survey*   Edward Nevin
4. *Demand Relationships for Ireland*   C. E. V. Leser
5. *Local Government Finance in Ireland: A Preliminary Survey*   David Walker
6. *Prospects of the Irish Economy in 1962*   Alfred Kuehn
7. *The Irish Woollen and Worsted Industry, 1946-59: A Study in Statistical Method*
                          R. C. Geary

8.	*The Allocation of Public Funds for Social Development*	David Walker
9.	*The Irish Price Level: A Comparative Study*	Edward Nevin
10.	*Inland Transport in Ireland: A Factual Study*	D. J. Reynolds
11.	*Public Debt and Economic Development*	Edward Nevin
12.	*Wages in Ireland, 1946-62*	Edward Nevin
13.	*Road Transport: The Problems and Prospects in Ireland*	D. J. Reynolds
14.	*Imports and Economic Growth in Ireland, 1947-61*	C. E. V. Leser
15.	*The Irish Economy in 1962 and 1963*	C. E. V. Leser
16.	*Irish County Incomes in 1960*	E. A. Attwood and R. C. Geary
17.	*The Capital Stock of Irish Industry*	Edward Nevin
18.	*Local Government Finance and County Incomes*	David Walker
19.	*Industrial Relations in Ireland: The Background*	David O'Mahony
20.	*Social Security in Ireland and Western Europe*	P. R. Kaim-Caudle
21.	*The Irish Economy in 1963 and 1964*	C. E. V. Leser
22.	*The Cost Structure of Irish Industry 1950-60*	Edward Nevin
23.	*A Further Analysis of Irish Household Budget Data, 1951-52*	C. E. V. Leser
24.	*Economic Aspects of Industrial Relations*	David O'Mahony
25.	*Phychological Barriers to Economic Achievement*	P. Pentony
26.	*Seasonality in Irish Economic Statistics*	C. E. V. Leser
27.	*The Irish Economy in 1964 and 1965*	C. E. V. Leser
28.	*Housing in Ireland: Some Economic Aspects*	P. R. Kaim-Caudle
29.	*A Statistical Study of Wages, Prices and Employment in the Irish Manufacturing Sector*	C. St. J. O'Herlihy
30.	*Fuel and Power in Ireland: Part I. Energy Consumption in 1970*	J. L. Booth
31.	*Determinants of Wage Inflation in Ireland*	Keith Cowling
32.	*Regional Employment Patterns in the Republic of Ireland*	T. J. Baker
33.	*The Irish Economy in 1966*	The Staff of The Economic Research Institute
34.	*Fuel and Power in Ireland: Part II. Electricity and Turf*	J. L. Booth
35.	*Fuel and Power in Ireland: Part III. International and Temporal Aspects of Energy Consumption*	J. L. Booth
36.	*Institutional Aspects of Commercial and Central Banking in Ireland*	John Hein
37.	*Fuel and Power in Ireland: Part IV. Sources and Uses of Energy*	J. L. Booth
38.	*A Study of Imports*	C. E. V. Leser
39.	*The Irish Economy in 1967*	The Staff of The Economic and Social Research Institute
40.	*Some Aspects of Price Inflation in Ireland*	R. C. Geary and J. L. Pratschke
41.	*A Medium Term Planning Model for Ireland*	David Simpson
42.	*Some Irish Population Problems Reconsidered*	Brendan M. Walsh
43.	*The Irish Brain Drain*	Richard Lynn
44.	*A Method of Estimating the Stock of Capital in Northern Ireland Manufacturing Industry: Limitations and Applications*	C. W. Jefferson
45.	*An Input-Output Analysis of the Agricultural Sector of the Irish Economy in 1964*	R. O'Connor with M. Breslin
46.	*The Implications for Cattle Producers of Seasonal Price Fluctuations*	R. O'Connor
47.	*Transport in the Developing Economy of Ireland*	John Blackwell
48.	*Social Status and Inter-Generational Social Mobility in Dublin*	Bertram Hutchinson

80. *An Econometric Study of the Irish Postal Service*   Peter Neary
81. *Employment Relationships in Irish Counties*
                                                  Terence J. Baker and Miceal Ross
82. *Irish Input-Output Income Multipliers 1964 and 1968*
                                                  J. R. Copeland and E. W. Henry
83. *A Study of the Structure and Determinants of the Behavioural Component of Social*
    Attitudes in Ireland   E. E. Davis
84. *Economic Aspects of Local Authority Expenditure and Finance*
                                                  J. R. Copeland and Brendan M. Walsh
85. *Population Growth and other Statistics of Middle-sized Irish Towns*
                           D. Curtin, R. C. Geary, T. A. Grimes and B. Menton
86. *The Income Sensitivity of the Personal Income Tax Base in Ireland, 1947-1972*
                                                  Brendan R. Dowling
87. *Traditional Families? From Culturally Prescribed to Negotiated Roles in Farm*
    Families   Damian F. Hannan and Louise Katsiaouni
88. *An Irish Personality Differential: A Technique for Measuring Affective and Cognitive*
    Dimensions of Attitudes Towards Persons   E. E. Davis and Mary O'Neill
89. *Redundancy and Re-Employment in Ireland*
                                                  Brendan J. Whelan and Brendan M. Walsh
90. *A National Model for Fuel Allocation – A Prototype*   E. W. Henry and S. Scott
91. *A Linear Programming Model for Irish Agriculture*
                                  Robert O'Connor, Miceal Ross and Michael Behan
92. *Irish Educational Expenditures – Past, Present and Future*   A. Dale Tussing
93. *The Working and Living Conditions of Civil Service Typists*
                                                  Nóirin O'Broin and Gillian Farren
94. *Irish Public Debt*   Richard Bruton
95. *Output and Employment in the Irish Food Industry to 1990*
                                                  A. D. O'Rourke and T. P. McStay
96. *Displacement and Development: Class, Kinship and Social Change in Irish Rural Com-*
    munities   Damian F. Hannan
97. *Attitudes in the Republic of Ireland Relevant to the Northern Problem: Vol. I:*
    Descriptive Analysis and Some Comparisons with Attitudes in Northern Ireland and
    Great Britain   E. E. Davis and R. Sinnott
98. *Internal Migration Flows in Ireland and their Determinants*
                                                  J. G. Hughes and B. M. Walsh
99. *Irish Input-Output Structures, 1976*   E. W. Henry
100. *Development of the Irish Sea Fishing Industry and its Regional Implications*
                           R. O'Connor, J. A. Crutchfield, B. J. Whelan and K. E. Mellon
101. *Employment Conditions and Job Satisfaction: The Distribution, Perception and Evalua-*
    tion of Job Rewards   Christopher T. Whelan
102. *Crime in the Republic of Ireland: Statistical Trends and Their Interpretation*
                                                  David B. Rottman
103. *Measure of the Capital Stock in the Irish Manufacturing Sector, 1945-1973*
                                                  R. N. Vaughan
104. *A Study of National Wage Agreements in Ireland*   James F. O'Brien
105. *Socio-Economic Impact of the Construction of the ESB Power Station at Moneypoint,*
    Co. Clare   R. O'Connor, J. A. Crutchfield and B. J. Whelan

Typeset by Wendy A. Commins, The Curragh; Make-up by Paul Bray Studio.
Printed by Criterion Press Limited, Dublin.